Kit Carson

The Oklahoma Western Biographies
Richard W. Etulain, General Editor

Last known photograph of Carson, 1868. Courtesy Denver Public Library.

Kit Carson
The Life of an American Border Man

By David Remley

University of Oklahoma Press : Norman

Also by David Remley

Erna Fergusson (Austin, 1969)

Crooked Road: The Story of the Alaska Highway
(New York, 1976; Fairbanks, 2008)

Bell Ranch: Cattle Ranching in the Southwest, 1824–1947
(Albuquerque, 1993; revised paperback edition, Las Cruces,
N. Mex., 1999)

(ed.) *Adios Nuevo Mexico: The Santa Fe Journal of John Watts in 1859*
(Las Cruces, N.Mex., 1999)

Library of Congress Cataloging-in-Publication Data

Remley, David A.
    Kit Carson : the life of an American border man / by David Remley.
        p. cm. — (The Oklahoma western biographies ; v. 27)
    Includes bibliographical references and index.
    ISBN 978-0-8061-4172-5 (hardcover : alk. paper)
    1. Carson, Kit, 1809–1868. 2. Pioneers—West (U.S.)—Biography.
3. Scouts (Reconnaissance)—West (U.S.)—Biography. 4. Soldiers—
West (U.S.)—Biography. 5. West (U.S.)—Biography. 6. Frontier and
pioneer life—West (U.S.) I. Title.
    F592.C33R46 2011
    978'.02092—dc22
    [B]
                                                              2010037350

Kit Carson: The Life of an American Border Man is Volume 27 in The Oklahoma Western Biographies.

The paper in this book meets the guidelines for permanence and durability of the Committee on Production Guidelines for Book Longevity of the Council on Library Resources, Inc. ∞

1   2   3   4   5   6   7   8   9   10

For Mother
—A book just for her—

In memory of
Waa-nibe, an Arapaho woman, wife of
Kit Carson

and their children:
Adaline
and a baby girl, name unknown

"Truth is an aspiration, not a possession."
—Drew Gilpin Faust
"Installation Address," first woman to serve
as President, Harvard University
October 12, 2007

At the edge of the parade ground at Fort Riley, Kansas, the Old Army's cavalry school, stands a bronze cavalry horse. Its ribs show. Its head hangs to the ground. The memorial is to the numberless horses, and mules, who have given their lives for soldiers at war. I acknowledge here the countless saddle, pack, and draft animals who gave their best efforts and their lives to their men and women over the many years Kit Carson traveled the mountains and plains of the West.

Contents

Illustrations

Illustrations

MAPS

Series Editor's Preface

Stories of heroes and heroines have intrigued many generations of listeners and readers. Americans, like people everywhere, have been captivated by the lives of military, political, and religious figures and intrepid explorers, pioneers, and rebels. The Oklahoma Western Biographies endeavor to build on this fascination with biography and to link it with two other abiding interests of Americans: the frontier and the American West. Although volumes in the series carry no notes, they are prepared by leading scholars, are soundly researched, and include a discussion of the sources used. Each volume is a lively synthesis based on thorough examination of pertinent primary and secondary sources.

Above all, the Oklahoma Western Biographies aim at two goals: to provide readable life stories of significant westerners and to show how their lives illuminate a notable topic, an influential movement, or a series of important events in the history and cultures of the American West.

David Remley more than achieves these goals in his valuable new biography of Kit Carson. In fact, he gives us what we need: a lively, balanced, and engrossing story of the man. Rather than swing toward the earlier romantic portraits of a larger-than-life Carson or toward the later revisionist treatments of Carson as an Indian killer, Remley presents a complex border figure. Here is a Carson whom readers will be drawn to, a person who displayed multiple facets in his frenetic, on-the-move, adventuresome life. Of note, too, Remley builds this exceptional biography upon his close reading of all the major published primary and secondary sources dealing with this complex westerner.

The author does not shy away from Carson's less-than-ideal attitudes and actions. We hear of episodes illustrating how much Carson contributed to frontier violence against opponents, especially Native foes and occasionally Hispanic competitors. In addition, Carson was sometimes so loyal to his commanders, military or civilian, that he infringed on the rights of others. When he was absent, often his family suffered. On other occasions, particularly early in his career, he acted precipitously, making mistakes that endangered himself and others. These human limitations are clearly displayed in Remley's portrait.

We are also treated to a Kit Carson of still other dimensions. Like that other notable man of the western mountains, Jedediah Smith, Carson came to know huge portions of a sprawling West. He was a skilled, intrepid explorer, a leader, and a man of the wilderness. He knew Indians, often negotiating with them for peaceful settlements and serving as a helpful agent for the Utes and other Native groups. On several occasions, he helped spare John C. Frémont and his expeditions from the potentially disastrous consequences of that self-centered, naïve leader's often foolish decisions and actions. Throughout his life Carson was a culture broker bridging societies, settlements, and leaders. Remley furnishes numerous examples of Kit's influence on the history of the American West from the 1840s through the 1860s.

A palpable sense of the trails, camps, and mountains of Carson's West pours from this lively biography. Readers experience life under the big sky, the dangers of frontier exploration, and

Preface

the humor, warmth, pathos, and daily human extravagance of a central participant in the opening of the West. Here's Kit Carson aplenty for general readers and scholars alike.

Richard W. Etulain
Professor Emeritus of History
University of New Mexico

Preface

Take U.S. Highway 491 north from Gallup, New Mexico. Turn west onto State Highway 264 toward Window Rock, Arizona, capital of the Navajo Nation. At the stoplight in the middle of town, go north to Fort Defiance, today a sprawling western town with a supermarket, ministore, burger joints, and fields of trailer houses called "manufactured homes." Ford and Toyota pickups wait among puttering eighteen-wheelers for the stoplight to change.

Find the U.S. Post Office. Ask the postmaster for directions to the site of "old" Fort Defiance, abandoned by the U.S. Army on April 25, 1861, then reoccupied in July 1863 and renamed Fort Canby. Some years later still, a U.S. government Indian hospital replaced the fort. Here in 1863, Col. Christopher Carson's First New Mexico Volunteers gathered up the Navajos for their "Long Walk" to Fort Sumner, located at the Bosque Redondo, an immense grove of cottonwood trees along the Pecos River far to the east on New Mexico's High Plains. A parallel to the Cherokee Trail of Tears, the Long Walk remains a profoundly important tragedy for Navajos. No historical marker points the visitor to the place where the soldiers assembled them. Truly, the Diné don't need a marker to remind them of this grievous gathering.

The postmaster tells you to drive west on the main road past the post office, cross a cut through a low ridge, then bear slightly to the right and turn hard right into the parking lot behind the old hospital, a great brown sandstone building, now long closed. Park the car. Scramble up the high ridge to the big water storage tank. At the water tank, turn around to face west. There you see the panorama that appears in the sepia-toned lithographs and penciled drawings of old Fort Defiance, or Fort Canby. These drawings were made about the time the Navajos began their dark journey from this very place.

None of Fort Canby's buildings remains intact. You can easily recognize the site, however, by the great slash in the mountain wall directly west of where you stand and by the massive outcrop of gray rock behind the Catholic church, just left of center view. The vast gray rock is exactly as it is in the browned lithographs and drawings. Otherwise, the entire site, including the parade ground, is cluttered with housing representing every period of American commercial architecture since the late nineteenth century. Here and there, nearly hidden in the clutter, stand old sandstone hospital buildings. Little white frame houses with Victorian trim sit in rows among the trees along the streets. The houses were built for hospital workers well before 1900. It was a time when children still played on the parade ground and in the streets after dinner on summer evenings while their parents sat in swings on their front porches so they could visit with neighbors out taking walks.

Col. Christopher Carson was here. Gen. James H. Carleton, commanding the U.S. Army's Department of New Mexico from Santa Fe, in General Orders No. 15 dated June 15, 1863, had ordered Carson's volunteers to establish a "defensible Depot" in the "Navajoe country," thence "to prosecute a vigorous war upon the men of this tribe until it is considered at this Head Quarters that they have been effectually punished for their long continued atrocities." This "vigorous war" would end with the Navajo "removal," a grossly euphemistic term for the Long Walk. The brutal journey continued from here and from nearby Fort Wingate until it ended at the Bosque Redondo. The entire experience proved to be a great loss and a great test for Navajos, who look back upon this trial as *the ordeal* that fused their identity as today's Navajos, Diné, The People. Although they could never recover what their ancestors remembered as the beautiful long-ago time of roaming, hunting, and raiding before the Long Walk, to have shared that calamity made them who they were afterward, and who they remain today.

Who was Colonel Carson? What responsibility did he have for the Navajo surrender and for other important events connected with the history of his time? A man of action rather than of a philosophical turn of mind, he performed duties that made a difference, for better and for worse, for the people he lived with and worked among. What does this fact suggest about his character?

Qualities other than sheer luck, good or bad, seem to have enabled him to play a part in an unusual number of important actions of his day. Unable to read or write, he eventually learned to scrawl his name, "C. Carson," when he signed letters he had dictated. In 1856 he told his life story to a clerk named John Mostin, who had a tin ear for Carson's border vernacular, and who apparently edited the dictation heavily for prospective readers. At the time of this dictation, Carson was the Ute Indian agent. He lived in Taos, New Mexico, and he was forty-six years old. Over the next twelve years he would perform many of the most important actions of his colorful, and, today, controversial life, none of it covered by the dictation of 1856. While he left a great deal of official correspondence, all of it dictated, during these later years, there is little about his personal life, except for a few letters to his wife, family, and close friends. He died on May 23, 1868, at Fort Lyon, Colorado.

Other important western figures of the day left many pages from their own pens. Supremely able mountain men Zenas Leonard, James Clyman, Osborne Russell, and Warren A. Ferris wrote their own accounts. These are packed with realistic detail and thoughtful reflection. From such recollections it is possible to describe their writers' actions, capture their thoughts, and summarize their principles. For Carson, however, it is necessary to rely heavily upon the accounts of those who knew him, described him in action, or remarked upon him in some way. Biographers have always had to struggle to *imagine* Carson as the singular human being he was. Writing about the man today remains a risky job, largely because (with the exception of what he dictated to his clerk in 1856) he himself was not at all helpful.

He certainly was *not* the dazzling frontier figure of the dime novels that began appearing well before his death. Writers of these fictions exploited his name ruthlessly. They marketed their books to readers in the East who, as an escape from their dreary daily lives, wished to relish spectaculars of bloody escapades in the Far West. Though Carson did in fact live actively in a dangerous West, almost all of what was written of him in the nineteenth century was fanciful. Traveling, trading, hunting, and living with American Indians, as he did, learning their languages, swapping clothing and tools, marrying Indian women and having children with them, fighting them and oftentimes beside them, were in reality a rather unheroic business seven days a week.

But eastern readers didn't want the real picture. They bought the heroic one. Actually, people of all cultures and of all races on the western borders in Carson's day had to struggle just to get by, whether they were in conflict or working together. They got dirty. They got sick. They got hurt. Many of them died young. They were often as not half starved or yellow with malaria. Women died in childbirth, children from every childhood disease, men from simple accidents. People went hungry. Horses and mules were bony and slab-sided.

Men and women worked at surviving on what Richard White called a "middle ground" between different cultures and languages.

All had to invent and reinvent themselves every day on the ever-shifting middle ground just to meet new conditions. The weather was changing for the worse. Hunting prospects were poor. Cholera or smallpox appeared in camp. Such diseases wiped out whole villages and settlements overnight. Accidents were always expected, with severe results. And outsiders, friendly *or* hostile, from God knows where, were likely to come charging into camp at any time of day or night. Mere survival burned up enormous amounts of energy and must have required an odd kind of understanding, even a cooperation of sorts, between all sides, whether they were on friendly terms or were fighting with one another.

Probably the first of the cheap fictions to appear with Carson's name in the title was Charles Averill's *Kit Carson, The Prince of the Gold Hunters.* This potboiler came out in 1849. Soon to follow were such spectaculars as *Kiowa Charley, the White Mustanger, or, Rocky Mountain Kit's Last Scalp Hunt; The Fighting Trapper, or, Kit Carson to the Rescue; Red Knife, or, Kit Carson's Last Trail;* and *Kit Carson's Bride, or, the Flower of the Apaches.* These fictions had a huge audience much like the people who watch TV thrillers today, interested more in rousing fantasy than in tedious truth. And the readers tended, like today's TV fans, to mistake the one category for the other, violent chimera for dull reality.

The popularity of this fanciful fiction spread rapidly from America to Britain and to Europe. Ireland's Mayne Reid, who served as a captain in the U.S. Army during the Mexican War, turned out romantic tales like *The Rifle Rangers* (1850), *The Scalp Hunters* (1851), and *The War Trail* (1857). Such "Westerns" swept up British readers. Irishman Charles M. O'Donel (the longtime manager of the great Bell Ranch in New Mexico) when he was just a boy was an avid reader of Westerns. Reid's work represented to the young O'Donel, and to many thousands of British readers during the late nineteenth century, "all the promise of the New World," wrote his grandson, Manus Sweetman. Germany's Karl May spun out thrillers with a blond hero called Old Sureshot and Old Shatterhand, who knocked around the American West with a handsome Apache pal named Winnetou. For years, May's fictions were popular with German readers and are still found on their bookshelves today.

Some of this widely read fiction included an idealized white-Indian pair. Long before Karl May dreamed up Old Shatterhand and Winnetou, James Fenimore Cooper had created the white Natty Bumppo and his Indian friend named Chingachgook in "The Leatherstocking Tales." Such fictional combinations carried over into the twentieth century with the Lone Ranger and his faithful sidekick, Tonto. These couplings in books and later in Saturday afternoon movies had a serious side in addition to entertainment value. Various scholars have suggested that such pairings relieved Americans of their guilt over the European-American assault on the New World and her Native people. In any event, such fictions and the Saturday afternoon Western movies they spawned were immensely popular.

Not the great white hero of the dime-novel West, Kit Carson was also not the figure he has become in the revisionist western history of our day. This recent image of "Carson as villain," to repeat Marc Simmons's words for it, is as simplistic as the earlier image of the white hero. By about 1990 Carson had acquired the widespread reputation of a man whose main motivation and usual daily business was to kill Indians. In an effort to "counter this pervasive, negative view," wrote Marc L. Gardner, the New Mexico Endowment for the Humanities invited speakers to a conference planned for Taos in the summer of 1993. The hope was that the speakers would present reliable evidence to support their points of view, and that participants might arrive at tentative conclusions about Carson's actual motivation in relation to Indian people. The object was, as Gardner put it, "to closely examine the fact and fiction of Carson's dealings with various Indian groups."

But the conference did not clear the air. The most painful subject was Carson's part in the Navajo Long Walk. One critic who had agreed to take part refused to attend, apparently after learning that someone who disagreed with him had also been invited. Tribal representatives who were asked to present the Navajo point of view turned down the invitation. Local newspapers made a big fuss out of all this. The *Santa Fe Reporter* ran an article headed "The Second Battle for the West." For months afterward, the *Taos News* ran opinion pieces with titles like "Seminar on Kit Carson Fueled Racism, Ignored Truth" and "History Reveals the Truth: Kit Carson Seminar Defended." A collection of the conference papers later appeared as a book, *Kit Carson: Indian Fighter or Indian Killer?*

The disapproving criticism of Carson began in the late 1960s. In 1972 a professor at Colorado College persuaded the college ROTC unit to remove a display honoring Carson because, according to the professor, Carson was "a terrorist and a killer." An informative book with a definite point of view, Clifford L. Trafzer's *The Kit Carson Campaign: The Last Great Navajo War* suggested that Carson was General Carleton's tool during the Navajo "removal" and that he ought to be remembered with other figures like Davy Crockett, Wyatt Earp, and Billy the Kid because he was an Indian killer. In retelling the story of the Long Walk and the tragedy of Bosque Redondo, two important books expressed Navajo views of Carson and the "removal." Understandably, these are extremely negative. Broderick H. Johnson's *Navajo Stories of the Long Walk Period* presented oral accounts of the Long Walk and of the Bosque Redondo by descendants of Navajo people who suffered the experience. The book also serves, as the foreword states, as a Navajo "version of their history as prepared and interpreted by their own people." The other noteworthy book, Noël Bennett's *Bighorse the*

Warrior, presented Tiana Bighorse's account from memory of her grandfather's experience of the Long Walk. Readers interested in the Navajo story, especially in understanding the effects of the Long Walk and the Bosque Redondo horror on the Navajos themselves, need to read these books.

Today the popular conception of Carson is largely negative. When I told a bright and articulate friend of mine that I was working on a biography of Kit Carson, he asked, "Have you got to the genocidal part yet?" A writer named Bob Scott dismissed Kit's vigorous criticism of Col. John Chivington's murderous action against a Cheyenne Indian camp on Sand Creek in Colorado in 1864 by asserting that Carson himself "was personally responsible for the starvation and freezing deaths of thousands of Navajos." Such heavy criticism has even reached public television. Tom Dunlay wrote that a folk-singer, after explaining on a TV program that he had talked with a Navajo about Carson's part in the removal, decided that Kit was a demon. "[His] song depicted Carson," wrote Dunlay, "as having undertaken the campaign against the Navajos on his own initiative, apparently knowing that he had thereby damned himself."

Even thoughtful scholars, generally well-informed people trained to consider a subject seriously, write of Carson as if he were little more than a scoundrel of the worst sort. In his recent best seller *Blood and Thunder: An Epic of the American West,* Hampton Sides called Carson "a natural born killer," a man who, though "loyal, honest, and kind," talked "with a clinical lack of emotion, and . . . a hit man's sense of aesthetics." Aaron Sachs, a highly respected young environmental historian from Cornell University, in his acclaimed book, *The Humboldt Current: Nineteenth-Century Exploration and the Roots of American Environmentalism,* defined Carson in just one sentence. "Trigger-happy Carson was one of [Frémont's] most trusted men," wrote Sachs, as if Carson were little more than a harebrained simpleton with a gun. If Kit had been trigger-happy, he'd have died young. The primitive powder and ball rifles border men used were slow to reload after firing. Every single shot had to count. Still, though, the one-liners continue to appear. In a new book from the Edinburgh University Press entitled *The American West: Competing Visions,* authors Karen R. Jones and John Wills wrote, "The gun skills of outlaws Kit Carson, Billy the Kid, and Jesse James made national folklore." Kit Carson, little more than another "outlaw" with "gun skills"? Serious scholars as well as general readers need to look at the evidence critically before deciding who Kit Carson was. Whoever he may have been, he surely was more than a simpleminded rascal with a rifle.

Of course he cannot be absolved of his responsibility for human life while he was a field commander during the Mescalero and Navajo campaigns, or elsewhere. Neither, if one respects the search for truth, should it be said that he was simply an Indian killer, plain as that. For years, as we shall see, he lived among and worked successfully with Indian people. He learned their languages. He represented the Utes as their U.S. government agent. He married an Arapaho woman named Waa-nibe. She and Kit had two daughters together. After Waa-nibe's death, Carson placed Adaline, the older of the girls, with his relatives in Missouri where she could receive schooling and a proper upbringing. In Missouri, Adaline learned to read and to write, a most unusual education for a half-Indian woman at that time.

Carson's treatment of Adaline was unusually responsible behavior for a father of his day and place. It appears he wanted his half-Arapaho daughter to have a more secure life than he had had, and he wanted her to learn to read and to write. He was then making a living as a hunter on the High Plains. Such men lived as nomads. They followed the migrations of buffalo and other big animals. They traveled among some very rough men, men who often deserted their children of Indian wives. Clearly, Carson chose not to drag Adaline around with him from hunting camp to hunting camp. And he never deserted her.

Preface

Like most human beings, he did have decent qualities. However, unlike other famous westerners such as Davy Crockett and "Buffalo Bill" Cody, he was characteristically self-effacing. He never advertised himself, for good *or* for bad. He certainly never presented a fictional self the public would buy, as Bill Cody did so successfully with his "Wild West Show." Thus the "real" Carson is hard to characterize largely because he seldom if ever took credit for decent things he did, never said much about himself either way. The biographer's job is to find the balance of qualities, good and bad, in this elusive man. David Roberts suggested the extent of the difficulty, "to disentangle the dime-novel hero from the real man. It is far easier to imagine Kit Carson as played by Clint Eastwood than by the historical Christopher Carson."

Today Carson's name appears everywhere in New Mexico and elsewhere across the West. There are Kit Carson Cafes; Kit Carson Motels; a Kit Carson Club in Carson City, Nevada; Carson National Forest in New Mexico; and Fort Carson, Colorado. The New Mexico Endowment for the Humanities sponsors an actor who impersonates Col. Christopher Carson as the commander of the First New Mexico Volunteers. The Masonic Grand Lodge of New Mexico offers the Kit Carson Award every year for public service, for Carson was a Mason and a founding member of the Montezuma Lodge of Santa Fe. Even at Fort Canby, where the Long Walk began, a street is named for the man. Edging the west side of the old fort's grounds, Kit Carson Avenue runs northerly up the ridge beyond. A green metal sign with white letters marks the street. The sign has been defaced on one side.

Ask people who Kit Carson was. Most suspect that he was not the great white hero of dime novels, but a real border man of some sort—a trapper, a guide, a hunter, a mountain man, a frontiersman. Some think that he was good and that he was larger than life, others that he was just a killer, even genocidal. Ask when he lived, and they aren't sure, except that it was a long time ago. Among adult Navajos, opinions

xxvi

usually remain extremely negative, based on the stories of the old peoples' recollections of the horrors of the Long Walk and of the Bosque Redondo.

Driving toward Canyon de Chelly on the Navajo Nation late one July morning, I picked up a teenage hitchhiker. Before he climbed out at a convenience store in Chinle, we had the following talk.

"You have any horses?" I asked.

"Three horses. My dad, he has eight!"

"Good horses?"

"Good horses!"

"You ever hear of Kit Carson?"

"Yep."

"Was he a good guy or a bad guy?"

"To white guys he was a good guy. To Navajos he was a bad guy."

So. Kit Carson. Who was he? This book-length essay presents him as a man of his culture and a product of his times. His ancestors were Scots-Irish. Thus he could be duty-bound and caring, but he could also take violent action quickly, for he grew up and lived among people whose ancestors all the way back to the Scots and English border country had used physical force and had even gone to war almost reflexively to defend themselves from enemies. My model is Bil Gilbert's fine biography *Westering Man: The Life of Joseph Walker, Master of the Frontier.* Like the Scots-Irish Joe Walker, Carson was a border man, one who mastered the rules of living on America's borders, those fluid, highly unstable regions where people of different races, cultures, and languages met, mixed, and lived together, and where they often fought, sometimes against each other, sometimes together, for possession of land, home, and hunting rights as well as for honor and rank within their group.

On such borders, Carson was skilled, thorough, scrupulous, pragmatic. Characteristically, he helped other people, whoever they might be, if they were harmless and in need. He helped women and children, and he mourned their death or injury. He killed if he considered it necessary to protect, to possess, or to punish, although such instances were usually in "kill or be killed" situations. Several times, saved only by sheer luck or destiny, he himself was very nearly killed. Upon occasion he appears to have killed with zeal, as if briefly out of control, for the moment lost or abandoned to an overwhelming pressure of dark internal hurt and rage. As a young man especially, he was not above getting revenge, customary with his Scots-Irish border people. So far as I can tell, however, he *never* killed simply because the opponents were of a different race or culture. It might be argued that his relations with the Blackfeet were an exception to this rule, but the Blackfeet of that day made it a point to be deadly enemies to *everybody*, a fact that was widely known and respected.

Besides telling the story of Carson's life, this essay states the case for my conviction that Carson, educated by his experience on America's western borders, matured intellectually and ethically as he grew older. To illustrate the story, to be fair to all sides, and to encourage readers to think before making up their minds, I have selected instances that reveal him as humane and responsible and others that show him as violent and aggressive. My hope is to stimulate more thoughtful writing about him than the cardboard fictions of the nineteenth century or the simplistic negative characterizations of recent years. He was, I think, a common man of mind and feeling, a human being of his day and place, misrepresented in his own time as a great white hero, and in ours as just another damned killer.

Acknowledgments

I shall always be indebted to the following people who provided essential help of many kinds over the past four or five years: Betsy Stepanovich, Jessie Tillman, Alex Ricciardelli, Bob Doeling, John Crow, Pamela Reeves, Andrea Jaquez, Terry Humble, Eileen M. Sullivan, Susan Berry, Curtis Fort, Joy L. Poole, Fred Brock, Robert White, Cherie Salmon, Dusty and Pat Hunt, Dean Foster, Elroy Limmer, Richard Felger, Silke Schneider, Julian Lee, John van Horn, Russ Kleinman, and Lee Burke, who gave me an important article on Carson in Missouri and a photograph of Carson's home in Taos taken in the nineteenth century. Marc Simmons, the *real* Carson scholar, gave me essential guidance and information. Freelance copyeditor Maya Allen-Gallegos, managing editor Steven B. Baker, and publicity manager Sandy See helped greatly in getting this book to publication.

Without the advice and continual support of the senior editor of this series, Dick Etulain, I feel sure that this book would never have been completed.

My niece Leslie Remley Wang and her husband, Gene Wang, bought a total of three computers for my use in writing *Kit Carson.* The first burned up because of a defective

Acknowledgments

battery, the second wore out, and the third, fortunately, is still operating. I shall always appreciate Leslie and Gene's help, as well as the love and support of their beautiful children, Andrew and Sally.

To all of these people, my thanks ever!

Also, in memory of those longtime friends who made my life better and my work easier—Dean Byron K. Trippett, Bob Petty, Bob Keedy, Aunt Sally Remley, Grandpa Remley, Guy Tremaine, Margie Jones, Bob and Mary Ellen Simpers, Phillip and Audrey Madrid, Dave Bedard, Larry Lancashire, Rusty Lancashire, Len Cox, Hugh Johnson, Prof. Russel B. Nye, Don and Abby Hofman, Evelyn Yates, and Frank Kirschner— and for Mike, Julie, and Sarah Nash. God bless them all!

Kit Carson

1

A Young Boy in the Schoolhouse

Born in Kentucky in December 1809, Kit spent his boyhood at Cooper's Fort on the Missouri River. In later years he joked about his days in the log schoolroom Captain Cooper had set aside for the children of the fort. John Savage was their teacher. Legend is that Daniel Boone himself had brought Savage and a box of books out to Cooper's on the way home from a trip to St. Louis to sell deerskins. No one knows how long Kit went to school, or what he learned. Probably he could "figger" with numbers using a stub of pencil on a board. Everybody could do that. As for reading and writing, however, he learned nothing. "I was a young boy in the schoolhouse when the cry came 'Indians!'" he said years later, smiling. "I jumped to my rifle and threw down my spelling book and there it lies!"

Instead of learning to read, Kit mastered the rifle and other simple tools required to survive on America's borders where he would live out his life. His illiteracy would become a severe handicap later, after he joined government service as a guide, courier, Indian agent, and soldier. Curiously, he had a knack for picking up spoken languages besides the backwoods English he learned as a child on the Missouri border. Within a year of running away from home to Santa Fe in 1826, he spoke Spanish just by having lived among Spanish-speaking people. Later he learned the languages of the mountain and plains tribes he would live among. With the universal sign language of these diverse Native people, he became a speaker, negotiator, and diplomat of great skill. He never forgot features of the landscape or the detail of things he could see or hear or put to use with his hands. But he could never write down any of his vast, thoroughly practical knowledge on paper or fathom anything on the written or printed page.

The daily realities of life in western Missouri, where men cleared land with broadaxes, plowed around stumps to plant corn, stood guard against American Indians, and hunted deer with long rifles, did not encourage growing boys to learn their books. Besides, Kit had a hard childhood. And he was a rebellious teenage boy. At age sixteen he broke contract with the saddlemaker his mother had apprenticed him to and ran away from home. One story has it that his father, Lindsey, wanted him to become a lawyer. The law was a good profession for getting rich in a time when land was cheap, border settlement was booming, and shifty speculators bought and sold vast acreages, sometimes at great profit. But Kit showed no interest in books, and Lindsey was killed in a terrible accident. Soon Kit's mother married again. Kit and his brothers quickly went head-to-head with their stepfather, and then moved out, or may have been kicked out. Kit went off to live for a time with an older brother who was farming nearby. But that arrangement soon ended too.

Trying to bring the boy up as best she could, his mother apprenticed him to a local saddlemaker in a line of work always in demand in Kit's time, especially in Franklin, Missouri, where his family lived. The Santa Fe Trail started in Franklin. Horses and mules passed through here by the hundreds, probably thousands, heading for or returning from Santa Fe, where manufactured goods from the East were easily traded for Spanish mules and silver coin. A saddlemaker spent most of his hours repairing saddles, stacks of broken harness, and busted pack equipment, all of it made of leather, hand-stitched over wooden saddle and pack trees. He also made bridles and halters, and harness and reins. There was always plenty of work for a saddlemaker and his apprentice around busy town centers like Franklin.

But Kit soon got bored stitching leather. He was unhappy over the contract his mother and a local judge had drawn up for him. Of course he had had no say in the matter. By the summer of 1826 he decided to run off with a caravan bound for Santa Fe. One late night, as the story goes, he "borrowed" a mule from a neighbor and lit out. Although it appears that he struggled with himself for a year or two afterward, feeling guilty about having run off or just being homesick, he did not return to Franklin until after his mother had died and after his sisters had married and had children of their own.

In 1856, thirty years after he ran away, Kit decided to tell the story of his life. Long before then, however, he was known locally in the West as an experienced hunter and trapper. His real prominence outside the West, however, began when John Charles Frémont employed him in the 1840s as a general hand, hunter, and guide to his first three western exploring expeditions. Frémont's colorfully written government reports of the expeditions went through several commercial printings, which circulated in the East and in Europe as best sellers of their day. They turned a plain and capable Christopher Carson into an early-day celebrity, the famous "Kit Carson." The reports pictured him in colorful scenes as *the* master horseman, always-fearless defender, and ever-reliable friend.

In one such scene, Frémont described Carson horseback, protecting the men of the expedition from hostile Native warriors. In Frémont's words, when a terrified member of the expedition of 1842 came "spurring up in great haste, shouting Indians! Indians," Carson leaped up bareback and rode off alone to look for the enemy. "Kit Carson," Frémont wrote, sprang "upon one of the hunting horses, crossed the river, and galloped off into the opposite prairies to obtain some certain intelligence of [the Indians'] movements. Mounted on a fine horse, without a saddle, and scouring bareheaded over the prairies, Kit was one of the finest pictures of a horse-man I have ever seen." By reading such prose, thousands of readers got the picture of Carson as the heroic horseman and fearless hunter of Indians. It hardly mattered that the report was false. The band of Indians turned out to be only a herd of elk. John Wayne himself could not have done more with less.

As early as 1847, when Kit traveled to Washington carrying official letters, Frémont's reports had made him famous, a fame multiplied by his connection (through Frémont) with Frémont's lovely wife, Jessie, and her powerful father, Sena-tor Thomas Hart Benton. An article that appeared in the *Washington Union* of June 16, 1847, and in the *Supplement to the Connecticut Courant* of July 3 described Kit as "one of the best of those noble and original characters" produced by the American West, a man of "genuine simplicity and truthfulness of disposition . . . generosity, bravery, and single-heartedness to a degree rarely found in society." Thus journalists placed Carson in the company of "the best" of westerners: capable, courageous, generous, humble, a true "original." He was Cooper's Natty Bumppo all over again, and more.

Soon the dime novelists began pumping out their fanci-ful Carsons. As early as 1848 one such invention appeared in *Holden's Dollar Magazine*. In 1849 came Emerson Bennett's *The Prairie Flower*, and in 1850 a sequel, *Leni Leoti, or, Adven-tures in the Far West*. Bennett's Carson kills two charging In-dians at the same time. He buries "his knife in the breast of one, and at the same moment, his tomahawk in the brain of the other." A moment later, "like an imbodied [*sic*] spirit of battle," Kit "thundered past . . . on his powerful charger," and seizing the scalp lock of a warrior "in one hand," with "the other [he] completely severed his head from his body, which he bore triumphantly away." Also in 1849—just in time to feed the gold rush fever—appeared Charles A. Averill's *Kit Carson, the Prince of the Gold Hunters, or, The Adventures of the Sacramento*. Now the pasteboard Indian killer became the pasteboard gold hunter, a line of work that Kit never seriously followed. But that didn't matter. Averill, like Bennett and the other fictioneers, never let truth block the way to book sales. They pictured Kit as an Indian fighter who killed "the red varmints" and slaughtered "the savage critters" left and right as if that were his mission in life. This was the flimflam Carson created for people with pocket change and the inclination to read.

Then in 1858 the first biography appeared. It was titled *The Life and Adventures of Kit Carson, the Nestor of the Rocky Mountains, from Facts Narrated by Himself.* The name DeWitt C. Peters appears on the spine and title page as author, although just who actually wrote the book remained a mystery for years, and there are still elements of mystery about its circumstances. Dr. Peters became acquainted with Carson during 1854–56 while both men lived in Taos. Peters was stationed there as an army surgeon, Carson as the Ute Indian agent. A handwritten manuscript of Carson's life story, which Kit dictated (it is now known) to his clerk, John Mostin, turned up many years after the publication of the 1858 biography in, of all places, Paris, France, inside a trunk that held papers left by one of Dr. Peters's sons, William, after William's death. This autobiographical manuscript, today located at the Newberry Library in Chicago, contains various changes, corrections, and suggestions in Dr. Peters's handwriting. It is supposed now that Peters used this autobiographical dictation as a basis for the 1858 *Life and Adventures of Kit Carson.* However that may be, the great Carson scholar Harvey L. Carter characterized this heavily padded biography as filled with "excessive panegyrics and tiresome moralizing." When someone showed Carson the book in 1858 or 1859, without doubt reading him a passage or two from it, he remarked that Peters had "laid it on a leetle too thick."

Long before that, however, people had told Kit about the Carson exaggerations circulating in print. He was embarrassed by these exaggerations because he was generally a soft-spoken man who did not want to be the center of attention.

Probably wishing to clear the record, he sat down with John Mostin in 1856 in Taos and began to dictate his own story as *he* remembered it. He said all that he had to say of his first year and a half in one sentence: "I was born on the 24 Decr. 1809 in Madison County, Kentucky."

Kit said nothing more of Kentucky or of his family's origins. Like Joe Walker, however, and a great many other border people of his time and place, he was of Scots-Irish ancestry. He was also a straight product of his ancestors' culture. The shared customs, beliefs, and practices of his forebears prepared him and his kind for life on America's borders. "The movement of people [westward] was more than simply the migration of individuals," wrote historian Malcolm Rohrbough. "It involved partly the transference of an old society, partly the creation of a new one." By "old society" Rohrbough meant the sum total of "the ways in which people related to one another, [their] common experiences, present circumstances, future hopes, and . . . shared values and priorities." Daniel Walker Howe put this matter even more simply and clearly. "Participants in the Great Migration [from the British Isles]," he wrote, "remained loyal, often fiercely loyal, to their cultural heritages and resolved to re-create them on the frontier."

Forced out of Britain by greedy landlords and English meanness of every sort, Kit's people had first migrated with masses of other "lowlanders" from the lowlands of Scotland and England to Northern Ireland (also called Ulster) during the seventeenth century. The lowlands lie along the border between the Scots highlands to the north and England to the south. Americans gave the name "Scotch-Irish" or "Scots-Irish" to these lowland Scots who came to America by way of Northern Ireland in the eighteenth century. The name was a way to distinguish them from the Scots and English immigrants who were also arriving in wave upon wave from elsewhere in the British Isles during the same years. The term set the "Scots-Irish" apart from the "Irish" proper, people largely of southern Ireland, mostly Roman Catholic, many of them urban. Most of these Catholic Irish arrived later. The Scots-Irish like the Carsons were Protestant, mostly Presbyterian, of very strong opinion and combative as hell about it, to put the matter mildly. They hated not only the English with their "Anglican" Church and their voracious landlords but also the Scots highlanders and the native Irish, both of whom were largely Celtic and Roman Catholic.

Kit's mother's name was Rebecca Robinson. His grandmother's was Eleanor McDuff. His father's first wife's name was Lucy Bradley. All of these were common Scots, Scots-Irish, and English names. The Robinsons, McDuffs, and Bradleys were probably from the lowlands and from Ulster, although it is possible they came from elsewhere in the British Isles. A rural people, the Scots-Irish were farmers, stockmen, and small tradesmen whose parents and grandparents had been forced to rent, or to steal, a piece of land on which to scratch out a living in the lowlands. Mostly refugees of warring tribes and clans, they had drifted onto the poorest and thinnest of soils. There they lived on a shifting borderland between testy Catholic Celtic Scots to the north and mean-spirited Anglicans to the south. Arriving in Ulster later, they survived on grit in a bind between their stingy English landlords and the embattled native Celtic Irish.

When not fighting the Scots, the English, or, later, in Ulster, the native Irish, they fought among themselves. Generation after generation of them in the lowlands had mastered few skills other than how to use their weapons. Violence rose quickly in their hearts. They made good soldiers, and still do. If they learned much more than how to fight, it was about handling bony livestock and scraping cabbages and onions out of a stony garden on poor land. As for "the arts" and "learning," they had none. Scotland had its Edinburgh, England its Oxford and Cambridge, but the lowlands had no university where borderland people might study the arts and sciences. In *Westering Man: The Life of Joseph Walker*, Bil Gilbert wrote of these people: "For centuries . . . as both participants and sullen bystanders whose welfare was inconsequential to either [the Scots or the English] they were regularly plundered, imprisoned, raped and massacred." Gilbert called the lowland Scots "the disposable people." These were Kit Carson's forebears.

Their rich English betters, considering them no more than a dangerous nuisance, had thought of resettling these disposable people somewhere else. Since titled Englishmen held the land in Northern Ireland, they decided to rent it to the scrappy lowlanders. If the poor could be resettled in Ulster, they might outfight the native Celtic Irish, born fighters themselves, and force them off the land. There was no one better suited to this nasty job than these ignorant, quarrelsome lowland Scots. Besides, these undesirable people were Presbyterians, born enemies of the Anglican Church, which harassed them continually. Kit's people, starting at least with his great-grandfather Alexander Carson, were resolute Presbyterians. Alexander Carson himself was a minister of that faith. Reverend Carson had served his church in Dumfries, a border county in the lowlands.

These Presbyterians were tough-minded Christians, not only because of the poverty and hardship they had endured, but also from the nature of their faith. They were followers of John Knox, the fervently ideological Calvinist thinker and leader, whose faction in the Scots Parliament had outlawed the saying of the Catholic Mass and abolished the pope's authority in Scotland. Parliament had also approved the so-called Scots Confession (1559) and the Westminster Confession (1644), which declared the "true Church," by which of course they meant *their* church, to be "invisible, known only to God, who alone knows whom He has chosen." The Calvinistic God these Presbyterians imagined was omnipotent, judgmental, and unbending without fail. He had from eternity "predestined" each one of his flock to hell or to heaven. All the "good works" performed in this life could avail a man or a woman *nothing* toward salvation in the afterlife. No one could ever know, until judgment day, to which group he had been assigned. Such a demanding faith in an inscrutable God coupled with their everlasting poverty kept believers in a perpetual state of anxiety. Dirt-poor followers of this strong faith, fighters to the core, the lowlanders and Scots-Irish were truly a hardscrabble people.

To add to their anxiety, the Church of England punished them for their nonconformist attitude, their stiff-necked refusal to give in. Nearly as powerful as the king himself, Anglican bishops saw to it that Presbyterians were denied the privileges of other citizens. They could not serve in the king's army and could not hold political or religious offices. Their ministers were forbidden to conduct public services, including marriage. Thus they were driven to be the most independent and resilient Britons of their day. It was first-rate training for a people who would soon be fighting the Indians for possession of land and scratching out a living in the cold forests of North America.

Such people customarily married among their own kind, to men or women from the same neighborhood, family, and clan. Clans carried over all but unchanged from the old country to America's borderlands, where they provided their members with essential support in threatening circumstances just as they had in the lowlands and later in Ulster. Clans consisted of related families who lived in the same region, county, or township, close enough to be reached on the information grapevine in times of trouble and for such essential ceremonies as marriages, baptisms, funerals, and reunions.

Members had the same surname or names. They knew one another as "kinfolk" or "blood kin." They claimed common ancestors, although collateral connections were more important to them than lineal descent. Often not knowing their actual relationship, people would call one another "shirt-tail cousins." Commonly, younger people called each other

"Cousin" so and so. Older members were simply called "Aunt" Mary and "Uncle" Jimmy. Remnants of this and of other clannish customs were still about in the community where I grew up in western Indiana where my Scots-Irish McCain ancestors had settled from Ohio in 1824, "when there were still Indians in the woods," as I remember my elders putting it.

The annual family reunion was an essential occasion. Held one year at Aunt Sally's in town, another year at Clayte and Jennie's farm, and still another out at Uncle Harry and Aunt Alice's place, it was always a great feast and a memorable visit. These gatherings acquainted everyone with new family members who had arrived by birth and by marriage since last year's reunion, while the stories of old times told and retold year after year gave the family its very identity. The tales kept the sense of shared ancestry, mutual belief, and unchanged custom alive and active in molding behavior and faith.

When I was in high school, my barber, when *he* was a young man, had regularly trimmed my Civil War great-grandfather's beard. The barber told me that everyone in town knew the old man. As a successful farmer, for years he and his five or six farming brothers had forgathered in town without fail each Friday (in a social room kept by the local bank for such occasions) in order simply "to visit," as the custom was known. The old veteran always drove his horse and buggy to the First Presbyterian Church on Sundays, and he drove to my great-grandmother's burial service. One of my aunts, a very little girl at the time, rode beside him on that last sad journey. When she started to cry, the old man put his arm around her shoulders and said quietly, "No tears now. No tears." His name was Ambrose, but everyone knew him as "Uncle Amberse." All of these men and women—all the chains of cousins, and uncles, and great-uncles and aunts—were deeply aware of a common bond that supported them. "*We* are farmers and stockmen, *we* are Presbyterian, *we* are family, and by God, *we'll fight ye!*" they might have said. It was that spiny attitude that had stirred their families from the lowlands of Scotland to Ulster, from Ulster to America, then westward on America's borders generation after generation. Kit Carson belonged to exactly such a family.

Preyed upon by the Anglican Church, by politicians, and by treacherous landlords, the fierce lowlanders by thousands had gone off from the lowlands of England and Scotland to Ulster to rent land, to squat on it, or to rustle up a meal somehow. Once in Ulster, they met the same intolerable living conditions as those they hoped to leave behind. Though Americans like to think their ancestors came to the New World seeking liberty and freedom, the Scots-Irish and lowland Scots came *fleeing from* unbearable living conditions back home. In Ulster these conditions had included several seasons of poor crops, higher rents, and a downturn in the linen industry, which employed many of them. "Poverty, Wretchedness, Misery, and Want are become almost universal among them," wrote a correspondent for the *Pennsylvania Gazette* in 1729. "Their griping, avaricious Landlords exercise over them the most merciless Racking Tyranny and Oppression. Hence it is that such swarms of them are driven over to America." Swarm to America they did, not only the Scots-Irish, but other Britons too. Between 1630 and 1660, remarked historian Bernard Bailyn, roughly 210,000 Britons sailed for the New World. And waves of them continued after that. During the 1720s alone, about 50,000 Scots-Irish left Ulster for America.

More than anything else, the Scots-Irish wanted to own a piece of land where they could be self-sufficient, and *be let alone.* They wanted no more rigid officials, established churches, ravenous landlords, or high taxes. "The lure was the land," wrote Malcolm Rohrbough. "[East] of the [Appalachian] mountains [very early] were worn-out fields, high prices, and quit-rents." In a letter to James Madison on November 20, 1784, Richard Henry Lee wrote of the "powerful emigration" of people from Virginia to Kentucky already in

13

the 1780s. He named two of the best reasons: "the desire of removing from heavy taxes and the search for land."

As for land, the cheapest and often the best of it was available beyond settled areas in western Pennsylvania and in Kentucky, Ohio, Indiana, Illinois, and later in Missouri. By taking up remote land, whether by purchase or by squatting on it, as they often did, the Scots-Irish and other European intruders would have to fight the Indians for possession. But experience had long ago taught them how to fight for what they wanted. Thus warring between settlers and Indians over control of the land on the borders would continue throughout Kit Carson's lifetime. One observer noted that the Britons "imagine they can still obtain land for themselves, and their flocks of Cattle at a trifling Rent, or of conquering it from the Indian with the Sword."

The Scots-Irish readily used the sword. Having been treated with violence of every sort in the old country, they had mastered all the ways of responding with it. David Hackett Fischer suggests that violent ways of trying to solve problems (including even wife beating and child thrashing) were an approved "cultural adaptation to the endemic violence" with which these people had lived. It can be said that an *ethic* of violence—of fighting not for the sake of fighting, but of fighting to *win*— was an important element of their culture. "Here was an ethic of violence which had been formed in ambuscades and border raiding," Fischer wrote. "It had nothing to do with combats of chivalry or the idea of war as a gentleman's game." It was fighting to get something they needed or wanted, or to punish for something they had lost, "endemic violence and retributive justice." Even their religion had a large element of violence in it. Their Calvinistic God, though they considered Him just, could be extremely harsh. "God's Mercy" was a blessing they seldom experienced and quickly learned never to expect.

Having gone first to Ulster sometime before 1700 (and perhaps briefly back to England), Kit's great-grandfather

Alexander Carson brought his family to Pennsylvania, where they settled in Lancaster County, probably before 1738. Reverend Carson may also have brought other families over, for ministers might gather their flocks and find passage for the entire group. With him came several sons. The third son, William, was born in Ulster about 1720. William was Kit Carson's grandfather.

When it came time to leave his father's house in Pennsylvania, William Carson followed the flow of Scots-Irish people southwestward from Pennsylvania up the Shenandoah Valley into the Carolinas. He eventually settled in Iredell County, North Carolina, where on December 1, 1761, he registered 692 acres of land from a vast English grant belonging to Lord Granville. William Carson's place lay along both sides of Third Creek in central-western North Carolina not far from present-day Statesville.

Considering that France would not give up her claim to the trans-Appalachian west until she had lost the so-called French and Indian War and had signed the Treaty of Paris (1763), William Carson settled this place very early. The rush into Kentucky over Cumberland Gap would not begin for another fifteen years. This pause was largely due to unresolved problems with France and to the conflict with the Cherokee, Creek, Choctaw, Shawnee, and other Native tribes who hunted over the ground west of the Appalachians. Not until 1775 could James Harrod establish Harrodstown, now Harrodsburg, the first permanent settlement in Kentucky. Daniel Boone founded Boonesborough shortly afterward.

Sometime before registering his Carolina land, William Carson married Eleanor McDuff. Little is known of her or of the couple's life together, but they had six children. Lindsey, born on August 1, 1754, would be Kit's father. One story has it that William married Eleanor in a log church. Very likely this is so, for wherever Presbyterians went, they took their faith with them. That meant holding services regularly, and it meant putting up a log hut for a church as soon as possible wherever a settlement sprouted. Because William Carson's father was a minister, it seems likely that William and Eleanor were married in a Presbyterian service, at home or in a log church.

During the so-called Great Awakening, a flood of intense religious fervor that swept through the American woodlands after about 1740 with George Whitefield's enthusiastic preaching, Protestant churches often split apart, one faction unhappy with others. Besides "Old Light" and "New Light" Presbyterians, there were Baptists of several persuasions for the thousands of English-speaking settlers to choose from. There was also a host of German, Dutch, and other northern European Protestant groups: Lutheran, German Reformed, Dutch Reformed, and so on, not to mention the Methodists, whose souls caught fire in England with the Wesleys' preaching. The immigrants, particularly the English speaking, were, if nothing else, an individualistic and an argumentative people. On the subject of religion they could be especially ornery, debating the fine points at great length. What someone said of Presbyterians might have been said of most other English-speaking Protestant churchmen in early America: "Take one Presbyterian and you have a theologian. Take two and you have a theologian and a reformer. Take three and you have a theologian, a reformer, and a dissenter."

Historian Bernard Bailyn noted that the number of Scots-Irish in America after 1717 and before 1760 reached 100,000 to 150,000. The U.S. census of 1790 indicates that 83 percent of Kentucky's population that year was "White." Of this, 42.8 percent was English, 20.6 percent Scots and Scots-Irish, 5.6 percent Welsh, and 7.5 percent Irish. Thus by 1790 an astounding total of 76.5 percent of the European population of Kentucky was from the British Isles! It can be assumed that the large majority of these Britons were non-Anglican Church Protestants. And that was in Kentucky about thirty years after Kit's grandfather William registered land in North Carolina. This information gives some sense of the overwhelming number of English-speaking Protestant people who engulfed the eastern woodlands and the Ohio Valley during this period.

Kit Carson was born of these people in Kentucky. Raised in Missouri among the same people, he absorbed their values and their culture. As his great-grandfather Alexander was a preacher of long experience, it can be assumed that he read his Bible. Very likely he could also write more than his own name. Perhaps he even outlined his sermons and wrote letters to family in Ulster and to friends in the ministry in England. If so, he would have kept quill pens, a bottle of ink, and sheets of paper on a shelf near the family's precious Bible. He would have read from the Bible to his wife and children daily, the children memorizing short passages and repeating them aloud. If father or mother could write, they taught the children to write more than their own names. Possibly the children had a few months of schooling from an itinerant schoolmaster as Kit is supposed to have had from John Savage at Cooper's Fort.

All the Carson children of each generation learned to work. Everyone "did chores." Hard physical labor and the risks that went with it were the way of life in the woodlands and on later American borderlands farther west. Eleanor and the girls did all the cabin chores and often helped with the field work too. Older girls looked after the younger boys and girls. Still breastfeeding the latest baby, Eleanor supervised her daughters while she spun woolen yarn and flaxen thread. She could do several things at a time. The cradle my Scots-Irish great-great-grandmother Sarah McCain put her children in is worn on one side where she touched it with her toe to keep it moving while she used her hands for other chores, like stitching torn linen or carding wool. Using homemade waxed linen thread, she stitched up the worn binding of a book of religious tracts she had treasured since she was a girl. This little book and her Bible, in which she entered the names and birthdates of her children as they came along, centered her down.

The older Carson children carried water in a wooden bucket from a spring or a creek nearby. Everyone pitched in, toting kindling in from outside, baking bread on the hearth, chopping wood, churning butter. In the summertime one of the girls put the butter and buttermilk in wooden bowls or in crocks beside the spring to keep cool. Eleanor and the older daughters washed clothes in the creek, or boiled them in a kettle with lye soap, made by boiling wood ash and hog fat together. They carded wool, spun thread from wool or from flax, then wove a lightweight cloth of a woolen weft and a linen warp. The cloth was called linsey woolsey, and it was used to make clothing for the entire family.

The girls learned to milk as soon as they could walk, for "keeping the cow" was a woman's business. A healthy girl with a good milk cow was a very marriageable young woman. My Scots-Irish ancestor James McCain died on his farm in Basking Ridge, New Jersey, in 1754. He is buried under the great oak tree in the Presbyterian cemetery there. He willed each of his two single daughters, Catherine and Nelly, should they be as yet unmarried at the time of his death, "fourty [*sic*] pounds in money or the value of it when she comes of age and a good Cow."

Kit's grandfather William and his sons worked his North Carolina farm from daylight until after dark. When William's son Lindsey was about nineteen, William died suddenly. According to a family story, his death came at the end of a day's work in the field from drinking too much water from a spring. Another story says that he died after he drank from a well in a churchyard. Summer weather in North Carolina is very hot. William may have had a heatstroke. If he was born in Ulster about 1720 and if Lindsey was about nineteen, then William was close to fifty-three years old at the time of his death about 1773. A family story has it that he was buried in Morrison's Cemetery, a half mile from Concord Church.

Biographers say that Lindsey served the American side during the Revolutionary War, although information is vague about exactly what he did. After the war he and his brother Robert went to South Carolina where Lindsey married Lucy Bradley. He brought her back to North Carolina where they settled and farmed and began raising children until about 1792. Following the pattern of the Carsons and of their Scots-Irish people, they moved west again in 1792 or 1793, this time to Madison County, Kentucky. There they settled near present-day Richmond, a little south of Lexington. Although they might be called early settlers in Kentucky, they were not among the earliest. Malcolm J. Rohrbough presents a table showing that from 150 inhabitants (presumably of European blood) in 1775, Kentucky's population grew to 8,000 in 1782; 30,000 in 1784; and 50,000 in 1787. According to the U.S. census of 1790, Kentucky's population had by then reached 73,677.

Lucy's fifth child, Sophie, was born in Kentucky in 1793. Lucy died not long after giving birth to Sophie, probably of what was called "childbed fever." She had come west from the Holston River in North Carolina, across Cumberland Gap over Daniel Boone's Wilderness Road, traveling with Lindsey and their four children, William, Sarah, Andrew, and Moses. Pregnant with Sophie, Lucy probably walked, then rode a horse when she needed to rest. In his classic *History of Kentucky*, Thomas D. Clark described these processions: "Adventurous men came westward walking at the head and rear . . . driving cattle, sheep, and hogs. Women and children formed the center, driving pack horses loaded with household necessities."

Since their days in the lowlands, the Scots-Irish had become a moving people. Their moves were nearly always toward the west. Speaking for most of them, Magdalena McCain recalled a day shortly after her marriage to Daniel McCain at Lebanon, Ohio, in 1826: "When we turned out to seek our fortunes in the world," she wrote, "we thought it best, while we were going, to emigrate still further west." Daniel and Magdalena McCain moved from Ohio to Carroll County, Indiana, in 1826, the

19

same year Kit Carson ran away from the saddlemaker in Missouri to join a wagon train bound west for Santa Fe.

In 1796 Lindsey Carson married again, this time to Rebecca Robinson of Greenbriar County, Virginia. Lindsey and Rebecca would have nine children, six born in Kentucky, the others in Missouri. In Kentucky, Elizabeth, Nancy, Robert, Matilda, and Hamilton preceded Kit. Apparently, ten children from Lindsey's two marriages lived at home when Kit was born. Such crowded cabins were very common in the woodlands. Anyone who couldn't be of help was only in the way, so the small children would be run outside, particularly during birth times. Small children being fascinated with such matters, Kit's brothers and sisters, cold as the weather was, no doubt huddled outside, whispering to each other, listening for baby's first cry. My mother's great-uncle George recalled my grandfather's birth in a woodshed on a farm in Michigan in February 1877. Run outside, little George waited, his ear to the shed wall. "I listened. I listened," he said, "and dreckly I heard him go Nyaaaaaaaa. And I knowed he was born!" Something like this scene must have repeated itself countless times outside log cabins and sod houses on America's borderlands.

For 250 pounds money, Lindsey bought 115 acres of land from John Berry on November 25, 1801. The land was located "at the corner of Tate Creek and Groggin's Lane in Madison County," Kentucky. Here Kit was born and lived for the first year or so of his life. Though an unconfirmed story has it that he was born in North Carolina while his parents were home on a visit, Kit was certain he was born in Kentucky.

Carson family reminiscence has it that Lindsey and his older sons starting logging to make an income about this time. If so, the Carsons joined other woodsmen in a common occupation of the day—harvesting the great middle-western forests of black walnut, cherry, oak of several varieties, American chestnut, and yellow poplar, locally called tulip poplar. Great rafts of oak, chestnut, and poplar logs were assembled, then floated down the Ohio and Mississippi rivers to Memphis, Natchez, and New Orleans, where the rafts were broken up and sold. Giant stumps marked the woodlands after the woodsmen's work in Kentucky, Ohio, and Indiana. According to my great-aunt Sally, her grandmother Sarah McCain remembered stumps big enough that two couples could dance a square to a fiddler's tune on just one stump on a Saturday night.

In the South the great logs that made up the rafts were sawn into lumber for framing houses, barns, and outbuildings. After observing the "peculiar institution" of slavery and sampling the sinful pleasures of New Orleans and of "Natchez-under-the-Hill," raftsmen returned home horseback or afoot over the Natchez Trace across Mississippi and Tennessee to Kentucky and the Old Northwest. Kit was a baby then. By the time he was four or five years old, he must have listened with wonder to the stories his brothers and half brothers told about their travels. Half brother Moses Carson had really good stories. Big Mose was a wanderer and an adventurer all his life, taking an active part in several important historical events. Listening to Mose's stories, Kit surely caught the travel fever.

Working in the timber and building rafts were obvious ways for Kit's enterprising father and older half brothers to make a living. Rafting, flatboating, and keelboating flourished in Kentucky where the streams drained northerly into the Ohio River. There were as yet no railroads. Thus in Kentucky, as in Ohio, Indiana, Illinois, and in Missouri where Kit would grow up, men made the network of rivers do what the railroads would do later—transport the country's resources to market. The rafts the men built might run an acre in size, or even more. Once made up, they were loaded with every kind of local produce, including livestock. Besides horses and cows, there were pens full of sheep, pigs, goats, and cages of chickens. There were barrels of pickled pork and kegs of whiskey, shelled corn, wheat and flour, bacon, hams, hemp, tobacco, apples, and walnuts. There was the exotic plant ginseng, called "sang." Dried, powdered, taken by the pinch, or added to food or water, sang was a seemingly magical cure for almost every ailment. Among other wonderful qualities, it was supposed to have the power "to make an old man young." People walking in the woods and children at play kept a sharp eye out for it because sang brought good cash money from local buyers and at markets in New Orleans, Wheeling, Pittsburgh, Cincinnati, and Louisville.

John Van Horn, whose Dutch Protestant ancestor moved from Pennsylvania to Kentucky's Big Sandy River in 1815, about six years after Kit was born, remarked that early Kentucky raftsmen started out by building a raft on the banks of the nearest creek. Then they built dams spaced along the network of larger creeks downstream until they had a series of ponds. By breaking the first dam, they caused a freshet that carried the raft down to the next pond, and so on until it reached deep water. Eventually the raft floated out onto a big river like the Tennessee, the Cumberland, or the Kentucky, and finally to the Ohio, the beautiful river the French had named "la Belle Rivière." Along the way, the size of the raft was increased as the ponds widened and deepened. This river trade was already well along by the time Kit's father, Lindsey, arrived in Madison County in 1792 or 1793. At the time, there was no other effective way for the woodsmen and farmers west of the Appalachians to market their products to the outside world except down the river system to New Orleans.

Kit's first home was his parents' cabin on Tate Creek. If Lindsey's family settled in Madison County by late summer after leaving the Holston River in the spring, they wintered like other newcomers, in a log lean-to with buffalo hides or deerskins hung so as to cover the open side and hold in the heat. A smoky log fire would be kept burning twenty-four hours during cold weather. As soon as winter broke in February or March, Lindsey and the older boys would be out with broadaxes, cutting and notching logs for the new cabin, before they went to clearing land for the plow. If it was a type very common on the borders, the cabin started as a one-room structure of logs notched on the ends, with a wattle and daub chimney on a flat hearth. Such simple one-room houses were common in the lowlands of Scotland. Most immigrants built in a style they were acquainted with. By cutting a door in the back wall and attaching a room with a shed roof, Lindsey could add covered space as needed. As the family grew, a loft could be floored for storage space or as a place for the children to sleep. A notched pole made it easy for the children to climb up to the loft at night and down again in the morning.

Another familiar type of cabin on the heavily wooded borders was the dogtrot or "turkey trot." Two one-room log structures were built twelve or fifteen feet apart. A roof was added covering the separate rooms and the space between them. A door opened out into the covered space from each room. This space served as a sheltered breezeway called the dogtrot. The dogtrot cabin was a great improvement over the one-room cabin. It provided a convenient shelter for a mother and her daughters when they were outside hulling beans, grinding corn, sorting dried apples, weaving, spinning, carding wool, or washing clothes in warm weather. In cold weather it protected the man or woman who split and stacked the firewood, butchered a hog, or skinned out a deer. In fall and winter, boys drove the team in under the dogtrot to unload firewood from a wagon or from a skid called a mudboat. Many a woman has milked her cow and watched over her new calf summer and winter sheltered by the dogtrot. Harvey L. Carter claimed that the Carson cabin had a puncheon floor of split logs laid side by side with the flat side up. If so, that would have been truly deluxe, for most cabins had floors of packed earth. "A puncheon floor in them days was somethin' folks bragged about!" Kentuckian John Van Horn insisted.

Another type of log house often seen was a two-story structure with a fireplace and a chimney on one end. This was also an improvement on the one-room style. In *Kit Carson: A Pattern for Heroes*, Thelma S. Guild and Harvey L. Carter describe Lindsey Carson's cabin with pegs on the walls for clothes, elk antlers hung up to cradle the rifle, and that deluxe puncheon floor. Such comfort, if it were so, suggests that the Carsons meant to stay put. If they did plan to stay in Madison County, they would certainly have planted peach and apple trees near the cabin. If they moved to an already settled area, grafts would have been available from someone who had arrived earlier. John Chapman, the famous "Johnny Appleseed," planted orchards from seeds on the fertile soils drained by the Muskingum River in Ohio at least as early as 1806.

Women often brought their own grafted stock with them, seeing to it that the bundle of grafts was tied with great care on top of the loaded packhorse before leaving camp each morning. Recently married, Sarah McCain carried a bundle of apple grafts all the way from Ohio to western Indiana when she and her young husband moved there in 1824 to build their cabin home. She wrapped the grafts in linsey-woolsey, then wet the cloth in camp every evening along the trail to keep the roots damp. Ancient remnants of apple, peach, plum, and apricot trees still can be found scattered across the Midwest as far as western Missouri and eastern Kansas where the woodlands fritter out into the Great Plains. They mark the many places where border men and women of Carson's kind long ago built their cabin homes, and decided, for a time anyway, to stay put.

2

The Only Use for a Saddle

Kit's father sold the homeplace on Tate Creek on October 6, 1811, for $1,000. He then moved his family to the "Boone's Lick" country along the Missouri River in Howard County, Missouri. The Boone's Lick was a region named for a salt spring where Daniel Boone's son Nathan boiled off salt from around 1805 to 1811. Carson biographers believe the Carson family left Kentucky in the spring of 1811 or 1812. In her book *The Road to Santa Fe*, Kate L. Gregg said that Lindsey Carson and Col. Hale Talbot went out to Missouri in 1810. If so, it was no doubt to look over the prospects for land farther west. After a year on Loutre Island, the two men went still farther west to the Boone's Lick. There they pulled into Kinkead's Fort, which was under attack by Indians at the time.

About 1811 Lindsey returned to Kentucky for his family, packed them up, and headed west again. Back in the Boone's Lick, he stopped in Cooper's Bottom near Cooper's Fort. There the family chose a site for a cabin and farm but couldn't settle on the place because of American Indian attacks. During the next few years Lindsey and his older sons Andrew and Moses fought in Capt. Sarshall Cooper's Rangers, as well as in a volunteer militia from Kinkead's Fort nearby. Kit spent his very early years in Missouri in the stockade with other small children while the grown men and older boys cleared land, planted corn, and fought Indians.

Leaving their Kentucky home must have been a melancholy occasion for the Carsons, as it was for other families moving west. People tried to be cheerful when the hour of departure arrived, but there were always tears. Neighbors knew there was little chance they would ever see each other again. Distances were great, travel slow, accident and illness common, medical treatment primitive. Typhoid, smallpox, cholera, and flu swept away entire communities, both Indian and white. Death hovered over young as well as old. Of leaving her Ohio home for the wilds of western Indiana, newly married Magdalena McCain recalled years later, "My husband [and I] accordingly made preparations, and on the 9th of November, 1826, we bade adieu to weeping friends and relatives and to our native country. With two ox-teams we slowly wended our way toward Indiana, which at that time was almost an unbroken wilderness, where the sound of the white man's ax was seldom heard." A move of many weeks by ox team or pack horse then is a five- or six-hour drive today.

Why would the Carsons have left their secure cabin home in an established community of friends and neighbors in Kentucky? Lindsey and Rebecca were by now middle-aged. Lindsey had two broods, those with his first wife, Lucy, and those with Rebecca. Why so restless? What drew them west again? Crop failures (like those of 1816) and land ruined by wasteful farming methods were major factors with many peoples' moving on, as were population growth and the rising cost of land in settled areas. But the risks of moving were always great. Historian Daniel Walker Howe observed that "their migration often took them [even] farther away from access to markets . . . and into conflict with the Native peoples." The Carsons were to suffer both these difficulties.

Daniel Boone's reasons for moving his family to the Boone's Lick apply also to the Carsons and thousands of other Scots-Irish and British settlers, especially from Kentucky and Tennessee. John Mack Faragher, Boone's finest biographer, answered the question thus: "The prospect of a new start in a fresh land, his family and friends gathered about him, lifted [Boone's] spirits." Border historian R. Douglas Hurt thought such people simply "made moving a lifetime habit." The Rev. Timothy Flint lived for a while at St. Charles on the Missouri River about the time the Carsons passed through. He watched the mass of travelers, probably talked with some of them, and was sure that they were answering a human need to pursue an illusion. In his classic *Recollections of the Last Ten Years*, Flint, a journalist, editor, and novelist, expressed his opinion of the matter at length. For the first few months, he wrote, "a charm of romance" hangs over the dreamed-of place, a charm soon dispelled by the reality of life there. A particular area "gets a name, as more desirable than any other." People talk far and wide of their expectations of this place. Their imaginations "get kindled" so that afterward, "the hills of the land of promise" are "not more fertile in milk and honey" than the currently "fashionable" place to go. While Flint lived in St. Charles, Boone's Lick was where everyone wanted to go. Thomas Jefferson would have called the entire phenomenon the pursuit of happiness on a mass scale.

What road did the Carsons take? One popular route from Kentucky was down the Ohio River by boat from Limestone on the Ohio. Daniel Boone's family had gone that way to Louisville at the Falls of the Ohio ten years earlier. (The Carsons knew the Boones well, as the two families were related by marriage.) Most likely, however, Lindsey, Andrew, and Moses Carson loaded up the family's possessions on pack horses at the cabin on Tate Creek, then took the much shorter road from Madison County through Lexington and Frankfort to Louisville. Crossing the Ohio River to Indiana at the Falls of the Ohio, they'd have taken the heavily used trail across southern Indiana and Illinois through Vincennes to St. Louis (Highway 150 to 50 today), the same as the Boones had. After watching Daniel Boone riding at the head of his family procession passing through St. Louis, Henry Dodge recalled, "[Daniel] rode a sad looking horse [with] saddle bags, rifle on his shoulder, leather hunting shirt, and a couple of hunting knives in his belt, accompanied by three or four hunting dogs." Lindsey Carson and most other border men moving their families west from Kentucky and Tennessee looked about the same.

Nathan Boone and his bride, Olive Van Bibber, had taken this popular route through St. Louis in October 1799. Starting from Limestone on the Ohio River, they traveled light, eating the parched corn they carried with them and the wild game Nathan shot along the way. Parched corn was the day's trail mix. The young couple had been married at Olive's parents' home in Limestone. Years later she recalled their trip with evident pride. "On the first of October, without any company but my husband, I started out to Missouri," she said. Crossing the Mississippi River, "my husband rowed and I steered and held the horses by the bridle. It was rather a perilous trip for so young a couple. I was just sixteen, my husband eighteen."

Twelve years later the Carsons also crossed the Mississippi at St. Louis. Probably there was a ferry by then, for countless people used this route. According to one story, Rebecca Carson held little Kit in her arms, resting the baby's bottom on the saddle pommel. If so, it was an appropriate beginning for Carson, soon to become a master horseman. From St. Louis the road ran northwest to St. Charles. From there it followed the Missouri River's course west. Later the main road left the winding Missouri to run slightly northwest from St. Charles past present-day Columbia to Old Franklin, which lay on a flat place across the river from present-day Boonville. Making the trip in 1827, George Champlin Sibley recorded the distance from St. Charles to Franklin as 149 miles (about the same as by I-70 today).

The Boone and Carson parties were typically plain, though some of the troupes passing through St. Charles were elaborate. Timothy Flint described one of these. "Between the second and third years of my residence [in St. Charles]," he wrote, "the immigration from the western and southern states . . . poured in a flood, the power and strength of which could only be adequately conceived by persons on the spot." He watched one of the big caravans, perhaps several related families, a clan, with their slaves. "I have seen nine wagons harnessed with from four to six horses [each]," he wrote. "We may allow a hundred cattle, besides hogs, horses, and sheep, to each wagon; and from three or four to twenty slaves. The whole appearance of the train, the cattle with their hundred bells; the negroes with delight in their countenances, for their labours are suspended and their imaginations excited; the wagons, often carrying two or three tons, so loaded that the mistress and children are strolling carelessly along, in a gait which enables them to keep up with the slow traveling carriage; the whole group occupies three quarters of a mile."

Like Kit's mother, women who were nursing babies rode horseback, or they walked along until they got tired, then climbed into a cart or a wagon with the milk cow tied on behind. After a few days travel, the cow learned to follow the wagon, the cart, or the pack horses. She grazed along slowly, then walked faster until she caught up, when she slowed down to graze along again. In processions like those of the Carsons and Boones, the family patriarch rode ahead. Other horsemen rode alongside as outriders. All of these watched the dark places for Indians and for wild-looking strangers, and they hunted game for the evening meal. Older boys or girls drove the loose cattle, hogs, sheep, and goats, which, like the milk cow, soon followed along out of habit. Little girls and boys walked. At least one man or older boy brought up the rear horseback to make sure that everyone, including the loose livestock, stayed together.

Insects could be terrible pests. When George Champlin Sibley made the trip in midsummer 1827, the flies on the Grand Prairie, he wrote, made it "impossible to travel through it in the day without very great injury to the horses. Even at Harrison's, we were obliged to keep the Horses Shut up in Stables." Over the next day or two, Sibley's "horses were very much jaded and worried." On another day he described "fighting the flies, if I Rode in the daytime, or else feeling my way in the dark as I traveled by Night." Lameness was a continual problem. A horse or a mule with a sore foot is useless. It could "throw a shoe" or go lame for any number of other reasons. Dr. Rowland Willard crossed Missouri to Franklin to pick up the Santa Fe Trail in May 1825. A few days on the road from St. Charles he noted in his journal, "Mare took lame . . . consequent to being hobble[d] to [*sic*] tight."

Women and girls did the camp chores, cooking, and cleaning up. Men and older boys, often helped by the women, guarded the livestock. Horses and mules have a strong homing instinct that they *will* answer to. Loose at night, even when hobbled, they outdistance a man afoot trying to run them down. If the horses got away, a halt had to be called to go after them, for they *were* going home. On May 22, 1825, Dr. Willard noted, "Two horses broke away last night. . . . They were followed back on the trail 9 miles[.] Returned without them and concluded to proceed having pack horses to carry the goods." On August 2, 1827, George Champlin Sibley wrote, "Horses all left us & Started back; they had got Six Miles before they were caught." John G. McCoy, a famous cattle buyer, traveled across northeastern New Mexico with mules in the winter of 1880–81. One late night in the snow he penciled in his diary, "Mules Stampeded with hobbles on and travel back eight miles. After a weary walk overtake the Mules at 10 P.M. Return to camp exhausted and weary." William Bratton, veteran of the Lewis and Clark Expedition, lost his horses one night in western Indiana while he was moving his family west. Leaving the family in camp, he followed the horses back to Ohio where they'd started from. By the time he gathered them up and brought them back again, "the family had gotten acquainted around the neighborhood," as his descendant Maude Bratton Chesterson told me when I was a very small boy. So the Brattons settled there in western Indiana near Waynetown.

Abington Public Library
781-982-2139
www.abingtonpl.org

Author: Remley, David A.
Title: Kit Carson : the life
of an American border man
Date due: 4/6/2015,23:59

Your receipt lists due dates.
The Library is not using
date
due cards in each item.
Due dates - www.
abingtonpl.org
Log on to your account.

When he dictated his story in 1856, Kit said little about growing up in the Boone's Lick. "My parents moved to Missouri when I was one year old," he remembered in his usual plain manner. "They settled in what is now Howard County." Fur trader Manuel Lisa traveled the Missouri River through Howard County with poet and novelist Henry Marie Brackenridge about the time the Carsons arrived. Brackenridge was an optimist and a romantic captivated by the West. John Mason Peck, another traveler, also described the Boone's Lick scene in 1818. Both men noted only the bright side of border life.

"This part of the territory will soon become the garden of Missouri," wrote Peck. Brackenridge described "a flourishing settlement" along the river, probably Cooper's Bottom, about where the Carsons pulled in. "As this is Sunday," he wrote, "the good people were dressed out in their best clothes, and came in groups to the [river's] bank to gaze upon us, as we passed by under sail. We put to shore, at the farm of Braxton Cooper. . . . The settlement is but one year old, but is already considerable, and increasing rapidly; it consists of seventy-five families, the greater part living on the bank of the river, in the space of four or five miles. They are, generally, persons in good circumstances, most of them have slaves." This was the Sunday scene at its brightest. Very likely the Carsons were among the people Peck and Brackenridge actually saw. Seemingly peaceful when the writers viewed it, Cooper's Bottom would not remain so. Everyday reality was different from the idyllic scene Peck and Brackenridge described.

The cousins Braxton and Sarshall Cooper had built Cooper's Fort. Born in Culpepper County, Virginia, the Cooper boys moved to Kentucky first. Like the Carsons and other Britons of their kind, they were always looking for something better. So in 1807 they moved farther west, this time to St. Charles County, Missouri. In 1810 they brought their families out to settle still farther west, in the Boone's Lick, near Arrow Rock on the Missouri not far from Nathan Boone's salt spring. Close by they built their fort, a common type of stockade in Kentucky and elsewhere in the Ohio Valley. These were simple log structures for protection from Indians in contested borderlands. Historian R. Douglas Hurt described Cooper's as "several log houses and a large stockade that could protect twenty families." This one and Kinkead's Fort were both in place or well under construction when the Carsons trailed in from Kentucky. Within two or three years, Kit was old enough to remember the forts and the foreboding forest surrounding them.

Oak and hickory forests covered the land in groves. Natural open meadows were scattered here and there. Somewhat farther west yet, the forest began to finger out into the tall grass prairies of eastern Kansas and the Great Plains. Daily life at Cooper's and Kinkead's was about the same as the Boones, Coopers, Carsons, and others like them had known since the Rev. Alexander Carson arrived in Pennsylvania before 1738. Hard labor was ceaseless. Grown men and boys felled logs and cut brush with broadaxes while others stood guard with long rifles. After limbing the logs, the men turned to notching them, then building the stockade on a spot prepared for it. Most such stockades, if ever finished, were square or rectangular clusters of huts or cabins connected by a palisade. Brush and trees were cleared all around the structure to provide a clear view in every direction as protection from hostile Indians. At least two corners of the palisade had rooms perched above them. These rooms hung over the log fences. Riflemen could kneel behind cover inside the room to sweep the entire field of sight right up to the palisade itself. One old border man described a fort in Kentucky or Tennessee simply as "20 or 30 steps square, a house at every corner, & a family in each house."

As soon as the simplest protection was up, men who could be spared from building turned to clearing land. They harnessed teams or yoked oxen to plow around the stumps of the newly felled trees. They planted corn or wheat among the green stumps the first year. Taking the logs they needed for the fort's construction, and for huts, cabins, and later for fence rails, they piled the rest of the limbs and logs with the smaller brush. During the second year, after the brush and trees had dried out, the men set the piles afire and burned the trash wood in mass. Such great burns went on without ceasing for months, even for years. The waste of trees that might have made lumber seems astounding today. Smoke from the burns covered the landscape for mile upon mile, month after month after month. "Never had civilization been so rich in wood," wrote ecologist Robert O. Petty. "By necessity, wood was used for every fashioned article of living. Even so, most of the trees were rolled together and burned. The greatest resource need [at the time] was land for crops."

Always ready to follow a strong leader, ever primed to fight to the death to protect their families, the Scots-Irish, Scots, and English settlers hung on in the Boone's Lick, as they had in Kentucky and elsewhere on earlier borders. "The two great defining characteristics of the Scots-Irish culture," wrote James Webb, "[were] a loyalty to strong leaders and an immediate fierceness [under attack]." These qualities made them all but invincible. Almost without exception, the settlers in the Boone's Lick when Carson was growing up had British names. Many, perhaps most, of these were Scots-Irish. Most came from Kentucky, Tennessee, or the Carolinas, where the percentage of their kind was very high. Traveling in 1818–19 through Missouri, John Mason Peck put down the names of the people he met along the way. A list of these is most impressive evidence of the high percentage of Britons on the border at the time, all of them with about the same cultural traits. Nearly in Peck's order, they are Callaway, Boone, Stevenson, McDermid, Smith, Coats, Darst, Roi, Fergusson, Henderson, McAllister, Jones, Doyle, Crump, Woods, Wilcox, McLain, Thorp, Wiseman, Cole, Brown, Gooch, Patton, Cooper, Head, Hempstead, Kincaid, Todd, Campbell, McMahan, Gregg, Busby, Still, Riggs, Hutchinson, McMillan,

Gillmore, Williamson, Green, Finlay, and Allen. With two or possibly three exceptions, all of these are British names.

Arriving in Franklin on December 28, 1818, just after Kit's ninth birthday, Peck witnessed daily life nearby. People stayed in the forts when, as he put it, "threatened danger required." Otherwise, they camped outside, cutting the forest, piling and burning brush and trees, hunting, handling livestock, plowing, planting, and gardening. Riflemen *always* stood guard. Workers "were divided into plowmen and sentinels," Peck wrote. "The one party followed the plows, and the other, with rifles loaded and ready, scouted around the field on every side, stealthily watching. . . . As [the guard] approached the end of the corn rows, where the adjacent woodland might conceal an enemy, his anxiety was at its height. When these detachments were in the cornfield, if the enemy threatened the fort, the sound of the horn gave the alarm, and all rushed to the rescue."

This was life as young Kit knew it. From second to second, night as day, a peaceful scene might suddenly explode into chaos. When he was older, Kit Carson would have remembered these scenes—men and women at hard labor outside, sentinels on watch in each clearing, the blast of a horn, rifle shots, a desperate race to the fort, lives saved, or lost, always the screaming, and, when someone was hit, the flow of blood. Such memories are stored deep in a child's head. "For two or three years after our arrival," Kit recalled to John Mostin in 1856, "we had to remain forted and it was necessary to have men stationed at the extremities of the fields for the protection of those that were laboring."

Unable to settle on the land they selected, the Carsons forted up as soon as they arrived. Lindsey, Moses, and Andrew worked the fields as they could and served in the militia organized at Kinkead's Fort. In one rifle fight Lindsey took a warrior's shot that smashed his rifle stock and mangled two fingers of his left hand. In the spring of 1815, when Kit was five years old, a warrior pushed a rifle through the chinking of a wall and shot old Capt. Sarshall Cooper dead as he sat by his own fireplace in Cooper's Fort. One story has it that he was holding a baby in his arms at the time. Cooper family members later recalled these early years. "The Indians were very friendly [at first]," said one. "They would occasionally steal our horses and put us to some trouble to recover them, until about March 1812, when they killed . . . Jonathan Todd and Thomas Smith . . . mutilated their bodies and [displayed] their heads and hearts . . . on poles."

At two or three years old, Kit may not have remembered particular events, but he certainly picked up the intense anxiety of his parents, his brothers, his sisters, and their neighbors. Tom Dunlay described Kit's boyhood world as characterized by "persisting insecurity." Both Cooper cousins were killed, Braxton in September 1814, shot while working up logs for a new building, and Sarshall was shot the next spring, inside his cabin. Almost from the time Lindsey and his family arrived in the Boone's Lick, Indians and settlers fought over every inch of ground. Both sides paid in blood for what they won, as well as for what they lost.

After the United States declared war on Great Britain in June 1812, border conflict in Missouri intensified for at least three reasons. One, the inrush of settlers, so well described by Timothy Flint and John Mason Peck, increasingly squeezed the Native people from their hunting grounds. Two, the declaration of war raised Indian expectations that England would support them in their battle with the settlers. Three, the powerful Shawnee chief Tecumseh and his brother, the spiritual leader called "the Prophet," raised the hopes of a great many Native people that they could unite with other tribes against the Americans and thereby defeat them.

But the Indians' hopes were to be crushed. In the fall of 1811 Tecumseh was off on a trip visiting southern tribes to promote Indian unity. While the great chief was away, William Henry Harrison marched an army from Vincennes on the Wabash River to "Prophet's Town," the main Shawnee village. Prophet's Town was located on the Tippecanoe River near present-day Lafayette, Indiana. Though warriors fought Harrison to a standstill on November 7, the soldiers burned the village to cinders the next day. Then in December 1814, England and the United States signed a peace treaty. That ended the War of 1812, and with it all Indian hope of British support in the struggle with the settlers. Afterward, the number of Americans in Missouri only increased. It is difficult to imagine the intensity of the Indians' anguish. No wonder Native warriors in a rage ravaged border settlements and isolated cabins and killed small parties and lone travelers.

Thus the Boone's Lick forts remained centers of life, such as it was, and provided hope of safety for settlers throughout Kit's boyhood. Women, children, and the elderly stayed close to shelter at all times. Sentinels stood guard while men and older boys cleared and plowed the land nearby. Everyone was ready to drop the plow, grab the rifle, and make a stand, or run for the fort. Trouble might be expected of any stranger or of any change from the ordinary. An odd sound in the night was a warning, a peculiar bird call on a quiet morning a signal, an unusual track an alert. Change triggered expectation. Anxious expectation could turn into bloody action quick as light. There had been enough violent clashes, costly to all sides over many years of border life by then, that settlers and Indians remained *always* watchful. They had developed a readiness to attack and repel never far from consciousness.

Thus the "persisting insecurity" as described by Dunlay. Everyone on the borders experienced it: "The fear and the hatred were based on the harsh and terrible experience of decades of intermittent border warfare." Such expectation caused people to imagine wildly and to spread rumor quickly. Malcolm Rohrbough calls "anxiety over the Indian" a "distinguishing feature" of the earliest trans-Appalachian borders. The same could be said of the Missouri border. People usually exaggerated their trouble reports. During the War of 1812, St. Louis residents rumored that British soldiers with ten thousand Native warriors were marching south from the Great Lakes to attack Missouri. Even people in a position to know better were affected. "God only knows what our fate is to be," wrote Julia Clark on January 1, 1814, after she heard this crazy rumor. Her husband was William Clark, former leader of the Lewis and Clark Expedition along with Meriwether Lewis, brigadier general of the Territory's militia, and principal U.S. Indian agent for Louisiana. If anyone ought to have felt secure, William Clark's wife should have. But that persisting insecurity was always at work, driving people to exaggeration, to rumor, and often to violent action.

When the Carsons arrived from Kentucky, there were at least three forts in the Boone's Lick: Cooper's, Kinkead's, and Hempstead's. Hempstead's and Kinkead's were located about two miles from the soon-to-be town of Franklin. Hempstead's was on the bluff, Kinkead's near the Missouri River. Of the three, Cooper's, on the river's bank west of the site of New Franklin by perhaps ten miles, was the most exposed. Floods soon washed away Old Franklin, the town where Kit would work in the saddle shop. New Franklin replaced the old town on a bluff nearby. By Christmas of 1818, when Kit was nine years old, the forts had increased to five. Head's Fort stood east of Franklin near the trail back to St. Charles, Cole's Fort on the right bank of the Missouri a mile below present-day Boonville.

In September 1818 Kit's father was killed. Kit was eight years old. While Lindsey was burning brush and trees, a flaming limb crashed down on him. His agonizing death would have marked his young son, although, characteristically, it appears that Kit never talked of it. Afterward, however, his life changed rapidly. Coming into adolescence, his strong father suddenly dead, his mother alone with a cabin full of children, Kit was a lost boy. He spent a short time in school, but book learning didn't take. In 1821 his mother married Joseph Martin, a widower with children of his own. According to one biographer, Kit and his brothers rebelled. Not willing to take orders from a stranger, the Carson boys moved out. Kit went to live for a time with his brother William, who was working on a nearby farm. William probably expected Kit to trade labor for his room and board. Whatever the arrangement between the two, it didn't work out. William soon lost patience with the boy.

At some point Kit was so troubled that his mother placed him in the hands of a ward, John Ryland, who later became a justice of the supreme court of Missouri. Kit's mother also apprenticed him to the saddlemaker David Workman. The year was 1824. An apprenticeship at that time was a familiar arrangement. It was a legal contract in which the persons responsible, Rebecca Carson and probably Ryland, offered so many years of a boy's service in return for the training he received. The choices and the terms of the agreement were not Kit's, but Rebecca's (and perhaps Ryland's). As might have been expected, Kit was unhappy about the arrangement. Years later one of his sisters, Mary Ann, is supposed to have recalled, "He didn't like it. About the only use he had for a saddle was on a horse's back." He knuckled under for a while though. He served the apprenticeship out until August 1826, when he broke off and ran away. One good thing to be said for certain of this period in his life is that Kit learned skills he would find useful later on.

Self-discipline? Work habits? Maybe. I doubt it. What he did learn was the basic skill of keeping saddle and pack gear in repair, a practical knowledge absolutely essential in the life he was to lead. As a grown man, the number of hours he would spend horseback "towing" a pack mule can only be imagined, never counted. In Carson's day a breakdown with saddle or pack stock and their equipment was like running out of fuel on the highway today. Much worse, actually, for no help was at hand, and none could be expected. As a teamster, mountain man, commercial hunter, Indian agent, and cavalry officer, all of which he was to be, Carson had to know how to keep his horse and mule gear in order, sometimes making repairs within a very few minutes, as often as not in emergencies. Given the distances traveled in the West, a man afoot was useless to himself and a burden to others if his livestock and leather gear were not in working order. Always!

A day in the saddle shop would have gone about as follows. According to old-time saddlemaker R. W. Doeling of Santa Rita, New Mexico, he'd have done "all the jobs the saddlemaker didn't want to do, building a fire in the stove first thing in the morning, sweeping out the shop in the evening, sitting on the stool of a stitching horse all day long pushing waxed linen thread through holes [he] hand punched with an awl." David Workman seems to have been unusually easygoing because Kit later remembered him as a decent man. "He was a good man," Kit told John Mostin. "And I often recall to my mind the kind treatment I received from his hands." Nonetheless, the boy would have been expected to arrive early in the morning and to work late, perhaps even staying over in the shop as a night watchman, for the tools of the trade were valuable and easily stolen.

Essential as an auto mechanic's tools today, these consisted at least of a few knives, kept well sharpened on a stone; a selection of awls; two or three leather punches; and a mallet. The shop would have had a cutting table for cutting saddle skirts, seats, jockeys, and latigo straps from oak-tanned cowhides. There'd have been a stitching horse, which looked like a wooden vice with a seat and a foot pedal for tightening the vice. The stitching horse gripped and held the "leathers" Kit was stitching at the time. The hand tools hung in leather loops pegged to the wall. The supplies were nearly as precious as the tools. There were saddle trees and "sawbuck" pack trees, both of them of lightweight wood, usually pine or cottonwood. The "trees" were covered with rawhide to give them strength. There were "sides" of cowhides that had been tanned in solutions of wood ash and oak bark in big tubs. And there were beeswax, rolls of thread spun of flax, a box of hog bristles for needles, and a box of iron buckles for the cinches and for other saddle and pack straps.

As it would turn out, probably the greatest benefit of Kit's apprenticeship lay in the saddle shop's location at the end of the Santa Fe Trail. Here the boy met teamsters and traders headed to far-off "Santee Fee." He heard their tales when they came in for repairs after they got home from a trip or prepared for the next. Or when they stopped in just to visit. For the saddle shop in the American West, like the barbershop and the small town café today, was a gathering place for workingmen taking a break. Here they exchanged their news of the trail and entertained one another with larger than life stories. If Kit hadn't caught the travel fever before his mother apprenticed him, he surely caught it in the saddle shop at the end of the Santa Fe Trail. As for the work itself, he stuck it out as long as he could, probably from his strong sense of duty, which was to be a ruling part of his actions all of his later life. By August 1826, however, after nearly two years in the shop, the "trail fever" got the best of him, and he left home to try to make it on his own.

He was in a prime location for a rebellious boy wanting to be independent. For Franklin was where the Santa Fe trade got its start. Josiah Gregg, known as the "Chronicler of the Trail," called the town "the cradle of our trade." And eleven-year-old Kit was there when it started. In the summer of 1821 William Becknell had gathered a band of men for exploring and trading toward the southwest all the way to the Rocky Mountains. Leaving Franklin in August with pack stock loaded with trade goods, Becknell traveled up the Arkansas River to its junction with the Purgatory River in southern Colorado (mountain men called this river the "Picket Wire"). Another trader, Jacob Fowler, came across the tracks of a party, probably Becknell's, on an island in the Arkansas River near present-day Dodge City. Fowler noted in his journal for October 26, 1821, "We Heare Con Clude them to be White men, there Horses being Shod." Beyond the Purgatory and far across the Raton Mountains in New Mexico, Becknell met a troop of friendly Mexican soldiers near San

Miguel on the Pecos River not far from Santa Fe. "Although the difference of our language would not admit of conversation," Becknell noted, the soldiers' "manifestations of kindness" assured the Americans "of their hospitable disposition and friendly feelings."

Meeting friendly Mexican soldiers here in 1821 was a great surprise. For years Spain had prevented free trade between Missouri and New Mexico. Spanish governors had usually jailed trespassers. In 1812 James Baird's and Robert McKnight's party from St. Louis had been held in Santa Fe at first, then marched off to prison in Chihuahua City for eight years. In 1817 Gov. Pedro Maria Allande imprisoned another party, which included Auguste Pierre Chouteau of the famous St. Louis trading family. Allande held them for six weeks. After threatening to have one of the party shot, he confiscated their trade goods and turned the Missourians loose. And there was the earlier hard luck of U.S. Army Lt. Zebulon M. Pike. Setting out in the summer of 1806 under orders to locate the sources of the Red River, Pike traveled up the Arkansas River into the Rockies from near present-day La Junta, Colorado. Clambering around in the mountains, which he called the "Mexican Mountains," Pike, with his men, nearly froze to death in heavy snows. Finally they built a stockade on the Rio Conejos. Mistakenly believing they were on the Red River, they had actually built their fort on a branch of the Rio Grande. Here a Spanish mounted patrol arrested them as trespassers in February 1807. They were taken into Santa Fe. From there Pike was marched off to Chihuahua. In June 1807 he was finally returned under guard to U.S. territory in Louisiana.

Prepared for the customary hostility, Becknell's party was happily surprised to learn that Mexico had recently overthrown Spanish rule. Traders from Missouri would henceforth be welcome in Nuevo Mexico under the new government! Hurrying into Santa Fe, Becknell shared a glass of the best local wine with Gov. Facundo Melgares in the old Governor's

Palace. The two men visited affably. Then Becknell swapped his goods for silver coin and Spanish mules and headed home to Missouri for another load of trade goods.

Back in Franklin by January 1822, his men made a great display of their success. Years later a Franklin man recalled the scene. "My father saw them unload when they returned," H. H. Harris said, "and when their rawhide packages of silver dollars were dumped on the sidewalk[,] one of the men cut the thongs and the money spilled out and clinking on the stone pavement rolled into the gutter. Everyone was excited and the next spring another expedition was sent out." Perhaps exaggerated, the account does illustrate Becknell's good fortune and suggests the excitement of his unlikely return from nowhere. If not gold, someone had at least found silver at the end of the rainbow! Shortly thereafter, Becknell, the so-called Father of the Santa Fe Trade, left for New Mexico again, this time with wagons. These would be the first wagons to roll over the Santa Fe Trail.

Although Becknell's return to Franklin happened before Kit was apprenticed to the saddlemaker, the boy certainly heard the news. Very likely he was in town the day the mules trailed in. If he was there, he saw the Spanish coin roll out onto the stone, and he heard the silver jingle. Just two years later he would be apprenticed to David Workman. Two years after that, at sixteen, he would leave the saddle shop to run off to Santa Fe himself.

He had plenty of time to think it over. Several men he knew from around Franklin had already gone west and then come home to tell stories of the mountains and the plains. Like news, the stories traveled fast. They grew with each telling and retelling: moccasin telegraph–style. Kit's brother Robert and his half brother Andrew had signed on with George Champlin Sibley's government-financed survey in 1825. The survey would mark a trail from Council Grove to the Arkansas River near the hundredth meridian. Sarshall Cooper's son, Stephen Cooper, guided this party. From his brothers and from other members of the Sibley survey whom he knew well, Kit must have learned much about the country farther west.

Then there was Kit's big half brother Moses Carson. Moses went up the Missouri River as early as 1819 with the Missouri Fur Company. Eternally restless, he joined Col. Henry Leavenworth's infantry soldiers who were ordered out to punish the Arikaras in the summer of 1823. The Arikaras had attacked the Ashley-Henry fur party in the tribe's village on the upper Missouri and had killed several trappers earlier that year. Moses would have enjoyed telling stories of his adventures when he came home to visit. His size alone had to impress pint-sized Kit. For Old Mose was big. Even at sixty years of age, he was a tough six feet tall and weighed two hundred pounds.

Multiply the effect of all that Kit actually learned in Workman's saddle shop times the big tales he heard there daily. The result? He would cut out to go west himself. As he recalled the break: "I remained with [Workman] two years. The business did not suit me and, having heard so many tales of life in the Mountains of the West, I concluded to leave him . . . taking into consideration that if I remained with him and served my apprenticeship I would have to pass my life in labor that was distasteful to me, and being anxious to travel for the purpose of seeing different countries, I concluded to join the first party for the Rocky Mts." So Kit left home and headed west, out on his own for the very first time.

3

Better Exchanges Than Gold

Kit said very little about running away from home. "In August, 1826, I had the fortune to hear of a party bound for that country to which I desired to go," he recalled. "I made application to join this party and, without any difficulty, I was permitted to join them." This was probably William Wolfskill's party. Andrew Broadus was certainly a member, and George Yount may have been. Later a mountain man and a pioneer rancher and farmer in the Napa Valley, Yount fought in the War of 1812. He first arrived in Santa Fe from Missouri in 1826 and headed on to California with Wolfskill in 1830. Wolfskill and Ewing Young, his longtime business partner, first trailed into Santa Fe with William Becknell. After trapping beaver for a time, they partnered up, trading horses and mules together across the Southwest all the way to Chihuahua. Of Wolfskill and Young, David J. Weber wrote that their joining Becknell in 1822 "began a profitable and lasting relationship which kept them in the vanguard of the Taos trappers." If Kit was with Wolfskill's party of traders and trappers on his first trip to Santa Fe, he could not have been in better company to learn a trade he would soon follow full time.

He struggled with himself, though, over quitting Workman and running off. His sister Mary Ann recalled years later that when he asked his mother if he could leave home, she told him to serve out his apprenticeship first. Mary Ann also remembered Kit's saying he'd heard traders in the saddle shop say that beaver furs in Santa Fe were "better exchanges than gold." He would have understood that breaking contract with Workman meant defying several important adults—his mother, Workman himself, and John Ryland, who had probably written the terms of Kit's contract. Other elders in the community would disapprove too, believing that the "good boy" was the one who "stayed put," who always did his job and performed his duty. Kit probably dreamed of leaving and agonized over it for weeks, perhaps months.

However that may be, he slipped out one night and disappeared. One story has him "borrowing" a neighbor's mule. If he did, it would have been at night. The story goes that he rode the mule to Independence where Wolfskill's party was in camp while they stocked up for Santa Fe. Once in camp, Kit would have turned the mule loose. He knew from experience that a mule would go home, grazing along the way. He also knew that in defying his elders, he had failed his responsibility as they saw it. A devotion to duty, sometimes carried to an extreme, was to become a trademark of his character, perhaps from a sense of guilt over this early break with traditional values.

Joining a Santa Fe–bound party at Independence made practical sense for a runaway. Kit couldn't have joined at Franklin where he'd have been nabbed for breaking contract and maybe even jailed. Independence was farther up the Missouri River (roughly 110 miles by modern highway, considerably longer by trail) and on higher ground than Franklin. It was far enough from home that he could feel safe. It was also quickly replacing flood-prone Franklin as the point where the Santa Fe Trail began. Kit undoubtedly knew men in Wolfskill's party he could trust, certainly Andrew Broadus, who had been a member of the Sibley survey with Kit's half brother Andrew. Of course Broadus knew Kit's adventurous half brother Moses. Everyone knew Mose. These men had all been in and out of Workman's saddle shop where Kit eagerly listened to their tales of adventure while he stitched leather.

Like Kit, Wolfskill was a Kentuckian, born in Madison County in 1798 not far from Kit's own birthplace. His family too had moved west to Missouri while he was just a boy. The two shared the same background. They knew the same people. Kit also had the kind of experience needed for a job with a Santa Fe–bound party. He knew horses and mules. He could handle livestock. Every trail-smart party carried along plenty of spare horses and mules besides the ones they worked regularly. So Wolfskill took the boy on as a wrangler. A wrangler looked after all the saddle and pack animals. He brought them in before daylight, checked to see that they were fed, watered, sound, and ready for the long day's work, ready to cover the miles.

The party left Independence no later than early fall 1826, in time to arrive in Santa Fe by November. The eight-hundred-mile trip was mostly uneventful. Early fall weather on the Great Plains is usually dry. The wind *always* blows, mostly out of the west. Now and then it brings up a shower, which often as not turns into a downpour of wind-blown rain choked with hail. Lightning crooks and crackles off here and there across the plains and ridges, waving and flattening the grass. Thunder booms and grumbles down, down, down from great white pillars of cloud. A rider could dismount and crawl under his horse for shelter from the hammering of the hailstones, or he might unsaddle and put the saddle over his head. Blue-stem, grama, and buffalo grasses were still plentiful in Kit's day, and for a time thereafter, at least well off the trail away from the campsites everyone used. The food value of these native grasses is very high.

Because travelers wanted urgently to get to Santa Fe, however, they grazed their livestock way too little. A man could always count his mules' ribs. Worn-out stock was customarily turned out to graze, with plans to gather them up again on the way home. A few years later, resupply posts like Bent's

Fort developed along the trail where jaded stock could be traded off for rested animals. As the Santa Fe trade grew in later years, grass, water, and firewood became very precious. Kit's early party, however, could still find plenty of grass for feed and sufficient wood for cook fires among the trees bordering the creeks that wandered across the tall grass prairies of eastern Kansas. Out on the short grass prairies of the High Plains, however, there were no trees except along the streams. Out here travelers had to pick up buffalo chips, called bois de vache by the French, for making fires to boil coffee and roast buffalo meat.

Kit's party took the "Cimarron Cutoff," the southern branch of the trail to Santa Fe, that "adobe brick outpost on a bleak and remote frontier," as T. R. Fehrenbach described the old Spanish town. The Cimarron Cutoff was shorter than the northern branch of the trail that followed the Arkansas and the Purgatory rivers up over Raton Pass between Colorado and New Mexico. The cutoff dropped southwest from the Arkansas River near present-day Dodge City, Kansas, clipped the northwest corner of today's Oklahoma Panhandle, and passed just north of present-day Clayton, New Mexico. People called the northern branch the "Mountain Route." A longer route, it followed the Arkansas River, then threaded mountain passes along dependable streams with plenty of water for livestock and groves of trees for shelter and firewood. The one great disadvantage of the Cimarron Cutoff was that it crossed a sandy, sunburnt prairie where feed for livestock was sparse at best and water holes were usually dry. Out here somewhere on this moonscape southwest of the Arkansas River a band of Comanche warriors were to surprise and kill even the great Jedediah Smith while he tried desperately to find water for his party one very bad day in May 1831. Water was a necessity. Men and women might suffer along for hours or days without it, but working livestock without water were today's eighteen-wheelers out of diesel fuel on the highway.

The one remarkable event of Kit's first trip across the plains was Andrew Broadus's shooting himself, although this kind of terrible accident was not uncommon. Kit later described the bloody scene in detail. Undoubtedly it reminded him of gunshot wounds back in Missouri, particularly of the time a Native warrior's shot mangled his father's hand. But Broadus's wound was much worse than Lindsey Carson's had been. The party's handling of the accident illustrates how experienced people of the time could treat a bad accident ably, successfully care for an injured man, and avert a worse disaster. These people were accustomed to facing possible calamity daily. They had developed ways of treating an accident effectively, and were ready to try anything that might work, even though they used medical techniques that today seem far below the primitive.

As Kit remembered it when he talked to John Mostin in 1856, Broadus "was taking his rifle out of a wagon for the purpose of shooting a wolf and, in drawing it out, [it] was accidentally discharged, [he] receiving the contents in the right arm. He suffered greatly from the effects of the wound. We had no medical man in the party. His arm began to mortify and all were aware that amputation was necessary. One of the party stated that he could do it. [Broadus] was prepared for any experiment to be tried that was considered of service to him. The doctor set to work and cut the flesh with a razor and sawed the bone with an old saw. The arteries being cut, to stop the bleeding he heated a king bolt of one of the wagons and burned the affected parts, and then applied a plaster of the tar taken from off the wheel of a wagon. The man became perfectly well before our arrival in New Mexico." Whether or not Broadus really got well in the next few weeks, the surgery impressed Kit so much that he remembered it in unusual detail.

When the party got to Santa Fe, Kit took the trail to Taos. A town of perhaps thirty-five hundred people at the time, Taos already attracted enterprising Americans. It was close to Rocky Mountain streams full of beaver and far enough north of Santa Fe that distillers of the famous local liquor called "Taos Lightnin'" could hide the fruits of their labor from Mexican customs officers. It also lay at the end of an alternate route to Missouri over Taos Pass. This route joined the Mountain Route of the Santa Fe Trail at Rayado, a little south of today's Cimarron, New Mexico, on the western edge of the Great Plains. Though steep and rocky, the alternate route bypassed Mexican customs in Santa Fe and shortened the distance to Missouri. Having arrived in Santa Fe in November, as Kit told his clerk, he proceeded to Taos "the same month, and remained during the winter with an old mountaineer by the name of [Kinkead]." Kit knew a number of Missourians and Kentuckians who had gone to Santa Fe and Taos earlier. These were all experienced border men by now, many of them from the Boone's Lick. They were men a teenage boy fresh out from Missouri could feel at home with.

Why Kit called Kinkead "an old mountaineer" instead of calling him by his name, however, is a mystery. This was Mathew Kinkead, son of David Kinkead, who had moved his family to the Boone's Lick from Kentucky before the Carsons made the same trip. Mathew's father, David, had built Kinkead's Fort. When Lindsey Carson first came to the area, he sought shelter at Kinkead's. Born in Madison County in 1795 not far from Kit's own birthplace, Mathew was a big boy of sixteen, already a man to handle an ax and a rifle by the time the Carson family arrived in Missouri. He had served with Kit's father and with Moses and Andrew Carson in the volunteer militia at Kinkead's Fort. There is no question whatever that Kit already knew Mathew well before the two spent the winter of 1826 together in Taos.

Away from his green and leafy Missouri home for the first time, Kit found himself in a brown land of mountains, where sagebrush, prickly pear, and junipers grew all about. People out here spoke a strange language and went to a different church: New Mexicans spoke Spanish and were Roman

Catholics. Missourians, if anything at all, were Protestants. Maybe sixteen-year-old Kit looked up to thirty-one-year-old Mathew as one of the men who had protected him when he was just a boy back in Missouri. Mathew had first packed a bundle of trade goods to Santa Fe in 1825, a year earlier, so Kit may have thought of him as already a man of the world, thus "an old mountaineer."

Biographers Thelma S. Guild and Harvey L. Carter believe that Carson's "never [speaking] appreciatively of Kinkead's help or hospitality" suggests that the two did not get along with each other that first winter. But Carson was never effusive. Throughout his life he revealed his respect and affection for his friends by his actions, seldom, if ever, speaking of them one way or the other. Not a man to get angry without good reason, he probably would have found another place to live if he and Mathew had argued, especially since he was clearly the junior of the two. It is also possible that calling his friend "an old mountaineer" was an instance of Kit's droll humor, for Carson could be whimsical. His quiet sense of humor has gone largely unnoticed by biographers, who seem to have a need to describe him seriously, either as frontier hero or as villain.

He was probably homesick that first winter in Taos. Maybe the judgmental Calvinistic religion of his ancestors and certainly the stern sense of duty to clan, family, and community that went with his culture weighed on his mind. He probably felt guilty about disobeying his mother and John Ryland and deserting Workman. Whatever his reasons, in the spring of 1827 he "started for the States" with a party of traders, as he later put it. He doesn't say whether he was employed with the caravan. What he did tell his clerk in 1856 suggests that he talked to no one about his decision, even that he traveled alone, although of course there were other people in the party. Perhaps he was feeling the isolation that comes with being without a useful purpose in life.

By the time he reached the Arkansas River, however, a little short of halfway home, he turned back west with another party headed to Santa Fe. Again, he gave no reason for changing direction and didn't mention any job. Possibly this westbound caravan was the one captained by Ezekiel Williams. If so, the travelers included David Workman, who by then had left the saddle shop, advertised Kit's desertion, and headed for Santa Fe himself. If Kit and Workman met on the trail, it may be that the easygoing saddlemaker forgave the boy. Since Kit had run off from Franklin, "being anxious to travel for the purpose of seeing different countries," as he put it years later, it is possible that by now his youthful restlessness had won the struggle with guilt about breaking contract and defying his mother's wishes. It may simply be that he had already grown attached to Taos, for Taos would ever afterward draw him back, and he would soon make it his home. Since Missourians traveled with this westbound party, meeting people of his kind who spoke the same border language probably made the turnabout easier. But there is no way of knowing what his feelings or motives were. Kit kept such things to himself.

During the next few months he followed the same pattern, wobbling between going off toward a strange place, then turning back toward the familiar. Like many a growing boy away from home for the first time, he took a step or two backward for every one forward. In the account he gave to his clerk in 1856, he remained detached from this early period by using the pronoun "I" or "my" in speaking of his actions, as if he felt that he hadn't at that time really belonged to *any* group. Not until he told of joining Ewing Young's party bound for California in 1829 did he begin saying "we," as if in joining this party he felt for the first time accepted as a member of a group of *purposeful* men. "Young . . . raised a party of forty men, consisting of Americans, Canadians and Frenchmen, and took command," Carson told his clerk in 1856. "*I* joined the party. *We* left Taos in August, 1829" (italics mine). These early years were years of searching, and a boy's search can be a lonely journey. Having broken a contract, disappointed his

51

elders, and stolen away from home, Kit may have been feeling the weight of duties failed.

Returning to Santa Fe with the party he had joined on the Arkansas River, Kit took a job driving a team of horses or mules for one dollar a day. He drove them down the Rio Grande to El Paso (today's Juarez, Mexico) where, he told his clerk in 1856, he took his "discharge" from the job and returned to Santa Fe. Was Kit fired in El Paso, did the job simply end there, or did he quit and walk away? If he quit, it would have been another show of the boy's developing independence. He never said either way.

From Santa Fe Kit went back to Taos where he "got employment" of Ewing Young, "to do his cooking, my board being the remuneration," he told his clerk. This was during the winter of 1827–28, his second winter in New Mexico. The job included cooking and probably doing other chores for Young, who kept a store in Taos with William Wolfskill. It certainly offered a practical education. The boy made friends with mountain man Ewing Young, who was later to depend heavily on Kit's skills. He could listen to the stories mountain men told as they came and went from the store, trading and visiting. Though all of them hoped to get rich, they wanted even more than that to see new country. They liked to talk about the adventures they'd had and to describe the things they'd seen. All of this was exciting for a young man like Kit. It also gave him information he could use later on.

Mysteriously, however, he quit the job and left again for "the States" in the spring of 1828. He must have given fair notice though. Clearly Young had been impressed with young Carson, for he never held his quitting against him later on. This time Kit turned back west at the Arkansas River with a caravan bound for Santa Fe. Instead of returning to Young's store, however, he took a job as an "interpreter" (undoubtedly in Spanish–English) with a man whose name he said was "Col. Trammell, a merchant." From Santa Fe the two went south to Chihuahua City. The man was probably Richard

Campbell, a Taos merchant, who made an early trading trip to California. Kit left Campbell (or Trammell) in Chihuahua, this time to hire on with Robert McKnight "to go to the copper mines near Rio Gila," as he put it. McKnight, who managed the Santa Rita Copper Mine (now the Chino Mine, near present-day Silver City, New Mexico) at this time, employed Kit "driving team" for a few months. "Not satisfied with this employment," however, Kit quit McKnight and went back to Taos in August 1828.

At the Copper Mine Kit must have learned a good many "border rules" from McKnight, a case-hardened old border man himself. Born in Virginia about 1789, McKnight, with James Baird and others, had packed several thousand dollars worth of trade goods to New Mexico in 1812, ten years ahead of William Becknell. Spanish officials arrested Knight's party as spies, however, confiscated their goods, and imprisoned McKnight in Chihuahua. He was at last released in late 1820 or 1821 during Mexico's war for independence. In and out of St. Louis for some time after that, McKnight was bitter that the government would not pay him for his lost trade goods. In 1824 he returned to Santa Fe, married a local woman, and became a Mexican citizen. Until at least 1838 he operated the Santa Rita mine. Carson biographer Edwin L. Sabin noted that Kit remembered the Apaches running off eighty of McKnight's pack mules, a disaster at the time, for these mules were used to pack the ore by way of Cow Springs to Janos, Mexico, where it was processed for copper. At Santa Rita, Kit no doubt began to learn the Apache language and customs, for the country all about here belonged to Mangas Coloradas, great chief of the Eastern Chiricahua, the Red Paint People.

Kit's first real opportunity came in August 1829, when Ewing Young chose him to join a band of hunters and trappers bound for California. Young had heard that California offered plenty of beaver streams and that Spanish horses grazed wild and fat over her golden hills. He had also heard that coastal schooners would buy beaver fur. If so, it would not be necessary to pack the furs all the way back to Santa Fe to market. By now a prominent Taos trader, Young had been born in Tennessee about 1792. Apprenticed to a carpenter, he too was a woods boy at heart. He and Kit were born of the same culture, sewn of the same cloth. Both were restless to go west. For Young this urge for independence seems quickly to have overcome any regret he may have felt about leaving home or breaking a contract. Disappearing from Tennessee as Kit would disappear from Franklin, he turned up again in Chariton, Missouri. In January 1822 he and a partner bought a farm on the Missouri not far upstream from Franklin. Only four months later, however, Young sold his share. It was May 24. The very next day he bought a bundle of trade goods and joined William Becknell as a junior partner in Becknell's second Santa Fe trading expedition.

Plainly Kit and Ewing Young had a lot in common and much to talk about when they spent time together. Not only did farming bore them, but the two had served apprenticeships. Both of them really wanted to see new places, to get outside the usual round. Young spoke for the two when he told a partner that what he wanted more than anything else was "to get outside of where trappers had ever been" before. Young and Kit had either been in Franklin or nearby when Becknell first packed in from Santa Fe with Spanish mules and silver coin. Discovering while Kit worked for him in the Taos store that the two were compatible, and probably also that Kit took orders, learned quickly, and was more dependable than the average, Young would later come to depend upon him on their trip to California. And what Kit learned from Young cannot be measured, for Young by the time the two met had mastered all the arts of survival in the border trade. When Howard R. Lamar wrote of Young, he might almost have been describing a grown-up Kit Carson: "Young almost ranks with Jedediah Smith in the range of his travels and the success of his enterprises."

By the time Kit joined the party bound for California in August 1829, Young had battled the American Indians of the Gila and Salt rivers whose land and streams he hunted and trapped. He had also taken hard knocks from Mexican customs officers. In 1826 his partner William Wolfskill led a party of Young's trappers from the Copper Mine down the Gila to its junction with the Salt River in today's Arizona. Considering the dangers they faced, the party was small, though composed of very brave and able men such as Milton Sublette, George Yount, Richard Campbell, and Tom "Peg Leg" Smith. Peg Leg later became famous for using an old meat saw and a butcher knife to cut off his own leg that had been shattered by a rifle ball. Then he'd carved an artificial "peg" from the limb of an oak tree. According to Smith, a band of Apaches played friendly with Wolfskill's men at first, then "shot an arrow into a [pack?] animal." Bang. The fight was on. Outnumbered, the trappers fought back, but had to retreat to the Rio Grande. Worse, they lost their precious traps and supplies.

In January 1827 Young put up another, larger party. This time he led it himself. There is little doubt he intended to teach the offenders a lesson and perhaps even to recover the traps and supplies Wolfskill had lost. Trapping down the Gila River from the Santa Rita mine, the men came upon the only three survivors of a thirty-man French-American fur party massacred by Apaches, Yavapais, or possibly Papagos (now known as the Tohono O'odham). Michel Robidoux, James O. Pattie, and one other man had by luck escaped being butchered. Young's men cleaned up the scene and buried the mutilated bodies. "A sight more horrible . . . I have never seen," Pattie said later. "They were . . . cut in pieces, and fragments of their bodies scattered in every direction."

Following the border custom of making the enemy pay in kind for damages, the trappers charged a local village the next morning. They killed as many Apaches as they could run down. Though the question has been raised whether these were the same people who had slaughtered the French-American fur party, Young couldn't have cared less. He had taught a lesson. The word would get around. Border men were quite capable of punishing people for what others had done in order to instruct someone else. What we consider an outrage of justice, they did not. The trappers' golden rule was "do unto others so that others will not do unto you."

After wrecking the village, Young's party trapped on down the Gila and eventually up the Colorado River. While working up the Colorado and then the Mojave River, they were attacked by Mojave warriors. After the trappers killed several of the Mojaves, they hung the bodies in cottonwood trees as a warning meant "to dangle in terror to the rest," as Pattie put it. The Mojaves got even though, for several of them were soon found, or so it was said, roasting and eating the body parts of dead trappers, probably both for revenge and as a way of borrowing the trappers' courage. Discovered in the act, they threw away their bloody meal, then ran off before Young's men could kill any of them.

Thereafter, by May 1827 Young's party returned to Santa Fe over a fantastic route, its trace now "lost in the confusion of dimming memories or fevered imaginations," Robert M. Utley wrote. Upon their return, Young learned that although Santa Fe officials had issued him a valid trapping license before he left for California, they had since revoked it. Thus they arrested him, threw him in jail, and went about confiscating his furs, amounting to twenty-nine cargas (or about 8,700 pounds). Hearing in advance of the trouble awaiting him, Young had left the furs with a friend named Luis Maria C. de Baca who lived at Peña Blanca on the Rio Grande (just below today's Cochiti Lake). Ordered to go get them, Mexican soldiers killed C. de Baca on his own property when he resisted their attempts, then took the packs back to Santa Fe. Such costly troubles only made combative, vengeful men like Young and his trappers harder and more dangerous than ever. "American trappers did not soon forget the confiscation of Ewing Young's furs," wrote David J. Weber. "Young's story must have been repeated on the trail and around the camp-fire for the next decade." These were the men who schooled the growing Kit Carson.

Having learned well from experience, Young changed his plan in 1829. He left Taos with Kit and others in August and headed north so as to make it look like he meant to trap the streams in Colorado. About fifty miles out of Taos, however, he turned southwest and aimed for the vast land beyond Zuni and the Mogollon Rim, toward the Salt River, the lower Gila, and, eventually, toward California. Somewhere along the Salt River, the party ran into the same Native warriors who, Carson told his clerk later, "had defeated the former party," by which Kit probably meant Wolfskill's party of 1826, though possibly Young's of 1827. Years later Kit described the scene that followed: "Young directed the greater part of his men to hide themselves, which was done," he said, "the men conceal-ing themselves under blankets, packsaddles and as best they could. The hills were covered with Indians and seeing so few, they came to the conclusion to make an attack and drive us from our position. Our commander allowed them to enter the camp and then directed the party to fire on them, which was done, the Indians losing in killed fifteen or twenty war-riors and [a] great number in wounded. The Indians were routed, and we continued our march." Of course the war-riors had to get revenge. "We were nightly harassed by the Indians," Carson added. "They would frequently of nights crawl into our camp, steal a trap or so, kill a mule or horse, and endeavor to do what damage they could."

Now Young divided the party. He chose Carson and sixteen others for the trek to California. He sent the rest back with the furs they'd already taken. Carson remembered making "tanks" of deerskins to carry water across the desert ahead. He described crossing "a country sandy, burned up, and not a drop of water." Men and animals "suffered extremely." The party crossed the Colorado River near today's Topock, Ari-zona, where they "procured . . . a few beans and corn" and

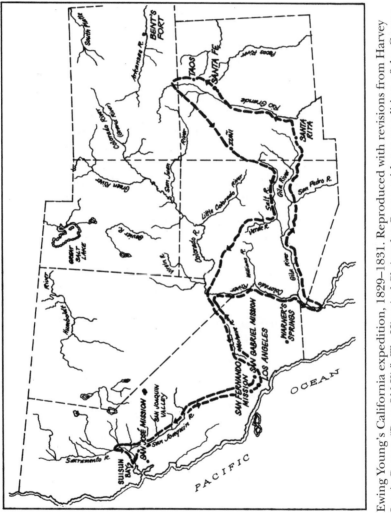

Ewing Young's California expedition, 1829–1831. Reproduced with revisions from Harvey Lewis Carter, *"Dear Old Kit": The Historical Christopher Carson*, with a new edition of the Carson memoirs (Norman: University of Oklahoma Press, 1968), 51.

"purchased . . . a mare heavy with foal" from Mojave people. The mare "was killed and eaten by the party with great gusto; even the foal was devoured," Kit told his clerk in 1856. Then, sweating their way up the dry course of the Mojave River for thirteen days, they at last reached Mission San Gabriel, south of Pasadena in today's greater Los Angeles complex. The party was received by "one priest, fifteen soldiers, and about one thousand Indians," all friendly, Carson recalled.

They stayed over one day to trade for what they needed, swapping four butcher knives for one beef, no doubt on the hoof. "They had about eighty thousand head of stock," Carson told his clerk, "fine fields and vineyards—in fact it was a paradise on earth." Founded in 1771 by Fr. Junipero Serra, Mission San Gabriel flourished among vineyards and live oak groves. Today it remains—a beautifully preserved museum of its former self, a green, quiet place in a sea of modern city. When Young's sunburnt men straggled in, the vineyards prospered and Spanish cattle and fine horses grazed all about. Fr. José B. Sánchez, a gracious, civilized man, was in charge. Harrison G. Rogers, Jedediah Smith's clerk, recalled Smith's visit three years earlier. Father Sánchez took good care of the ragged visitors who had just crossed the Mojave. "I ever shall hold [him] as a man of God," Rogers said, "taking us when in distress, feeding, and clothing us, and may God prosper him and all such men."

From Mission San Gabriel the party left for the San Joaquin and Sacramento river valleys. They traveled by way of Mission San Fernando. Northwesterly down the San Joaquin drainage they discovered signs of other trappers. These turned out to be a Hudson's Bay Company fur brigade of sixty men under Peter Skene Ogden. By then on his sixth expedition to penetrate what would become the American West, Ogden was Hudson's Bay's point man in the struggle between Great Britain and the United States to control the huge basins of the Columbia and Snake rivers. The Jedediah Smith of Canadian fur men, Ogden had a reputation for ruthlessness unknown to Smith's character. Working first for the North-west Fur Company, he had joined Hudson's Bay after the two competing companies merged. He then rose to the position of chief factor. Ogden took it as his mission to trap out the California and Oregon country so completely that American fur men, and, hopefully, the United States, would have no reason to want it. As William H. Goetzmann wrote of him, "Ogden was to create a fur desert, a burned-over district into and beyond which it would not be profitable for rival American traders to pass." He was also something of a diplomat, for these competing bands of trappers, Young's Americans and Ogden's Canadians, traveled peaceably together down the San Joaquin River and up the Sacramento as far as the Pit River. Finally separating, Ogden rode north to the Columbia, Young back down the Sacramento. During this summer in California, Young's party, like Ogden's, hunted "game plenty, elk, deer, and antelope in thousands," Carson recalled. Hunting thrilled these men hugely. For them, a day in the field, beyond all borders, rifle in hand, game boundless, was happiness itself.

Later, Young's party stopped over at Mission San José (Carson confuses Mission San José with Mission San Rafael). The priest was friendly. He also needed Young's help. A band of Native converts had run away from the mission and was hiding out in the hills among hostiles. Fifteen people were sent to bring the converts in, but the hostiles drove them off. Then the priest asked Ewing Young for help. Years later, Carson told his clerk about the ugly affair that followed. According to Kit, Young "directed" him and eleven other trappers to go get the converts. After a day of fighting, the trappers routed the Natives. "[They] lost a great number of men," Kit said. "We entered the village in triumph, set fire to it, and burned it to the ground."

Upon returning to the mission with the runaways, Carson's party was "well received." The priest introduced Ewing Young to don José Asero, captain of a schooner lying offshore.

Better Exchanges Than Gold

Captain Asero bought Young's furs. Not only did the sale provide the money to buy horses and beef from the friendly priest, it proved what trader Richard Campbell had believed, and what Young had hoped for: there was a ready market for beaver on the California coast!

But why the extreme measures? Why the killing and burning? Undoubtedly the hostile Natives and the runaway converts fought hard and fought to kill, for as Carson says, the battle lasted all day long. In such situations, these trappers and most such border men were prepared by culture and by experience to kill or be killed, then to burn the enemy's village and supplies. That had been common practice in Missouri, Kentucky, and the Ohio country, and on the Scots and English border before that. In situations like this one, such men seldom, if ever, considered the humanity or the ethics of the circumstances and of the action they were taking. On this occasion, they probably had what they considered to be practical reasons too. Young needed to sell his furs, and he needed to buy horses and beef. It was probably essential that he please the priest, who provided him with beef and horses and introduced him to Captain Asero. A certain diplomacy was needed. Whether or not he approved of the killing and burning, the priest was little doubt pleased with the return of the converts.

Predictably, the violence was repaid in kind. During the night Native warriors ran off sixty head of fresh horses Young had just bought at the mission. "Twelve of us saddled and took the trail of the lost animals," Carson recalled, and "pursued them upwards of one hundred miles into the Sierra Nevada." Coming upon the thieves feasting on horse meat, he told his clerk later, "We charged their camp, killed eight Indians, took three children prisoners and recovered all our animals, with the exception of six that were eaten, and returned to our camp." Harsh punishment! Men of both sides depended upon horses for transportation and for status. Horses and mules were their pickup trucks and their evidence of rank

61

and power. These warriors would have killed anyone who stole *their* horses, and they could expect to be pursued and killed for stealing other men's horses. Vengeance was the custom of the time and place. As we shall see, all sides on such borders practiced it. "Justice" as we define it today was not often a question.

Striking camp on September 1, Young headed south for Los Angeles. The men desired a night out on the town. Once they got there, Mexican officials demanded their passports. Of course they had none. So, Carson later said, the Mexicans sold them liquor, thinking it would be easy to arrest drunken men. This was a mistake. Trappers fight. Drunken trappers fight mean. Some were crazy fighters. Quite sober himself, Young "directed" Carson "to take three men, all the loose animals, packs, etc., and go in advance," while he stayed behind, trying to bring the others along. "If [Young] did not arrive at my camp by next morning," said Carson, "I was directed to move on . . . and, on my return [to Santa Fe] to report the party killed, for Young would not leave them."

Then, for no apparent reason, James Higgins got off his horse and shot James Lawrence cold dead, "deliberately" Carson said. Observing this craziness, the police backed off. "They departed in all haste, fearing that if men, without provocation, would shoot one another, it would require but little to cause them to murder [the police]," Carson said. Afterward these violent Americans trailed their way back home to New Mexico. Good riddance!

Headed for Taos now in earnest, Young and the others caught up with Carson and the pack stock near dark that evening. After recrossing the Colorado River, they had another fight with Native warriors. Carson proved now that he could think clearly and speak persuasively when he and men with him were in grave danger, a developing trait that was to serve him well later on.

Most members of the party were out checking their traps while he and others guarded camp. Pretending at first to be friendly, a body of warriors approached them. Carson recalled that they came in "large numbers" and "concealed" their weapons. Thus "it became apparent to us that their design was to murder the party." As one of the warriors spoke Spanish, Carson directed him to order all the others out of camp "inside of ten minutes." If even one stayed behind, "he would be shot!" Before ten minutes were up, every warrior had left.

Heading east again, near the junction of the San Pedro River with the Gila, the trappers amused themselves by stealing horses from Indians who had no doubt stolen them from Mexican ranchos down in Sonora. After killing and drying ten horses for meat, the trappers turned the others loose and departed for the Santa Rita Copper Mine. Bluffing, stealing horses, fighting with rifles and knives, and threatening other men made good sport for these trappers, as well as for Native warriors. The more danger a man could face, the more courage he showed. And everyone gained in status.

At the Copper Mine, Young hid the furs in a drift. While Robert McKnight guarded them, Young and Carson rode on to Santa Fe to buy a trader's license. Young then sent back for the two thousand pounds of fur he had "traded for," as Kit put it. Selling these "to advantage" in Santa Fe must have cheered Young considerably. Cheating the Mexican officials who had earlier cheated him no doubt cheered him all the more. Then he paid off his men. It was April 1831. Carson returned to Taos, where he and his friends spent their pay, he recalled, like sailors on shore leave. "Trappers and sailors are similar in regard to the money that they earn so dearly, daily being in danger of losing their lives," he told his clerk later. "They think not of the hardships and danger through which they have passed, spend all they have and are ready for another trip."

Not flamboyant like mountain men Joe Meek, Tom Fitzpatrick, or Jim Bridger, Carson at twenty-one years of age was already revealing traits he would be known for later. His earlier jobs had been boy's jobs, trials, learning times: saddler's apprentice, cavvy boy, teamster, interpreter, cook. But Ewing Young had expected him to think clearly, act decisively in fluid, dangerous situations, and carry out orders, never whining, never letting his comrades down, and performing, without fail, even the toughest jobs assigned to him. And though he had yet to learn caution, Kit had performed well. Young had even used him as second-in-command in very demanding situations. He also undoubtedly enjoyed Kit's companionship. Years later in his book *The Old Santa Fe Trail*, Col. Henry Inman described an older Carson as "brave, but not reckless. . . . Under the average stature, and rather delicate-looking . . . nevertheless a quick, wiry man, with nerves of steel, and possessing an indomitable will . . . full of caution, but show[ing] a coolness in the moment of supreme danger that was good to witness." Kit Carson was clearly developing these qualities during the trip to California with Ewing Young.

This little man—plainspoken, firm, cool under fire, protective of his friends and of others in need, as a young man sometimes impetuous, even reckless, willing to use violence—joined a Rocky Mountain Fur Company brigade in the fall of 1831 after he arrived back from California. Led by famous fur man Tom Fitzpatrick, the brigade rode north from Taos into Colorado. "We traveled north till we struck the Platte River and then took up the Sweetwater," Kit recalled. "We trapped to the head of the Sweetwater and then on to Green River, and then to Jackson's Hole, a fork of the Columbia River; and from there on to the head of Salmon River [where they went into winter quarters] . . . During winter we lost some four or five men when out hunting Buffalo. They [were] killed by the Blackfeet Indians."

Thus Carson outlined his travels over much of the West in one season, the fall and winter of 1831–32. He had now survived, and had learned from, experience that would become familiar to him over the next ten years: trapping, traveling the Rockies and the Far West, fighting with and living among Indians, getting revenge, killing while being shot at, recovering stolen horses, wading freezing rivers, hunting game, and surviving short days and long nights in snowbound winter camps.

4

"Shuch Thing Never Has Been Known until Late"

By Kit Carson's day, New Mexico and the trans-Mississippi West drew people from everywhere. There were the attractions of the Santa Fe trade. There was the promise of beaver on a thousand miles of mountain streams, and the pleasure of exploring the big open from Mexico to Canada, from the Great Plains to California and the Pacific Northwest. The fur market in the East and Europe grew throughout the 1820s and early 1830s because men's fashion required beaver fur for manufacturing men's hats. Until about 1850, when silk began to replace beaver felt as the cloth of choice, every small businessman, politician, and preacher from every town or city, European and American, had to have a felted beaver hat. The great surge of exploring the West between about 1820 and midcentury went along with the thriving beaver trade and the manufacture of fashionable hats. In 1831 young Carson rode into the middle of this hazardous business with a brigade of beaver trappers led north from Taos by Tom Fitzpatrick, a partner in the Rocky Mountain Fur Company.

The trip marks the beginning of Kit's life as a serious trapper, or "mountain man" as they were called. Mountain men must be understood in relation to the lives of the American Indian people with whom they daily associated. They lived with Indians, fought against them, and often beside them.

They were on the alert for them day and night, without pause. Kit's diplomatic abilities developed, along with his fighting skills, throughout these years as his complicated relations with men and women of several tribes expanded. Now he began to practice skills he would later use as the government Ute agent in Taos. In learning their languages, in marrying an Arapaho woman, in looking to the raising of his half-Arapaho daughter, and in hunting, trapping, and fighting, Kit became a dynamic and unusually capable diplomat, as well as a fighter. At times he seemed overzealous when he and other trappers fought Indians, in one instance provoking an unnecessary fight with Crow horse thieves. In another instance he led trappers into an ambush. Biographers have suggested that his fighting zeal was the result of his youth and inexperience. This may be partly true. But the conflicts of his boyhood on the Missouri border, the values of his Scots-Irish culture, and his capacity to learn from experience in the field definitely shaped his behavior and his actions as he grew to manhood.

Indian people were everywhere Kit and other trappers worked. Men of these tribes made a point of becoming proficient warriors. They proved their manhood and earned tribal status by displaying skill at fighting. Desirable territory belonged to a tribe or to a loose confederation of tribes as long as they could defend it. Each group knew its hunting range, and each would fight to keep it. Trappers, if they happened to be white men, were highly visible and usually outnumbered. Thus, cultivating cooperation, and even friendship, enabled them to hunt desirable land and trap productive waters. Working as they did in small parties of three or four men, trappers were at the local Indians' mercy unless they had the goodwill of the tribe. In what might seem the friendliest of situations, however, fighting could break out quick as a prairie fire. Among combative men, all wanting the same ground and all proud of their fighting skills, negotiating was far more difficult than starting a fight. During these years Kit learned to be an able fighter and an effective negotiator in every kind of potentially explosive situation.

A few generalizations about Indian people and outsiders' views of them apply here. First, the European concept of "Indians" was completely foreign to American Indian thinking. People knew themselves as Nez Perce, Crow, Flathead, Jicarilla, Papago, Chiricahua, or Navajo, not as "Indian." A parallel would be the German citizen who thinks of himself as a "Salzburger" rather than a "German," or as a "German" rather than a "European." Second, relations between trappers and Indians, when they were not fighting against each other, were thoroughly pragmatic, based upon mutual need or perceived need. As Tom Dunlay summarized it, "Indians and mountain men not only traded and fought together but interacted in virtually every other way." Trappers needed good beaver streams, and thus required the goodwill of local tribes. And they needed Indian companions and wives to do the camp chores and the packing.

From their side of it, Native people came to need iron knives and axes, wool blankets, trade beads, metal cook pots, muskets, rifles, gunpowder, and lead. As Indians acquired such tools, especially as the rifle replaced the bow and arrow, they had to learn to use them. This process needed traders to supply the goods, and hunters and trappers willing to teach their proper uses. Thus a need for practical education, learning the "how-to" of the technology of the day, helped foster a complex of cooperative efforts, community living arrangements, and trading all around. One of several downsides to this continual close contact was the spread of smallpox, flu, measles, and other diseases deadly to Native people with little or no immunity. One historian believes that European diseases sadly "destroyed as much as ninety percent of the Native population of North America." Another downside for Natives was the devastating pleasure of whiskey.

Third, certain tribes were usually hostile, others usually friendly, still others friendly or not, depending upon circumstances. After Arikaras attacked and killed several of William F. Ashley's trappers at the Arikara village on the upper Missouri River in 1823, trappers and Arikaras hated each other. The Blackfeet were famously hostile to everyone. Some think that this pattern began with an incident on the Lewis and Clark Expedition when a small party traveling with Lewis killed a Piegan warrior and wounded another caught stealing rifles in camp. The Blackfeet, however, were unusually warlike among all the mountains and plains tribes. Inveterate enemies to the trappers, they also continually harassed their neighbors the Nez Perces, Shoshones, and Flatheads. Expert John Ewers observed that "they were the dominant military power on the northwestern plains, feared by all neighboring tribes." By supplying them with firearms as a means of blocking American traders and trappers from mutually desirable territory, British and Canadian trading companies increased Blackfeet efficiency at war making, and probably also their love of power over their neighbors. The Blackfeet were the known bad guys of the northern plains. They liked it that way.

On the other hand, the Nez Perces, Shoshones, and Flatheads were generally friendly to Americans. Delawares and Shawnees, master scouts and hunters, had fought the Europeans and Americans bitterly in the East and in the Ohio Valley in earlier years. By Carson's day, however, they often scouted for the Americans and fought beside them. Other tribes had mixed reputations. The tall, handsome Crows would shake your hand, embrace you, offer you a pipe, and steal your horse. They were the legendary horse thieves among the Plains tribes. Almost any Plains Indians might be friendly to a large, well-armed group. The same Indians were likely to kill anyone caught out alone, poorly armed, or poorly mounted.

Fourth, tribes formed alliances out of mutual interest and convenience for long or short periods just as trappers and other people did, and do. Fifth, tribes had fought among themselves for years just as Europeans had. Making war was not an activity Europeans introduced to Native people. Their styles of warfare were very different, of course, and the European newcomers had to learn the Indian ways of fighting to combat them effectively. "The mountain men were not intruders in a peaceable kingdom," Tom Dunlay wrote. "Tribes fought for possession of horses, for control of hunting grounds, and for revenge. This state of affairs had existed for centuries, long before the appearance of the whites, though their presence and their trade may have . . . complicated, changed, and intensified intertribal warfare." Sixth, there were always special considerations. Dunlay described this aspect of it clearly: "Behavior . . . appropriate with one [tribe] was wholly inappropriate with another. People with whom one had socialized, traveled, shared winter quarters, hunted and eaten buffalo, fought alongside, and who were perhaps relatives by marriage, were to be regarded and treated very differently from [others]."

Finally, there was the perplexing practice of "justice" in the mountains and on the plains. Where there was no written legal code (or codes) covering the vast area in which people of different cultures and languages competed for the right to hunt and to roam, tribes operated by their own laws. The principle generally followed was "an eye for an eye, a tooth for a tooth." Call it the Law of Retribution. In general, an *entire tribe* would be held responsible for the wrongdoing of any *one* of its members. Thus if a Cheyenne warrior stole a horse from a Crow, the Crow Nation held the entire Cheyenne Nation responsible. This principle appealed especially to competitive young men working their way up the tribal ladder of success. It was even easier to pick a fight with a party from another tribe when the adults of your own tribe approved, cheered you on, and gave you status. Successful retributions were celebrated with tribal dances, which included a circle of women, swaying and clapping their hands as they stepped along in a sort of cheering section for the young warriors. Later, as the U.S. government expanded its power across the West and the army arrived as "the protector," the entire system of "justice" would be greatly complicated by the over-lap of Native, federal, territorial, state, and army law and enforcement methods.

After wintering in 1831–32 with the Rocky Mountain Fur Company (RMFC) on the headwaters of the Salmon River in Idaho, Carson trapped the Bear and Green rivers during the spring. While on the Green, he learned that a party under John Gantt was trapping in "New Park" (also called "North Park," today's Jackson County, Colorado). He and three companions thereupon quit the RMFC to join the Gantt and Blackwell company. This act of quitting angered Fitzpatrick, whose RMFC competed fiercely with Gantt and Blackwell's company. Feeling mean and wanting to hurt Gantt's business, "Ole Fitz" apparently started a rumor that Gantt and Blackwell were going broke. If they were going broke, free trappers would be discouraged from trading with them.

Like all trappers, Carson could work for a company at a fixed wage, or by an agreement to sell his furs to that company only. Or he could work independently as a "free trapper," which Kit would soon do. Proud of his independence, the free trapper sold his furs where he chose and at the best price he could get. Now, however, locating Gantt after about ten days, Carson trapped the New Park, the Laramie, and the South Fork of the Platte for the rest of the season. The party then went into winter camp for 1832–33 on the Arkansas River near today's Pueblo, Colorado. During the winter a fight occurred with Crow horse thieves in which Carson played a leading role. The fight illustrates the kind of conflict for which he was noted in dime novels as an American hero, but today is marked as an easy killer, "a natural born killer," as Hampton Sides put it. This change from iconic hero to smooth killer suggests more about the transformation in Carson's audience than it does about Carson himself.

Both Carson and George Bent later described the fight with the Crows in detail. An examination of the two accounts raises questions about Carson's character and his possible motivation. Keep well in mind that while Kit took part in the battle, Bent did not. The two accounts, though they offer extensive detail, report the events leading up to the battle and its development as differently as if the two men were reporting different fights. Biographers' views of Carson's actions in this and other fights also differ. Edwin L. Sabin described him simply as young and impetuous. Biographers Guild and Carter remarked that he was a young man "for whom danger and daring swelled the heart irresistibly." They suggest that we ought to let him off because of his youthful zeal and inexperience. More recent writers suppose that, youthfulness aside, his actions reveal that he was at least trigger-happy, at most genocidal.

Carson dwelt on this fight in what he told his clerk in 1856 as if recalling this particular battle defined something important to him. How did he feel about the fight while it was happening and immediately afterward? How did he feel in looking back upon it years later? Was he proud of his part in the action, or did he regret it? Since he doesn't say, we can never really know. There are possibilities, however, other than that he was simply young and impetuous or that he was psychopathic. George Bent characterizes him as "the leader" of his party in this battle. One writer suggests that as budding leader, he "may have been unwilling to shrink from combat in his first command," certainly a plausible explanation of Kit's dynamic action in this fight. Another possibility is that first leadership might well be the reason he pondered it later on. If, in looking back, he considered his part in this battle an episode in his growth to manhood, or in the history of his country, he would have been more inclined to dwell upon it, as in fact he did. Without any doubt, he was also creating a *public* Carson in his own account in 1856. Aware by then that the fictioneers were exploiting his good name, and also aware that he would be known for what he said of himself, he'd have stressed those qualities he wished to be remembered for: bravery, decisiveness, skill in battle situations—all the qualities his culture stressed as important to manhood. He certainly would have wanted to correct the exaggerated picture appearing wholesale in the dime novels of his day.

However that may be, according to what Carson said in 1856, a party of about fifty Crows stole nine of his party's horses one night in January 1833. The next morning, twelve men took the trail of the thieves. They followed them in deep snow for about forty miles. According to George Bent, two Cheyenne warriors, Black White Man and Little Turtle, were among those tracking the horses. Both men performed very good service. Carson does not mention the two Cheyennes.

According to Kit, his men followed the Crow thieves until they saw fires four miles ahead. They then tied their horses, waited until after dark, and "took a circuitous route for the Indian camp." Crawling to within a hundred yards of the Crows, who had built two "forts," they watched the thieves "dancing and singing, and passing the night jovially in honor of the robbery." Though "suffering severely from the cold," said Carson, "let come what would [we] were bound to get our horses."

Accordingly, he and five others then crawled in among the horses, "the snow being of great service to us for when crawling we were not liable to make any noise." They "cut the ropes and, by throwing snowballs at [the horses], drove them to where was stationed our reserve." By his account, in keeping quiet his men avoided waking up the warriors, or their dogs. Next, said Carson, his men "held council taking the views of each in regard to what had best be done." Those who had recovered their horses favored calling the campaign off and returning to camp on the Arkansas. Those who had "lost no animals . . . wanted satisfaction for [their] trouble and hardships." Carson said he took this latter side of the argument. "Myself and two more were the ones that had not lost horses and we were determined to have satisfaction, let the consequence be ever so fatal. . . . Seeing us so determined for a fight (there is always a brotherly affection existing among the trappers and the side of danger always being their choice) we were not long before all agreed to join us in our perilous enterprise," Kit said, according to his clerk.

By now the horses had been gathered and driven off the field in charge of three men. Nine others then stole upon one of the forts, but woke up a barking dog. "The Indians were alarmed and commenced getting up," Kit said. "We opened a deadly fire, each ball taking its victim. *We killed nearly every Indian in the fort*" (italics mine). "The few that remained were wounded and made their escape to the other fort, the Indians of which commenced firing on us; but without any effect, we keeping concealed behind trees." The remaining Crows now charged from the second fort, but according to Carson, lost "*five more killed*" (italics mine). Again the Crows charged. This time Carson's party backed off. "We had to retreat," he told his clerk years later.

The Americans then returned to their winter camp on the Arkansas by that evening, according to Carson. "During our pursuit for the lost animals we suffered considerably," he said, summing up the affair in 1856, "but, in the success of having recovered our horses and sending many a redskin to his long home, our sufferings were soon forgotten." For reasons known only to them, the embattled Crows did not pursue. For reasons known only to Carson, he did not mention any injury to his men and did not say why they had to retreat. He gave only the number of "redskins" killed. This, he said, was nearly every warrior in one fort, and five more in the other, surely a high percentage of the number in the Crow party. If Carson was correct and if his clerk was not stretching the truth, the trappers truly decimated the Crow band.

Carson's expression of pleasure in "sending" these "redskins to their long home" and his desire for "satisfaction," even though he himself hadn't lost any horses, sounds today like ready-made evidence of the man's pure joy in killing Indians. Thus it may seem decent and right to condemn him as psychopathic, even genocidal. But think of the calamity awaiting anyone caught out in the Rocky Mountains in dead of winter in 1832 when his horses were stolen! Not only were horses (and mules) *the* means of transportation, they were often a party's *only* food source. This was a fact for all sides, whether American Indian or Euro-American. If the animals could not be used as riding or pack stock, their owners killed and ate them to keep from starving. In any event, death was the customary punishment for stealing horses and setting men afoot on America's borders, places where there was no written law and no judges or juries to slow the process down. These Crows were fully aware of this custom. They regularly practiced it themselves within their own culture and with other tribes. They would have killed with zeal anyone caught stealing *their* horses.

Some years after the fight, George Bent got the story as Black White Man told it. He also claimed to have heard it from Carson "just before he died in 1868." Bent knew Carson for years and considered him an old friend. George was William Bent's son and the nephew of Charles Bent of Taos fame. He lived all his life among the Cheyenne people and must have heard their stories many times over, for the Cheyennes told stories around their lodge fires in the evenings to entertain themselves and to pass on tribal history and tradition. Beginning in 1905 Bent wrote letters to George E. Hyde, who published the book *Life of George Bent Written from His Letters.* These letters give Bent's and the Cheyennes' version of this particular battle with the Crow thieves. It is a very different story from Carson's. Unlike Carson, Bent was literate. Like Kit, he was considered reliable by those who knew him. Anthropologist George Bird Grinnell, author of *The Fighting Cheyennes* and *The Cheyenne Indians,* thought highly of him and often used him as an interpreter.

Bent's account has Little Turtle and Black White Man, who was George's uncle, staying over in camp with Carson's party on the night the Crows stole the horses. It represents Carson as leader of the trappers, a role Kit may have been assuming about that time. In Bent's version, the two Cheyennes kept their own horses picketed overnight. After Carson sent them out the next morning to bring in his party's horses, Little Turtle came back, "riding fast." Many moccasin tracks in the snow, he said, showed that a big war party had stolen the trappers' horses.

According to Bent, Carson then "gave his orders at once." During the pursuit that followed, the two Cheyennes rode out ahead in deep snow, scouting, while "Carson and his eleven Americans" followed along afoot, "flounder[ing] about in the drifts," said Bent. When the Cheyennes "picked up two arrows in the snow," they recognized the thieves as Crow. Then Little Turtle and Black White Man spotted the Crow camp ahead and pointed it out to Carson, who gave orders to attack "at once." Kit ordered the two Cheyennes to "keep out of the fight," but to "stampede the stolen herd" if they saw a chance. Ever heard horses stampede? Even in deep snow, a stampede would have raised a half-dead Crow and his half-frozen dog. "Carson knew that the Crows outnumbered his men five or six to one," Bent said, "but he did not hesitate to attack them right out in the open." He said nothing about pitching snowballs at horses, about any attempt to preserve quiet, or about the democratic conference in the snow, all of which Carson described at length to his clerk in 1856. Bent did say that the Crow thieves had not expected to be pursued. "They were astonished," he said, "that such a weak party should dare to approach them."

Bent's account, seemingly a composite of what Bent got from the Cheyennes and of what Carson told him in 1868, differs substantially from Carson's version of 1856. Bent said that "sixty" Crow warriors charged Carson's twelve Americans *first* and surrounded them. But when the Americans "turned loose with their rifles the Crows had a big surprise." The Americans ran the Crows off the field. Then "Carson and his men came tumbling into the bushes, firing right and left with their rifles and pistols and giving the warriors no time to make a stand." Meanwhile, Little Turtle and Black White Man had gathered the loose horses. Harvey L. Carter added to this information years later that Black White Man told George Bird Grinnell that the Americans killed only two Crows, "the two Cheyennes accounting for the other deaths."

The most striking of several differences in the two accounts occurs in Bent's report (backed by Grinnell) that Carson's men killed only two of the thieves, while Carson reports "nearly every Indian" in one fort killed, then shortly afterward "five more killed" in the other fort. "It is a strange thing that Carson's men, all armed with rifle and pistol and all good shots, should have killed only two Indians in this fight; and queerly enough, not one of the Americans was even wounded," Bent said. This and other sharp discrepancies in the two accounts simply cannot be reconciled. It is as if Bent and Carson described two different fights. Bent's distance from the event surely accounts for some of the difference. He got all his information by word of mouth from participants.

As for Carson, it is possible that he was describing the *public* Carson, the man he wanted people to remember. Possibly his memory for detail was failing him when he dictated the account in 1856. Possibly the clerk John Mostin stretched the truth here in order to "improve" the story for prospective book sales. It is even possible that Kit himself stretched the truth now and then. After all, he'd sat around many a campfire visiting with the West's most infamous storytellers—the mountain men. There is no reason to suppose he couldn't "improve" a story for the fun of it now and then too. His tedious description of the democratic conference in the snow is certainly hard to take straight. These trappers had just trailed the Crow thieves for miles in the snow, then spent the night trying to collect their horses without waking the Crows up. Their buckskins were wet. One has to ask: did they have the inclination for a long discussion in the snow?

Over the next few years, Carson saw as much of the Rocky Mountains as any man ever did. He soon left Gantt and

Blackwell to work as a free trapper, going wherever he wished, selling his furs wherever he chose. He trapped with Hudson's Bay Company men and with Lucien Fontenelle, whom Hiram Chittenden described in his classic *The American Fur Trade of the Far West* as "one of the best examples of the Rocky Mountain 'partisan,' the leader of a [fur] 'brigade.'" He trapped the Blackfeet country on the Missouri River's headwaters and the Yellowstone with Jim Bridger. He attended several fur rendezvous, including some of the most colorful on Horse Creek and the Green River. He fought the Blackfeet many times. "We were determined," he said, "to try our strength to discover who had [the] right to the country."

He came within an inch of getting himself killed several times. In February 1835 trappers he was with were trying to re-capture stolen horses. While covering a partner named Mark Head, Kit fired and was left with an empty rifle. Seeing a warrior "sighting for my breast," he recalled, "I could not load in time so I commenced dodging as well as I could. He fired; the ball grazed my neck and passed through my shoulder."

Another instance occurred in June 1838 in what Carson called "the prettiest fight I ever saw," a phrase that seems to today's readers to suggest that he lacked any hesitation about killing Indians, even that he thoroughly enjoyed the act of killing. In a fight with Blackfeet, he had dismounted to help a friend named Cotton Mansfield, whose horse had fallen on him. Carson fired at a warrior who was running in to kill Mansfield. At the same instant, his own horse spooked and broke away and he was left afoot, surrounded, with an empty rifle. Showing great presence of mind, he waved to a nearby comrade named White. "As soon as he saw the predicament I was in he came to me," Carson recalled. "I mounted his horse [behind him] and we continued our retreat." Meanwhile, Mansfield's horse got up. Mansfield was able to mount and to ride off.

Carson was remarkably steady under fire, as in this instance with Mansfield. If he were alive today, he ought to make a first-rate Army Special Forces line officer. If he felt any fear, it was after the danger had passed. He once admitted to being afraid after two grizzlies put him up a tree, recalling that he had "never. . . been so scared in my life." But he never admitted to feeling, and never showed, the kind of fear that "freezes" a man from quick action in combat. On this particular day, trappers and Blackfeet kept up the fight. "We finally routed them," Carson recalled, "took several scalps, having several of our men slightly wounded." His use of the phrase "the prettiest fight I ever saw" doesn't necessarily mean that he relished the act of battlefield butchery. It may well mean simply that he and two companions, Mansfield and White, survived a very close call with death. It may mean that everyone on both sides fought well, as they apparently did. No one showed cowardice. No one flinched. Or, because both sides, trappers and Blackfeet, were determined to win the right to hunt and to trap this country, it may mean that Carson believed the trappers had successfully asserted that right.

After leaving Gantt's employ in 1833, Kit set out independently with two other trappers. As usual, he didn't give his reasons. It can be assumed that he had discovered he was experienced enough by now to be able to travel successfully with a small party. The chances of taking beaver with a small party were far better than with an entire brigade although the dangers were much greater. He knew that as a free trapper he stood a better chance of making a profit on his risk, and he enjoyed his independence. On this venture all turned out as he had hoped. "We trapped nearly all the streams within the mountains, keeping from the plains from fear of danger," he recalled. "We had very good luck; having caught a great amount of Beaver, we started for Taos to dispose of it and then have the pleasure of spending the money that caused us so much danger and hardship to earn." It seems clear that he had not as yet married. He was still throwing his hard-won earnings away on a few days of fun after the danger had passed and after the work was done.

In the fall of 1833 he left Taos again. This time he traveled with Capt. Richard Bland Lee, a U.S. Army officer in the West, on an unknown assignment. Lee reported leaving Abiquiu, New Mexico, on November 19, 1833, with twelve men. Carson was one of these. They took the Old Spanish Trail northwest. Acting as a trader, Lee trailed to northeastern Utah along the White and Uinta rivers, tributaries of the Green. On or near the Uinta they met Antoine Robidoux of the prominent St. Louis trading family. Robidoux kept two trading forts, one at the site of present Delta, Colorado, the other near White Rocks, Utah. One was called Fort Uinta (trappers called it Fort "Winty"), the other Fort Uncompahgre. Both were sometimes called "Fort Robidoux." In late February Lee left to pursue his own plan. According to what he later told his clerk, Carson stayed behind to winter "on the mouth of the Winty" with twenty of Antoine's trappers and traders. Here, he said, "We found a place that answered every purpose. . . . We passed a very pleasant winter."

Here occurred another of that kind of action for which Carson has been called cold-blooded in killing Indians. During the winter a man Kit identified in his 1856 account only as "a California Indian" who worked for Robidoux "run off with six animals, some of them . . . worth two hundred dollars per head." Robidoux then "came to me," Kit said, "and requested that I should pursue him." Deserting the party and stealing the horses in such a place in 1833 were both considered unpardonable crimes. Everyone involved understood this hard fact. The thief knew that he had signed his death warrant, that execution was the price he would pay if he were caught. The outcome can be foreseen.

Carson chose a Ute man "from a nearby village" to go with him on the chase. Robidoux "furnished" them with "two fine animals." Together they rode after the thief, who headed toward California. After a hundred miles by Carson's account, the Ute's horse gave out. Carson rode on alone. The rest can be told in his own words as his clerk put them down in 1856:

"But I was determined not to give up the chase," he said. "I continued in pursuit and, in thirty miles, I overtook the Indian with the horses. Seeing me by myself [he] showed fight. I was under the necessity of killing him, recovered the horses, and returned on my way to our camp and arrived in a few days without any trouble."

Chilling. Considering Carson's usual candor and especially the situation, there can be no doubt the thief "showed fight." By border custom, by the rules of border justice, the man had to fight to win, or die in the attempt. If there was any slightest chance he'd go free by turning the horses loose and making a run for it, his fighting stance ended that. Carson had just ridden horseback at speed an estimated 130 miles and had to return over the same distance alone, with no help, leading supremely valuable horses. He'd have had no way of picketing them safely to graze while he caught a few moments' sleep. He could hardly have been in a gracious mood. He still was not when he recalled the incident years later. It was not the fact that the thief was a "California Indian" that was against him. It was not a racial matter. The hard fact was that a man had stolen very precious horses from a party he deserted in a time and a place where the penalty for such acts was death, often with torture first. That was unwritten law. The thief understood this law as well as Carson did.

Carson was also exhausted. Mountain men in dangerous country caught little sleep. When they did, they slept with their loaded rifles by their side. They got up at night to change guard, looked over one shoulder to set the traps, and always stayed out of the firelight. If they slept, it was on rock, cold ground, or packed snow. A saddle blanket worn slick with sweat, a flea-ridden buffalo robe, or a grubby rag of point blanket provided what cover they had. Their buckskin leggings were always wet, unless they slept too close to the fire, when the buckskins dried crisp. In 1847 Lt. George W. Brewerton traveled east with Carson from California. He described the daily routine: "We rode from fifteen to fifty miles a day, according to the distance from water," he wrote. "Among our men there was but little talking and less laughing and joking. . . . The gloomy land by which we were surrounded, scanty food, hard travel, and the consciousness of continual peril, all tended to restrain the exhibition of animal spirits. Carson . . . scarcely spoke; his keen eye was continually examining the country . . . his whole manner that . . . of a man deeply impressed with . . . a sense of responsibility." Such conditions affected the emotions. Native warriors suffered the same conditions. Carson's tiring chase after the horse thief had to have colored his attitude at the time, and little doubt his later description of the incident.

At the 1835 rendezvous on the Green River he had his famous duel with "Shunar" or "Chouinard," the drunken bully. Probably at this rendezvous he also courted Waa-nibe, an Arapaho girl whose name seemingly means "Singing Grass." Although the evidence is conjectural, Carson biographers think it possible the duel occurred because Chouinard also showed an interest in Waa-nibe. Carson told his friend Smith H. Simpson later that "he and Shunar were rivals for the favor of an Indian girl, and [Simpson] understood it was the Arapaho girl that Carson married soon afterward." Kit described the ugly affair in some detail to his clerk years later, but left out the background.

According to what Carson told his clerk, Chouinard was a great bully. Carson described him as "overbearing" and "very strong." After beating up "two or three men" on this particular day, he bragged that he could "flog" all the "Frenchmen" in camp with no trouble at all, "and as for the Americans, he would take a switch and switch them." Tired of hearing such talk, Carson made the customary challenge. "I told him that I was the worst American in camp," he said. "Many could t[h]rash him, only [they did not] on account of being afraid [of him], and that if he made use of any more such expressions, I would rip his guts."

Both men went for their horses and their guns. Chouinard reappeared on the field in front of the camp armed with a rifle, Carson with a pistol. By Carson's account, the horses were touching, probably shoulder to shoulder as horses would do, when Kit "demanded if [he] was the one [Chouinard] intended to shoot." Chouinard "said no, but at the same time drawing his gun so he could have a fair shot. I was prepared," said Carson, "and allowed him to draw his gun. We both fired at the same time; all present said but one report was heard. I shot him through the arm and his ball passed my head, cutting my hair and the powder burning my eye, the muzzle of his gun being near my head when he fired. During our stay in camp we had no more bother with this bully Frenchman."

There are at least two other early descriptions of this incident. One by trapper Isaac Rose was retold in James B. Marsh's *Four Years in the Rockies; or, The Adventures of Isaac P. Rose* (1884). The other is an account by Rev. Samuel Parker in *Journal of an Exploring Tour Beyond the Rocky Mountains* (1838). Parker was a Protestant missionary on the way to Oregon. His party had stopped over at the rendezvous where he learned what he told of the duel, which he may not have actually seen. Both accounts add interesting detail and raise questions, but do not change the substance of Carson's account.

As for Waa-nibe, the probable cause of Carson's anger, she must have been pretty. Carson would have courted her after the custom of obtaining her father's permission with a gift of horses, a point blanket or two, and, if she was exceedingly precious, even a rifle. Though very little is known of her or of the marriage, the scant evidence suggests that she and Kit made a healthy union. The couple had two daughters. The first, named Adaline, was probably born in 1837, either while Carson was hunting out of Fort Hall, or at the rendezvous on Horse Creek that summer. She was named for Kit's favorite niece back home in Missouri. Waa-nibe and her baby would have packed along with Kit on his trapping rounds in the fall of 1837 and during the spring of 1838. When he rode down to Fort Davy Crockett in Brown's Hole (a valley enclosed by mountains was called a "hole") on the Green River (in northwestern Colorado) by September 1838, she and Adaline would have been with him.

After he made a trading trip from Brown's Hole to the Navajo country with other men that fall, he returned to hunt for Fort Davy Crockett during the winter of 1838–39. In October a traveler named E. Willard Smith saw him nearby with a hunting party, "composed of seven whites and two squaws." Very likely Waa-nibe was one of these wives. Starting out in the spring of 1839, Kit hunted and trapped the rest of the year. He covered mountains and streams from southern Wyoming north to the Yellowstone and Salmon rivers. Marc Simmons believes that Waa-nibe's second baby was born during these months and that Waa-nibe died shortly afterward, during "the winter of 1839–1840, possibly at Brown's Hole." Her death was most likely caused by complications following childbirth. The old fort in Brown's Hole, where she had probably lived happily for a time, and where she probably died, sat among immense cottonwood trees along a deep blue river flowing through a green, very remote Colorado valley rimmed in mountains.

Both girls survived their mother. More about Adaline later, but the baby died in a tragic accident when she was about three years old. Carson had left her in Taos with Charles Bent's family and their servants while he was off on a trip. Teresina Carson, Kit's daughter with his last wife Josefa, told a researcher in 1908 that the baby girl fell into a kettle of boiling soap about 1843 in Taos during her father's absence. Rural women commonly made lye soap by boiling wood ash and scraps of hog fat in open kettles of steaming water over a fire outdoors. They would turn away from the fire to do other chores, then check to add firewood as needed. Perhaps the little girl, fascinated by the bubbles in the steaming kettle, clambered onto a stool or a wobbly chair nearby while no one happened to be watching and tumbled over. One can only imagine the worst. Carson himself, ever tight-lipped about personal and family matters, apparently never spoke of it. He did speak of Waa-nibe on one known occasion. While in Washington, D.C., as a dispatch carrier for the army, he told his friend Lt. Edward F. Beale, "She was a good wife to me. I never came in from hunting that she did not have the warm water ready for my feet." Considering that he provided for his family by hunting game and by trapping beaver in icy mountain streams, this was a sincere compliment. Husband and wife had taken care of each other's needs.

In 1840 Carson attended the last of the big fur company–sponsored rendezvous on the Green River. Streams were trapped out by then and men's fashion in hats was changing, so there was little market for beaver. As a mountain man's annual "fair," the rendezvous this year was a bust. Everyone looked ahead toward a dim future. How does a trapper make a living when the streams are trapped out and the market is dead? Everybody was cranky, swilling and sleeping it off, or looking for a fight. No one had any zest for the usual foot-races, hatchet throwing, wrestling matches, or target shooting. The only good thing going was the presence of Fr. Pierre Jean de Smet, who was passing through with missionaries bound west on a peace mission to the Flathead people. Here Carson would have met the priest, soon to be known for founding St. Mary's Mission in Montana's Bitterroot Valley and a convent and school run by Catholic sisters in Oregon's Willamette Valley. Father De Smet even concluded a peace treaty between the Blackfeet and their neighbors the Flatheads, who had always warred with each other. Biographers Simmons and Bernice Blackwelder both suggest that Kit brought his daughters to Father De Smet for baptism.

Waa-nibe had recently died. Kit had two helpless little girls to worry about. They were probably with him, and if so, cared for by a friend's Indian wife. Kit later told an acquaintance, James F. Meline, "I remember [Father De Smet] came once

85

among the hunters and trappers up in the mountains, and baptized forty odd children." That would have been the rendezvous of 1840. Perhaps two of those children were Kit's daughters, but Carson never spoke of it either way.

Of Father De Smet, Carson did tell his clerk in 1856: "I can say of him that if ever there was a man that wished to do good, he is one. He never feared danger when duty required his presence among the savages[,] and if good works on this earth are rewarded hereafter I am confident that his share of glory and happiness in the next world will be great." Kit's awareness of the practical value of "duty" and "good works" comes through very strongly here. He may even have been thinking about his own religious faith. Notably, his words echo another side of a stern principle that his Calvinistic great-grandfather, the Presbyterian minister, would never have compromised. As a believer in a predestinarian faith, Rev. Alexander Carson believed that "good works" in this life can avail a man or a woman *nothing* toward salvation. Kit's phrasing, however, suggests a more hopeful faith popular in Kit's day. This was the "New Light" way of Protestant evangelicals who were thriving on the borders. New Lights believed that because God is infinitely forgiving, "good works" may well influence his judgment of men and women as they prepare for the afterlife. There is no reason to think that Kit, widely as he traveled, would not have been aware of these new ways of believing. In any event, he clearly used the words of a more hopeful faith in his account of Father De Smet's work.

Becoming acquainted with Father De Smet may even have influenced decisions Carson would soon have to make about his own life. For within just a year and a half, Fr. José Antonio Martínez would baptize him into the Roman Catholic faith. A few months after that, Kit would marry the young Josefa Jaramillo in her church. Perhaps Waa-nibe's death, his responsibility for his two daughters, and the meeting with Father De Smet had set Kit to thinking seriously about his own actions, his responsibilities, and about matters eternal. Some such thinking, in addition to his love of Josefa, had to precede his Roman Catholic baptism and his marriage in Josefa's church.

Just a year before the last rendezvous, Kit was involved in an unusual event at Fort Davy Crockett. A handful of deadbeat trappers had been loafing around the fort in 1839. They stole horses from a band of friendly Shoshones to replace their own that had been stolen by traveling Sioux. Carson and like-minded trappers were outraged by this meanness, and they knew if the Shoshone horses weren't returned, their own horses could be in danger. Whether from outrage or from more practical considerations, or both, the fact is that the trappers took action quickly to redress the wrong. These included Joe Walker, Robert Newell, Joe Meek, and Kit Carson. They formed a group, ran the deadbeats down, took the stolen horses back, and returned them to their owners.

Who knows how Kit felt about righting this wrong? His attention at the time was probably on family matters since Waa-nibe had just died, or was near death. All we can know for certain is that he joined the others in making this ugly matter right. It was a new turn from the old kind of "border justice." Mountain man Robert Newell expressed his feelings in no soft words. "Shuch thing," he wrote, "never has been Known until late." The traveler E. Willard Smith said considerably more: "The trappers remaining at the fort expressed their displeasure so strongly at this act of unparalleled meanness that [the deadbeats] were obliged to leave the party." When mountain men kicked out members of their own brotherhood for stealing horses from Indians, "justice" was taking on new meanings on the borders.

5

A Clear Steady Blue Eye

By the time Waa-nibe died, trapping as a way of life was already in steep decline. After attending the 1840 rendezvous, Carson trapped in Colorado the following spring, then summered around Fort "Winty" in Utah in 1841. With other trappers, he pondered the future. Like any workers being laid off, they would have to find new jobs.

A problem of chronology now arises because of Carson's habitual failure to clarify dates in what he told his clerk later. "Returned to Robidoux Fort [Fort Uintah] and disposed of our Beaver and remained till September," he recalled. "Beaver was getting scarce, and, finding it was necessary to try our hand at something else, [we] concluded to start for Bent's Fort on the Arkansas." Whether he meant September of 1840 or 1841 remains uncertain, although most people accept Harvey L. Carter's opinion that the year was 1841.

Kit's married friends would have brought their American Indian wives and children with them, their families trailing along on quiet horses, the women doing the packing, camp work, and child caring while the men hunted game and watched out for enemies. At Bent's Fort the sociable party found themselves out on the Great Plains east of the Rockies, those faraway mountains that had provided their living for so many years. Maybe here they could all make a new start. Some of the old trappers would take up hunting, others scouting or piloting, still others farming and ranching, and even politics. Joe Walker and George Yount eventually settled in California, Ewing Young and Joe Meek in Oregon, John Colter and Andrew Henry on farms back home in Missouri, where William H. Ashley became a U.S. representative and ran twice for governor of Missouri. Most of the old-timers, however, simply disappeared.

No sooner did Carson arrive at Bent's Fort than William Bent offered him a job. It was steady work for wages, something Kit hadn't known as a trapper. He held this job for nearly eight months. "I was kindly received at the fort by Messrs. Bent and St. Vrain, offered employment to hunt for the Fort at one dollar per day. Accepted this offer, and remained in their employ till 1842," he said. Bent's Fort lay on the mountain branch of the Santa Fe Trail on the left bank of the Arkansas River. It was about twelve miles from the junction with the Purgatory River, on the line people generally accepted as the border with Mexico. By terms of the Transcontinental Treaty (or Adams-Onís Treaty) signed February 22, 1819, Spain had officially recognized the Louisiana Purchase. The boundary of this land empire had been set along the Arkansas, the Red, and the Sabine rivers.

Besides refitting travelers going east and west, William Bent traded successfully here for many years with the Northern Plains tribes: Cheyennes, Arapahos, and others. The firm named Bent, St. Vrain and Co. also maintained a satellite post on the South Platte River to the north, and another to the south on the Canadian River in the Texas Panhandle. This post soon failed due to the hostility of the Southern Plains tribes, Comanches, Kiowas, and Plains Apaches, who refused to come into the main post on the Arkansas because their traditional enemies, the Northern Cheyennes and Arapahos, traded there. Quickly falling into disrepair, the southern post's rotting walls were known everywhere on the plains as the "Adobe Walls." Two major battles with Indians later occurred here. One of these would involve Kit Carson.

For years Kit had known the Bent brothers, owners of Bent's Fort. Charles Bent and Ceran St. Vrain had founded their trading company as early as 1830. In September 1846 Gen. Stephen Watts Kearny would appoint Charles Bent to the position of New Mexico's first civil governor. Early on a cold January morning in 1847 a crazed mob led by a Taos Pueblo man, Tomasito Romero, were to break into Governor Bent's home in Taos. Though Bent would try talking sense to the gang at the door, they rushed him with arrows and knives. As he made his stand, the women in the house used a poker and a big iron spoon to hack an escape hole in the adobe wall of an inside room. Those who crawled out included Bent's common-law wife, Maria Ignacia Bent, and her daughter, fourteen-year-old Rumalda Bent Boggs, recently married to Thomas Boggs. Ignacia Bent's sister, Josefa Jaramillo, by this time Kit Carson's wife, was also there. She too would escape. A neighbor hid the women by dressing them up as servants grinding corn.

After scalping Bent, the mob would go on a wild spree. They killed several more people, including Pablo Jaramillo, Josefa's brother and Kit's brother-in-law, and his friend, Narciso Beaubien, heir apparent to the great Beaubien-Miranda Grant, later famous as the Maxwell Land Grant. Young Narciso Beaubien had been home on vacation from school in St. Louis. His violent death that day changed New Mexico's history forever by placing his sister, Luz, and her husband, Lucien B. Maxwell, in line as heirs to her father's immense grant of land. Others killed were Sheriff Stephen Louis Lee, District Attorney J. W. Leal, and Josefa's uncle, Prefect Cornelio Vigil. Outside Taos, mobs killed Carson's old mountain man friend, Mark Head; Lawrence Waldo at Mora; and six other men at Turley's Mill.

Charles Bent's brother William had overseen construction of Bent's Fort in 1833–34. As a partner in Bent, St. Vrain and Co. he remained a remarkably successful manager for many years. He married an elite Cheyenne woman named

Owl Woman. The two lived in a tepee in a Cheyenne village in a cottonwood grove along the Arkansas River near the fort. There they raised their children. The story of their life together is an idyllic picture of the ideal suburban arrangement of the time. The family could stay at home during the day. Owl Woman did the domestic chores and visited with the other women while the children played in the river's sand under the cottonwoods. Meanwhile, their father, William Bent, walked or jogged along horseback to the office at Bent's Fort each morning.

Though Carson was well qualified for the job as hunter when he arrived at Bent's Fort, he also had "connections." He had known William Bent since 1829 and Charles probably even longer than that. Taos was Charles Bent's home. Kit had been drawn to Taos since he first arrived in New Mexico in 1826, and the people of Taos had become his friends. Charles Bent's wife was the older sister of Josefa Jaramillo, the lovely girl Carson would later marry. Josefa was indeed beautiful. English traveler and writer Lewis H. Garrard, who could not keep his eyes off New Mexican women, saw her at the trial of Governor Bent's murderers. "Her style of beauty was of the haughty, heart-breaking kind," he wrote, "such as would lead a man with the glance of the eye to risk his life for one smile. I could not but desire her acquaintance." Kit had already seen her at work or at play when he stopped to visit the Bents from time to time. Perhaps he had even asked them about Josefa and they had introduced the two, she as Ignacia's favorite little sister, and he as a friend from among their wide circle of acquaintances.

As always, however, now means now, and Kit had things to do. Waa-nibe had died. Kit's first duty was to provide for their two daughters. He worked as a hunter for Bent's Fort at a dollar a day, but such a job could not be expected to last, and there were no "benefits" as we know them. A commercial hunter lived a nomad's life. He had to follow herds of wild animals whose populations fell off here and rose somewhere else. He might be gone on the hunt a week at a time, or much longer. What would such a man do with growing girls? Also, if hunting was "man's work," child caring was considered "woman's work." One option was to leave the girls with an older woman. Another was to marry again. Kit would try both ways. Hearsay had it that Jack Robertson's Indian wife, Marook, took care of the girls while Carson was still at Fort Uintah.

At Bent's Fort, Kit could easily have left them with a Cheyenne woman from the nearby village. One legend has it that Charlotte Green, a Bent family slave and head cook at Bent's Fort, looked after them for a time. In Marc Simmons's words, Charlotte "commanded a small army of Indian kitchen helpers, and it would have been a simple task to have one of them keep a constant eye on the children." Undoubtedly many children played noisily—just imagine how happily—around the fort by day, all of them running hither and yon in bunches, the girls screaming those earsplitting little-girl screams and hugging corn shuck dolls, the boys hiding in the grass, jumping on half-wild horses, and shooting at birds and rabbits with kid-sized bows.

While he hunted for the fort, Kit married a Cheyenne woman named Making Out Road. Like his earlier marriage to Waa-nibe, this one was in the so-called Indian way; that is, in agreement with the custom of the culture, a couple chose to live together in the same tepee. Little is known of this brief marriage. Carson would not speak of it. According to Teresina Bent, Charles Bent's daughter, he even denied that it ever took place. Said Teresina, "Uncle Kit was very angry when [a man who had interviewed him] said that he was married to . . . Making Out Road. He said there was no truth in that story." Much later in 1908, however, Kit Carson's niece Susan Carson's husband, Jesse Nelson, told the interviewer Francis W. Cragin of the marriage to Making Out Road. And the ethnologist George Bird Grinnell, who also heard of the marriage from Cheyenne elders he was interviewing in 1917, published the information in 1923. It is said that Kit and Making Out Road had a baby daughter who died soon after her birth, but the evidence is insubstantial. As so often, the truth about Carson remains elusive. In any event, much later George Bent told George Hyde about Carson and this unfortunate marriage to Making Out Road. "While living at the old fort he married a Cheyenne girl," Bent wrote Hyde, "but they had no children."

According to Grinnell's informants, the couple quickly grew apart. Marc Simmons, who offers the most plausible account of this mysterious affair, suggests that Making Out Road, beautiful, independent, and determined, probably refused to put up with Kit's long absences from home, as well as with Adaline, the older of his two daughters, whom Kit often left with her. The name Making Out Road may mean "one who lays down the law." If she was indeed such an independent woman, she must have had a difficult time in the Cheyenne world, where wives did all the work while the men put in their time visiting, hunting game, stealing horses, and preening themselves for war.

Carson's motives and his part in the failure of the short marriage can only be imagined. Clearly his two daughters, Adaline and the baby girl, needed a stepmother or a female caretaker, and Making Out Road was attractive. But satisfaction of the basic needs of surrogate motherhood and of romance could not carry the marriage. Working as a hunter, Kit was away from home for weeks at a time. He also had the habit of visiting Taos often, where rumor was that he had a fling with Antonina Luna, mountain man Jim Beckwourth's former girlfriend. It was not a rumor, however, but a fact that he had fallen in love with Josefa Jaramillo. When in Taos, Kit never failed to visit Charles Bent and Maria Ignacia Bent, Josefa's sister. He knew the Bents well, and trusted them as much as he trusted anyone in the world.

Meanwhile, back at Bent's Fort, Making Out Road was increasingly unhappy about having to keep Adaline while

Carson was away. Before leaving New Mexico to take Adaline to Missouri to board her with relatives who could give her schooling, Kit was baptized by Fr. José Antonio Martínez in Our Lady of Guadalupe Church in Taos on January 28, 1842. Marc Simmons suggests that Carson "submitted to" baptism for thoroughly practical reasons. He had fallen in love with Josefa Jaramillo by then and intended to marry her. Of course her parents would have insisted that any prospective husband be Roman Catholic. Although Kit had never seriously attended church, his great-grandfather was a minister, and the Scots-Irish culture was marked by its sternly Protestant character. Traveling preachers were all about during Kit's childhood, and baptisms were common practice on the borders. Possibly Kit had already been baptized. His religious leanings, however, whatever they may have been, were surely not per se toward the Roman Catholic faith.

Not until February 6, 1843, exactly a year and one week after he baptized Carson, would Father Martínez marry this odd couple. Meanwhile, Carson had been back to Missouri, placed Adaline with caring relatives, met Lt. John C. Frémont, and held a job as guide to Frémont's first expedition. He had traveled from Taos to St. Louis, from St. Louis all the way to South Pass, back to Bent's Fort, then home again to Taos. He had just crossed a third of the continent. Whatever was going on in his romantic life during this time, the situation was complicated, and it was loaded. Any discerning person might have foreseen the outcome. When he returned to the Cheyenne village at Bent's Fort to pick up Adaline to take her to Missouri, he discovered all his belongings piled outside Making Out Road's tepee, the Cheyenne way of divorce.

The briefest account of the failed marriage is biographer Edwin L. Sabin's: "In about a year," he wrote, "Carson, no hero to his wife, found himself and all his personal possessions including Adaline thrown out of his lodge." Making Out Road did not stop with Carson. After marrying and divorcing two Cheyenne husbands, she married Charlie Rath, a well-known freighter, trader, and hide merchant. They had a daughter named Belle who attended the Darlington School in Oklahoma, then married a soldier. Belle's school superintendent recalled that Making Out Road was "a very determined woman, and was able to put Belle's husband in his place."

Recently divorced Cheyenne style, newly baptized as a Roman Catholic, in love with Josefa Jaramillo, and out on the road again in the spring of 1842, Carson left Bent's Fort for Missouri to place Adaline with his family and to take care of other matters. From Bent's Fort to Westport he traveled with Bent's annual caravan that carried the year's yield of buffalo robes and beaver bales. The caravan arrived at Westport no later than the middle of May, though the exact date is unknown. Charles Bent and Lucien Maxwell were also with the caravan. Kit picked up five-year-old Adaline at Bent's Fort from either William Bent and his wife, or from another Cheyenne woman caring for her since Making Out Road had put her out of the tepee. From Bent's Fort to Westport, a trip of about five weeks, Adaline rode with others in a light carriage called a Dearborn. It is probable that while he was on this trip his baby daughter left in charge of the Bents in Taos died tragically.

Evidence is conflicting about Adaline's next years. Although John C. Frémont later wrote that Carson "had just placed [Adaline] in the shelter of the St. Louis convent-school" when he and Carson first met in 1842, others sternly disagreed. Kit's sister Mary Ann insisted that the girl "was not sent to a convent in St. Louis as reported [by Frémont]." Others thought she attended both the St. Louis convent *and* Rock Springs school near Glasgow, Missouri. One report was that she spent six years on a farm near Glasgow with Mrs. Leander Amick, a daughter of Kit's sister Elizabeth. While there, she reportedly attended Rock Springs school. Mrs. Amick's daughter said that her mother "refused to accept any money for caring for" Adaline and that Kit consequently "purchased many presents for her; among them . . . a mahogany rocking chair which I still have." Marc Simmons suggests, as have others, that Kit may simply have left Adaline with his favorite sister, Mary Ann Carson Rubey, who lived not far from the site of Franklin, by that time washed away in river floods.

Kit's travels during the summer of 1842 are very difficult to trace. The importance of this period in his life, however, cannot be overstated. On this trip he first met Frémont, who was bound west leading the first of five expeditions. Kit would serve on three of these as a guide. Many of the events of his later life would be intertwined with Frémont's fame. Marc Simmons put the importance thus: "There can be no question that the beginning of Carson's association with Frémont . . . was a turning point in his life, one that set his course on a new road leading to lasting fame." What Kit himself said of this period, however, is not only tantalizingly little, but also confusing. In Simmons's words it amounts to little more than that "luck had brought him together with Frémont at the very time he was at loose ends and looking for something to do." Kit doesn't mention Adaline, whose care and education were a primary reason for the trip. He did tell his clerk in 1856, "It had been a long time since I had been among civilized people. I arrived at the States, went and saw my friends and acquaintances, then took a trip to St. Louis, remained a few days and was tired of remaining in settlements, took a steamer for the Upper Missouri, and—as luck would have it—Colonel Frémont, then a Lieutenant, was aboard of the same boat."

Arriving in Westport no later than mid-May, Kit and Adaline stayed at David Yoacham's inn, where Yoacham's daughter Susannah got acquainted with her. Kit apparently left Adaline with Mrs. Yoacham, who over the next few weeks outfitted her with "civilized" dresses to replace her buckskins.

From this point on, his movements and time schedule enter heavy fog. Recent research by Lee Burke reveals that, as a matter of record, the steam packet *Col. Woods* arrived at the Port of St. Louis on May 18 "from Mo. River," bearing "CONSIGNEES . . . Bent and St. Vrain." The St. Louis

Missouri Republican of May 19 reported her burden as "Santa Fe Traders.—Yesterday morning [May 18] a part of Messrs. Bent & St. Vrain's company of Santa Fe Traders, arrived here; bringing as part of the proceeds of their labors and the reward of their toils and privations, 283 packs of buffalo robes, 30 packs beaver, 12 sacks tongues, and 1 pack deerskins." Undoubtedly Carson was among these "Santa Fe Traders," for on the very next day, May 19, he appeared in the office of P. Chouteau, Jr., and Co., who were by then serving as disbursing agents for Bent and St. Vrain, to draw his pay. Wrote Lee Burke, "On the 19th when the hands gathered for payday at the offices of P. Chouteau, Jr., a partner [by then] with Bent and St. Vrain and de facto keeper of the books, Carson was at the head of the line and was first paid, and in full." Chouteau's ledger reveals that Carson received exactly $495.02, a huge sum for a border hunter to pocket in 1842.

Burke next finds Carson in Howard County where on May 31, 1842, he signed a legal paper giving a brother power of attorney to sell a parcel of land. Burke concludes that Carson used the nearly two weeks after he was paid off in St. Louis to return to Westport, pick up Adaline, settle her in with family in Howard County, and sign the legal paper before he boarded the *Rowena* bound upriver with Frémont's men. Marc Simmons follows the line that Kit could have taken care of these matters in Westport and Howard County (except for signing the legal document on May 31) *before* his trip to St. Louis. Either way appears possible, if thorny. His timing would have had to be exact. He'd have had no time to tarry. The trip by packet from Westport to St. Louis took about four days. If, say, the Bent–St. Vrain caravan had arrived in Westport as early as the first week of May, which is entirely possible, Kit could have had the time to proceed to Franklin, settle Adaline's affairs, then board the *Col. Woods* in Howard County bound downriver so as to arrive in St. Louis on the eighteenth. Unfortunately, the date of the arrival of the Bent caravan in Westport is presently unknown. However all that may be, Carson *was* aboard the *Rowena* on her run upstream to Westport when he and Frémont first met.

Adaline? The spotty evidence of later years suggests that she had a hard life, even for the time. Arriving for the first time in Missouri with her father, she was clearly very much out of place in the local culture. One scene suggests the pathos of American Indian females, in this instance a young girl, when first thrust into contact with white females from the East. Carson had left Adaline at Yoacham's hostel in Westport while he went about business of his own. "He brought this little girl with him to be educated," wrote Susannah Yoacham, daughter of the hostelry's keeper. "He bought her outfits in Westport, and had her dresses made in our home. She came to us dressed in buckskin and left dressed in as fine good[s] as could then be bought on the border. She was about my age, but uncivilized. She pulled up all my mother's vines and was chewing the roots when we found her at it."

After Adaline was schooled in Missouri, where she apparently lived with relatives, Kit brought her and his niece Susan Carson to New Mexico in 1851. He was returning home to Taos from a buying trip to St. Louis for Lucien Maxwell. Sometime later Adaline married "grizzled ex-trapper" Louis Simmons, an acquaintance of her father who had accompanied him in 1848 on his last trip to Washington with dispatches. "Louy" Simmons would tell S. P. Dillman later that he had asked her father's consent and that Carson had agreed to the marriage. Sabin dates the marriage as occurring in 1852, although no record of it has appeared.

No doubt Adaline was pretty. James Hobbs, in a fanciful book of "personal adventures" entitled *Wild Life in the Far West, 1834–1870*, much of which is clearly exaggerated and perhaps wholly fabricated, called her "Prairie Flower" and described her as "a noble looking woman, of mixed complexion; black eyes and long black hair, and could excel most men in the use of the rifle." Another described her as "handsome and in form and features resembling her mother." Marc

Simmons noted, "Observers tended to notice that she was well-educated, in sharp contrast to her father." Adaline and Louis Simmons were to go to California later with Carson, probably drawn there by the fever sweeping people westward since sawmill foreman James Marshall, while his workmen were at breakfast one morning in late January of 1848, spotted pea-sized specks of yellow metal in the millrace of John Sutter's new sawmill in the Coloma Valley on the south fork of the American River. After the discovery of gold in California, no one's world would ever be the same.

In 1853 Adaline and Louis would accompany Carson and his friend Tom Boggs on a sociable ride from San Francisco through the Napa Valley for a Boggs family reunion, then go on to the Russian River for a reunion with Kit's youngest brother, Lindsey, Jr., and half brothers Moses and Robert. Sometime thereafter, the marriage broke up. Jesse Nelson, a pal of Louis Simmons, told an interviewer years later only that "she didn't do right and he had to leave her." Adaline turned up next in 1859 at Mono Diggings, a gold camp near Mono Lake, California. She was traveling with a family named Wilson. By then she had found herself a new husband, one George Stilts, said by James Hobbs to be "a half-way 'fiddler'" and "a reckless man" who "turned out to be a regular desperado." An unconfirmed rumor is that she worked now as a prostitute. Adaline died about 1862, cause unknown, and was buried on the shore of Mono Lake. She was twenty-four, perhaps twenty-five years old. Today there remains a marker at her grave site.

When Kit had taken her to Missouri in 1842, Adaline and he traveled with Lucien Maxwell on the Bent–St. Vrain caravan. Lucien was to be Kit's lifelong comrade and friend, sometime business partner, and even, on one very important occasion, his personal adviser. To understand Kit, it is important to know something of Lucien Maxwell. Carson was remarkable for making lasting friendships with people of extraordinary ability and influence. Besides Maxwell, there were John Charles Frémont, his wife Jessie Benton, and Edward F. Beale, all of them exceptional people. Although Kit and Lucien shared many of the same interests, their families, their cultures, their talents, and their early experiences could hardly have been more different.

Born in 1818 in Kaskaskia on the Mississippi River below St. Louis near the colonial French village of St. Genevieve, Lucien Maxwell was the son of the prominent local merchant Hugh Maxwell. Unlike Carson, who was of a hardscrabble Scots-Irish Protestant family, Lucien was Roman Catholic, he was French and Irish, he was educated, and he was born to wealth. His mother, Marie Odile, was the oldest daughter of Pierre Menard, a prosperous French trader. Lucien's stepmother, Angelique Saucier, was the granddaughter of Pierre Dugué de Boisbriant, builder of Fort Chartres, completed in 1720 about fifteen miles north of Kaskaskia. From Fort Chartres, the French governed Upper Louisiana and the Illinois country for years. Angelique Saucier's sister had married Jean Pierre Chouteau, patriarch of the famous St. Louis trading family.

Lucien attended St. Mary's of the Barrens school near his home. He worked for Bent, St. Vrain and Co. and by 1839 may have been stationed at Bent's Fort as a supervisor. He then worked for a time at Bent–St. Vrain's northern post, called Fort St. Vrain, on the South Platte River. According to Lawrence Murphy, he was in Taos during the winter of 1841–42. Carson too was in Taos for at least part of this time. He had to be there no later than January 1842 in order to be baptized by Father Martínez on January 28.

Then as now, Taos was a small town. Everyone knew everyone else. The daily news consisted of talking about the weather and about other people's secrets. Both Kit and Lucien had hunted the mountains and plains, had lived among Indian people, and had learned their languages. Both had worked for Bent–St. Vrain. Both spoke Spanish fluently. They had mutual interests, mutual friends, mutual haunts.

The two would have visited the Bents, the Beaubiens, the Jaramillos, and other important Taos Catholic families during late January before Kit's baptism. Kit was already hoping to marry Josefa Jaramillo, while Lucien was hoping to marry Maria de la Luz Beaubien, Carlos Beaubien's daughter and mistress-to-be of the great Beaubien-Miranda Grant. Both men were to marry their chosen brides in Taos in the same cathedral.

Luz Beaubien's father, Carlos Beaubien, was a wealthy Taos trader. He and Guadalupe Miranda, Mexican collector of customs, had acquired the Beaubien-Miranda Grant through connections with Gov. Manuel Armijo in 1841. After her brother Narciso was murdered in the Taos revolt, Luz and her husband-to-be Lucien Maxwell would in time become the grant's owners. This twist of events happened not only through inheritance, but by the management skills of Luz and Lucien. After he worked as the manager for his father-in-law at the Rayado ranch in the early 1850s, in 1857 Maxwell and Luz bought from her parents twenty-two square miles of land centered around Cimarron. There they built their mansion, its style influenced by Pierre Menard's grand home on the Mississippi. Next they bought the Miranda half of the grant from Guadalupe himself for $2,745.

After Carlos Beaubien died, Luz and Lucien acquired, besides her inherited share, the undivided shares of her five siblings. With various other land deals and quieting of titles, they eventually became owners of the entire grand sweep of land. From home at Cimarron, Lucien for years managed this empire. It lay along the Cimarron and Rayado rivers on the mountain branch of the Santa Fe Trail in northeastern New Mexico and extended north into Colorado.

As young comrades during the winter of 1841–42, lifelong Roman Catholic Lucien Maxwell and soon-to-be Catholic Kit Carson were hoping to marry into two very influential New Mexican Catholic families. They were in the right place at the right time. They had much to talk about. If Kit ever discussed private affairs with any other man, it was with Lucien Maxwell during January 1842 in Taos.

After Lucien parted from Kit and Adaline in the spring of 1842 at Westport, he hurried on to Kaskaskia to visit his family. There he talked with his grandfather, old Pierre Menard, for the last time. Pierre Menard's magnificent home (today a beautifully restored Illinois State Historical Site) sits on the left bank of the Mississippi River across from Kaskaskia and St. Genevieve. When Kit and Lucien rode east from Taos and Bent's Fort with Adaline, they undoubtedly talked of returning home to New Mexico. Perhaps they also talked about meeting at the office of P. Chouteau, Jr., and Co. in St. Louis, where Kit would be paid off on May 19. They probably talked of taking a packet to Westport to ride home together on the Santa Fe Trail.

In any event, both men were aboard the *Rowena* when she arrived upstream from St. Louis at Chouteau's Landing near present-day Kansas City. By then Frémont had hired them both. Chances are that he had signed up Maxwell as a "hunter" at Chouteau's office in St. Louis *before* his expedition boarded the *Rowena*. "Without doubt Senator Benton had written ahead of Frémont, to the Chouteaus in St. Louis, requesting them to be getting good men together for the expedition," wrote biographer Sabin. Clearly a "good man" with plenty of plains experience, Maxwell was a prime candidate for a job with Frémont. Once hired, he was also in a strong position to recommend his reliable friend Kit Carson.

And there was still another factor in Lucien's favor, and therefore Carson's. Frémont already knew the Chouteaus well. This great business family had outfitted the Nicollet expeditions of 1838–39, upon which Frémont had served as the "disbursing agent" and as Joseph Nicollet's personal assistant. Besides his other qualifications for influence with Frémont, Maxwell was himself, by marriage, a member of the Chouteau family.

Frémont described the likable Maxwell in his *Memoirs.* "Maxwell was about twenty-eight years of age, about five feet ten inches in height, and strongly built," he wrote. "He was personally known, by trading among them, to the tribes who ranged the country toward New Mexico, accustomed to the life of the prairies, and a resolute man and good hunter." Frémont added that Maxwell and Carson were "close friends." Both men clearly fit his standards for employees. "For this journey, which would be exposed to serious contingencies," he added, "good men and fitting animals were a first necessity."

Lucien Maxwell was aboard the *Rowena* when Kit appeared at an upriver port on the Missouri River where the packet tied off. This was probably New Franklin or Arrow Rock, which lay a little above the site of old Franklin on the Missouri. In 1856, fourteen years after this first meeting with Frémont, Kit told his clerk, "I spoke to Colonel Frémont [on the packet], informed him that I had been some time in the mountains and thought I could guide him to any point he would wish to go. He replied that he would make inquiries regarding my capabilities of performing that which I promised. He done so. I presume he received reports favorable of me, for he told me I would be employed. I accepted the offer of one hundred dollars per month and prepared myself to accompany him." Little doubt it was Maxwell whom Frémont consulted. No one else aboard knew Kit as Lucien did. Nor was anyone else aboard with Lucien's family connections, always a very important matter to Frémont, who was a social climber of the very first order. There can also be no doubt that, when asked, Maxwell would have recommended Kit Carson for the job.

Frémont recalled this first meeting in his *Memoirs.* "On the boat I met Kit Carson," he said. "He was returning from putting his little daughter in a convent-school at St. Louis. I was pleased with him and his manner of address at this first meeting. He was a man of medium height, broad-shouldered and deep-chested, with a clear steady blue eye and frank speech and address; quiet and unassuming." After mentioning "the simple honesty of [Kit's] character," Frémont closed with, "I had expected to engage as guide an old mountaineer, Captain Drips, but I was so much pleased with Carson that when he asked to go with me I was glad to take him." Andrew Drips, fur trader, special Indian agent for the Upper Missouri, and Chouteau employee, would have been an excellent man for the job. If Frémont had met Drips first, Carson's name would little doubt have passed into obscurity as did the names of most old mountain men. "On no chance meeting in the long history of the American West," wrote David Roberts, "would more doings of high consequence depend."

Though this first of Frémont's expeditions covered much less ground than the later ones did, it foreshadowed the best, and the worst, in the coming four. It offered Carson and Maxwell the chance to prove their unusual talent and experience as hunters, guides, horsemen, and interpreters to the tribes they met. Both were exceptional all-around utility men in every kind of border situation. Lucien earned his entire year's pay on one occasion alone by saving the expedition from disaster. Somewhere along the South Platte River, with a small party of only three or four men out on the open prairie mounted on worn-out horses, Frémont and Maxwell spotted "two or three hundred" Indians "naked to the breech cloth . . . sweeping across the prairie," Frémont wrote. "Before we could reach [the timber] down came the Indians upon us. . . . We had jerked the covers from our guns, and our fingers were on the triggers. . . . Just as he was about to fire, Maxwell recognized the leading Indian, and shouted to him in the Indian language, 'You're a fool, God damn you, don't you know me?' The sound of his own language seemed to shock the savage, and, swerving his horse a little, he passed us like an arrow. He wheeled, as I rode out toward him, and gave me his hand, striking his breast and exclaiming, 'Arapaho!'" These Arapahos turned out to be from a village where Maxwell had lived as a trader a year or two before. They were also Waa-nibe's people. One almost might ask what Frémont would have done without the service of these two expert border men, Maxwell and Carson.

But what of Lieutenant Frémont? No other one person, with the exception of Josefa, would have a greater influence upon Carson's life.

A young officer of the Corps of Topographical Engineers (reorganized from the old Bureau of Topographical Engineers in 1838), Frémont seemed driven by a willful self-centeredness that caused him to attempt projects beyond official orders, and at times beyond reason. The result was that he thrust himself and his men into one excess after another. Sometimes the risks worked. Sometimes they ended in disaster, as in the privately financed winter expedition of 1848–49 to map a Pacific railroad route across the Rocky Mountains. This expedition came to grief in Colorado's San Juan Mountains. It was an ill-planned junket in which, fortunately for him, Carson had no part. Frémont did have lasting achievements, however. The most important was his second expedition (1843–44), in which he and his men circumscribed the entire Great Basin before returning east. Carson would play an important part as guide and adviser on this expedition.

A ruthless self-promoter, Frémont presented himself as *the* central figure among the others in whatever grand endeavor they might be about. The upside of this dangerous talent was that, in promoting himself, he promoted good men under his command, men like Maxwell and Carson. As he saw it, however, such highly skilled men were important for the part they played in the great drama of his own achievements for the nation. His official reports, starting with the *Report* of the 1842 expedition (1843), followed by the very widely read *Report* of the first expedition *and* the second to Oregon and California of 1843–44 (1845) propelled Carson toward a fame he never sought and otherwise would not have known.

Frémont's commanding officer, Col. John J. Abert, was chief of the Corps of Topographical Engineers. Senator Thomas

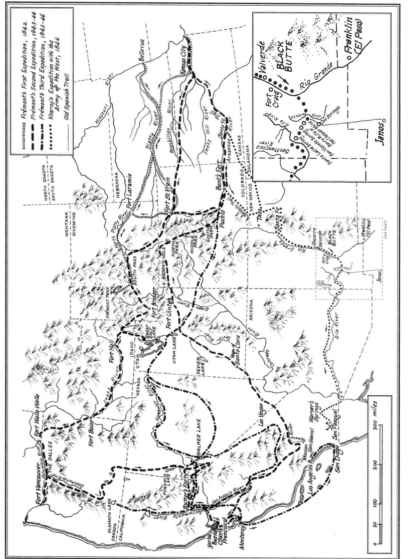

Frémont's expeditions and Kearny's route west. Adapted from Carter, "*Dear Old Kit*," 108–109.

Hart Benton, Frémont's father-in-law, was his unofficial supporter and defender. The great proponent of America's Manifest Destiny, Benton, with the cooperation of other senators, tied the Topographical Corps' purse strings. That potent fact put Colonel Abert under considerable pressure to oblige both Benton and Frémont. Cleverly, though unofficially, he modified the first expedition's plan in order to suit Benton, without changing the orders and without putting his own reputation at risk. Formal orders were that the expedition survey the route along the Missouri, Platte, and North Platte rivers east of the Rocky Mountains. Both Frémont and Benton, however, were unhappy with this modest plan. So in an undated letter, Benton urged Colonel Abert to change the orders so as to allow his son-in-law to proceed to "the great pass through the Rocky Mountains, called the South West Pass [because it] will be a through fare [*sic*] for nations to the end of time." Without rewriting the orders, Colonel Abert sent a *private* note to Frémont dated April 28, 1842, adding, "If you can do what he [Senator Benton] desires this season, without hazarding the work committed to you [in official orders], it is extremely desirable that it be done."

So began the first of Frémont's expeditions. After hiring Charles Preuss, a gifted German-born topographer, Frémont signed on Maxwell and the French voyageurs in St. Louis, then hired Carson on the packet *Rowena.* Proceeding to Chouteau's Landing, and from there a few miles up the Kansas River to Cyprian Chouteau's trading post, "six miles west of the Missouri line," the expedition paused for supplies. These included, as reported by Frémont, two rifles, 286 pounds sugar, 188 pounds coffee, coiled rope, halters, dressed deerskins, "tug ropes," twilled bags, "1 double-barreled shotgun," and "12 boxes percussion caps." There were "4 mules bought of L. Maxwell" and many other items, including wheeled carts and saddle and draft stock. Frémont spent $4.21 for "repairing guns" and $6.95 "to blacksmithing," probably for shoeing horses and repairing cart iron. Since the government hadn't advanced the funds, Chouteau put the bill of more than $1,000 on tab and charged the government a commission.

Departing Cyprian Chouteau's trading post on June 10, the expedition took the Emigrant Road (later called the Oregon Trail) across the prairie, then split into two parties near the forks of the Platte. A handpicked group including Frémont, Maxwell, Baptiste Bernier, Honoré Ayot, and Basil Lajeunesse followed the South Platte to Fort St. Vrain just east of Long's Peak. Their object was "to explore and report upon the country between the frontiers of Missouri and the South Pass in the Rocky Mountains, and on the line of the Kansas and Great Platte Rivers." Frémont also scouted locations for future military posts. Along the way his men met three traveling Cheyennes who drew a map of the country for Frémont and remained with him all the way home to their village on the South Platte. From Fort St. Vrain, Frémont trailed northerly in just five days to the old American Fur Company post of Fort Laramie, in Wyoming near the North Platte River. Meanwhile, the main party under Clement Lambert traveled directly to Fort Laramie on the Emigrant Road. Here the two parties regrouped. Then the expedition rode on to South Pass, as Frémont and Senator Benton had wished, and as Colonel Abert had *unofficially* agreed they do.

Beyond South Pass, Frémont acted entirely outside orders, even beyond the unofficial permission of Colonel Abert. From South Pass he marched the expedition north up the Green River along the western slope of Wyoming's Wind River Range, planning to cut eastward across the mountains, then march south again to the Sweetwater River. Changing his plan midcourse—putting at risk the lives of his men and all their animals and equipment—he decided to climb what he called "Snow Peak," which appeared to him to be the highest mountain in the range, though in fact it was not. He chose Carson to lead a small group up the frosted peak, got mad at him for climbing too fast, then got sick, overcome by the altitude. Carson awkwardly apologized, although he had done precisely what he had been hired to do, guide. He had moved along sharply at it, as any good man chosen for that purpose would have done.

Frémont's official *Report* of this and the second expedition (1845) is packed with useful information about the country. It is engagingly written and was widely read. Academically, the science of the mid-nineteenth century was still a branch of the humanities. Thus scientific writing had a strongly literary side. In America as in England, leading scientists such as Asa Gray, to whom Charles Darwin mailed an advance copy of *The Origin of Species*, wrote supremely well, exactly as they had been trained and were expected to do. Frémont's 1845 *Report* follows in this tradition.

The effect on most readers was as a compelling piece of literature. The style was "tinted" with what William H. Goetzmann called a "larger-than-life sublimity which has obscured [its scientific] achievement down to the present day." The *Report* enabled readers to "see" in their imaginations the western places Frémont described by comparison with familiar scenes at home in the East. Thus Frémont described the wildflowers along the Big Blue River of eastern Kansas: "the [A]rtemisia, absinthe, or prairie sage . . . glitters like silver, as the southern breeze turns up its leaves to the sun"; and "everywhere the rose is met with, and reminds us of cultivated gardens and civilization." Read somewhat as a travel guide might be read today, the *Report* not only encouraged an already growing interest in the Far West, but highlighted the names of men such as Lucien Maxwell and Kit Carson.

People by thousands read it, gave in to "Oregon Fever," packed the wagon, hitched the faithful team, and headed west. Recalling reading the *Report* as a teenage boy, poet Joaquin Miller wrote, "I fancied I could see Frémont's men hauling the cannon up the savage battlements of the Rocky Mountains, flags in the air, Frémont at the head, waving his sword. . . . I [was] inflamed with a love for action, adventure, glory and great deeds away out yonder under the path of the setting sun." Thus "literary" were the official reports of the expeditions Frémont hired Carson to guide. So Kit's name entered the public's mind and, shortly afterward, the folklore and popular literature of the day.

In contrast to Frémont's "tinted" style, Kit's description of his own work and exertion on the first expedition was plain as mud. Taking no credit, he gave it all to his leader. "We continued our march[,] arrived at the South Pass," he said. "Frémont accomplished all that was desired of him and then we returned." Of himself, he added only, "I performed the duties of guide and hunter." His recollections of the South Pass expedition show little more than the influence of his Scots-Irish devotion to duty and loyalty to the leader. "Arrived at [Fort] Laramie sometime in September," he told his clerk in 1856. "I, at Laramie, quit the employ of Frémont."

6

"Life Yet, Life Yet"

After leaving the expedition, Carson almost disappeared from September 1842 until January 1843. He did turn up in St. Louis on October 31 to draw his pay "for services as guide and hunter at 100.00 per month for 3 months, from 1 June to 1 Sept. 1842." His total was $300.00 plus $40.00 for "1 mule," total $340.00. For this amount, paid by "Voucher No. 19, St. Louis, 31 Oct. 1842[,] U.S. to Christopher Carson," a clerk witnessed Kit make his mark. Probably he visited Adaline and may have spent Christmas with her and other members of his family. Then he headed home again after the New Year. "I went to Bent's Fort in January 1843," he told his clerk in 1856, "[then] departed for Taos." One wonders if he ever had time to court Josefa or whether the marriage was managed *entirely* by arrangement with priest and parents.

He had to move along now, for back in Taos on February 6, 1843, he married Josefa. The two had not seen each other for about a year. She had probably never been farther from home than Santa Fe. By the day of their marriage, she was all of fourteen years old, nearly fifteen. Carson, a very mature thirty-three, was already twice married. He had had two children, perhaps even three. Characteristically, he gives little detail of this personal matter. "In February of same year got married to Señorita Josepha Jaramilla [*sic*], a daughter of Don Francisco Jaramilla," he told his clerk. "I remained in

Taos till April [1843] then started for the States with Bent and St. Vrain." During their short two months in Taos together, the newlyweds probably moved into their home a few doors off the plaza. No one knows how they came by this flat-roofed adobe building, which would be their home and Carson's office for much of their lives together. The Jaramillos may have presented it as the bride's dowry. Or Kit may have bought the property with cash from the Frémont expedition. Records have not been found.

Now, however, using wilderness skills he had long ago mastered, Carson set out to make a living for his new family. Josefa and he would eventually have eight children together. When he signed up as a hunter for the Bent–St. Vrain wagon train headed for Westport in April 1843, she stayed behind, as she customarily did. Depending upon *la familia* for work and companionship, she made the house comfortable. *Carpinteros* built pine furniture. Community women and children gathered to replaster the outside walls every two or three years. The mud plaster kept the adobe bricks from weathering away. *Trabajadors* changed inside walls, rebuilt the kitchen fireplace, and regularly hauled in loads of seasoned juniper and piñon on tough little burros. About as surely as a Peter Hurd painting of New Mexico contains a corral and a windmill, an old lithograph of Taos or Santa Fe has a string of burros packing firewood. Over the years Josefa grew even closer to her sister, Maria Ignacia Bent. The two women often spent nights together at the Bents' home.

Out in the middle of Kansas with the Bent–St. Vrain caravan eastbound, Kit tested his courage and his famous horsemanship. At Walnut Creek in the Great Bend of the Arkansas River his party met Capt. Philip St. George Cooke with a troop of U.S. Army dragoons. They were guarding a train of westbound wagons owned by Mexican traders. A gang of Texans led by border thug Jacob Snively had terrorized the traders by threatening to attack them as soon as they crossed the river onto Mexican soil, where they were beyond the protection of the dragoons. The traders offered $300 to any volunteer to ride to Santa Fe to request protection of Governor Armijo. Kit took the job.

As he passed Bent's Fort headed west, his friend William Bent lent him a fast horse, "a fine horse which I could lead and, in case I should fall in with any Indians, could mount him and make my escape," he recalled. Long-shouldered, long-hipped horses of the English Thoroughbred type, these big speed horses had been bred in Virginia since the early eighteenth century for one purpose alone, to scatter hell itself when asked to run. Crossed with tough little mustang mares, these prepotent English stallions produced big colts and fillies that could run just like their fathers, while they retained the hardiness of their little mothers. Such colts were priceless in a trade with men who needed them for their size, speed, and endurance, called "bottom." Wealthy traders like William Bent, who often traveled far from home, could afford them. Scarce on the northern plains at the time, these horses at a steady lope could raise the dust all day long out in front of a band of Plains Indians quirting their willing little mustangs all over the ribs and yelling like demons.

Such horses were beyond all value in a race for life, when losing meant paying the price of slow death by torture. One such horse saved John C. Cremony in a race with Apaches before the Civil War. Cremony crossed the Jornada del Muerto, a waterless desert in New Mexico between Socorro and Doña Ana near Las Cruces on the Rio Grande, running his horse without rest for the last seventy miles. Cremony later wrote, "I reached Doña Ana about twelve o'clock midnight, having made the distance of one hundred and twenty-five miles [from Socorro] on one horse, in the space of twenty-one hours, the last seventy miles . . . at a run." Capt. Richard King of the King Ranch in Texas and Lucien Maxwell imported Thoroughbreds. Maxwell crossed them on native mares for racing and saddle stock at his famous stables at Cimarron. The only downside to the big horses was that they needed high-quality hay and grain. Good wild grass hay could be cut locally, but until farming developed in the West, grain had to be shipped out in wagons from Missouri at a premium price. The big horses also had to be shod. The best thing about the smart little mustang mares was that they prospered on indifferent grass in the summertime and got by on cottonwood bark and twigs during the winter, no grain required. And mustangs had very hard hooves. Few of them were ever shod.

To loan Carson such an icon of an animal was a measure of William Bent's respect for the man. But Carson got lucky this time. He passed the Utes in the night without having to use the horse, rode on to Taos, forwarded the request to Governor Armijo at Santa Fe, and took precious hours with Josefa at home. After hearing back from the governor, he and a Mexican companion rode east again. This time hostile Utes blocked the road.

With great courage, Kit's Mexican companion urged him to take the fast horse and go on alone. "The Mexican advised me to mount my horse and make my escape," Carson recalled, "that the Indians had no animal that could catch him and, as for him, he thought the Indians would not injure him and they, in all probability, would kill me. I considered the advice very good and was about to mount my horse. I changed my mind and thought how cowardly it would be in me to desert this man that so willingly offered to sacrifice his life to save mine. I told him no, that I would die with him." As it turned out, the two men stared the Utes down. "They kept up among themselves a loud talk," Carson recalled. "We watched them closely, determined that the first that would raise his gun would be shot. They remained around us for about a half hour and seeing but little hopes of their being able to kill us without losing two of themselves, they left." Regrettably, Carson did not give his companion's name. Truly, the man deserves a monument.

When Carson arrived back at Bent's Fort, he learned that Frémont had just passed through, leading a second expedition westbound. Having received praises for his first, he had the full support of Senators Benton and Lewis F. Linn of Missouri for another. This time Colonel Abert ordered him to make a great "circuit" of the Northwest, in Abert's words to "embrace within its limits the heads of the Colorado, the Columbia, some of the heads of the Missouri proper, the Yellowstone and the Platte." He was supposed to explore the headwaters of the Kansas and the Arkansas rivers and to seek a pass across the Rocky Mountains south of South Pass, which he had visited on the first expedition. Orders also were to explore the vast country south of the Columbia River toward northern California, there to "join on to Lieut. Wilkes' Survey" and "from that point to return [east] by the Oregon road."

In 1841, two years earlier, parties under navy Lt. Charles Wilkes had gone up the Columbia to the Snake River while U.S. Navy ships explored Puget Sound and the Strait of Juan de Fuca. Meanwhile, an overland party led by Lt. George F. Emmons had gone up the Willamette River into California. Emmons traveled down the Sacramento River to Sutter's Fort and visited the San José and Santa Clara missions. As for Senators Benton and Linn, their interest was primarily in the development of the Oregon country and beyond. Senator Linn was more drawn to its agricultural potential, Benton to its use as a gateway to expanding trade with the Orient.

Carson recalled in 1856 that when he learned Frémont was only about seventy-five miles from Bent's Fort, he "wished to see him and started for his camp. My object was not to seek employment. I only thought that I would ride to his camp, have a talk, and then return. But when Frémont saw me again and requested me to join him, I could not refuse, and again entered his employ as guide and hunter." In spite of saying he didn't "seek employment," Carson seemed delighted to accept the job. Frémont's recollection of this meeting of July 21, 1843, suggests how compatible the two had become by then. Frémont could always use a man with Carson's skills. In his words, "I had here [at the site of Pueblo, Colorado, on the Arkansas River] the satisfaction to meet our good buffalo hunter of 1842, Christopher Carson, whose services I considered myself fortunate to secure again; and as a reinforcement of mules was absolutely necessary, I despatched [*sic*] him immediately, with an account of our necessities" to Bent's Fort.

Frémont had already hired a guide for the trip. He was Tom Fitzpatrick, Kit's old employer with the Rocky Mountain Fur Company. Charles Preuss served again as topographer. Thirty-some laborers, "Creole and Canadian French, and Americans," made up the workforce. Frémont had hired two Shawnees as "hunters" as far as Fort St. Vrain, misnaming them Delawares. "Two Delaware Indians—a fine-looking old man and his son—were engaged to accompany the expedition as hunters," he wrote. According to pay records, these were James Rogers and his son Thomas Jefferson Rogers. Also along were a Benton family slave, Jacob Dodson, and two free riders of society's upper ranks, Frederick Dwight of Massachusetts and Theodore Talbot of Washington. Talbot would turn out to be a useful member of the expedition, Dwight mostly a sightseer. Along the way, Frémont would also pick up Carson's old friend, mountain man Alexis Godey, and William Gilpin, the Oregon promoter and Colorado's first territorial governor. This expedition was an all-American blend of ethnic, cultural, and racial types—St. Louis Creole, French Canadian, African, Shawnee, Scots-Irish, English, Prussian, French, and Irish (Fitzpatrick was Irish-born). To borrow words from Elliott West's *Growing Up with the Country*, such a diverse but cooperative group of individuals represented a "particularly important element" of the "far western frontier." They were an example of "the human mix that constituted western society." In reality, border life and warfare were almost never as simple as "the whites" against "the Indians" as portrayed in the movies and in so much popular literature.

This time Frémont brought along a controversial piece of equipment, a horse-drawn bronze cannon called a mountain howitzer, supplied by the St. Louis Armory at his request. He then hired Louis Zindel, a former Prussian army artillerist, and three other men to operate the field piece. Learning of this matter, Colonel Abert accused him of poor "discretion." An apparent conflict of purpose, as well as the additional cost of the howitzer and crew, caused the problem. Abert had intended a *scientific* expedition, not a *military* foray. He grumbled over the hostile look of a geographical expedition towing a howitzer. "If the condition of the Indians in the mountains is such as to require your party to be so warlike in its equipment[,] it is clear that . . . geographical information cannot be obtained," he wrote Frémont. "The object . . . was a peaceable expedition, similar to the one of last year, an expedition to gather scientific knowledge." Mad as hell, Colonel Abert even threatened to call the trip off. If "the only objects" for "which the expedition was planned" could not be accomplished, he wrote Frémont on May 22, 1843, "you will immediately desist in its further prosecution and report to this office."

At Senator Benton's home in St. Louis, Frémont's wife, Jessie, intercepted this letter. Fortunately for him, her husband had already departed for the West and was out of reach. But Abert reported the affair to Senator Benton in a letter of July 10. The howitzer "appeared to me not only a useless, but an embarrassing weapon to such an expedition, requiring well instructed men for its Management, and a serious increase of means for its transportation," he wrote. Eventually Frémont's party abandoned the little howitzer on an icy slope somewhere in the Sierra Nevada, and so the ruckus seemed to end. Carson, however, usually a sensible man, was involved with a leader of flawed judgment who also ignored orders. Looking back on this affair, one can see that a scientific expedition's pulling an artillery piece foreshadowed Frémont's later problems. Unaware of such matters, Carson, however he may have felt, said nothing. In character as ever, he followed his leader.

Back at Bent's Fort on the Arkansas, Kit traded for ten mules, then trailed them to Fort St. Vrain on the South Platte where he joined Frémont again on July 23. By then the expedition had surveyed much of the upper Arkansas and the South Platte, but had not found another pass through the mountains. In fact, there was no other like the South Pass, though few knew that then except for local tribesmen and a few mountain men. Frémont's description of the reunion with Fitzpatrick and with Carson at Fort St. Vrain suggests why he had come to rely upon these two for their broad experience and absolute dependability. "We found Mr. Fitzpatrick and his party in good order and excellent health, and my true and reliable friend, Kit Carson, who had brought with him ten good mules, with the necessary pack saddles," he wrote. "Mr. Fitzpatrick, who had often endured every extremity of want during the course of his mountain life, and knew well the value of provisions in this country, had watched over our stock with jealous vigilance, and there was an abundance of flour, rice, sugar, and coffee in the camp; and again we fared sumptuously."

Now Frémont split the party again. He sent Fitzpatrick with pack mules, supplies, and carts via South Pass directly to Fort Hall on the Snake River, near present-day Blackfoot, Idaho. Boston fur trader Nathaniel Wyeth had built Fort Hall in 1834. The Hudson's Bay Company purchased it in 1837 and operated it until about 1856. It sat a few miles from the fork in the road where the California Trail later split off from the Oregon Trail. Having sent Fitzpatrick off, Frémont took Carson with several other men up the Cache la Poudre to near present-day Fort Collins, Colorado, in one last attempt to locate that "south-of-South-Pass" wagon route that was not. Finding instead very challenging mountains and increasingly threatening weather as the elevation increased, he bent off toward the northwest by July 30 and took an easier route to the Sweetwater River. Moving up the Sweetwater, he crossed South Pass again.

Kit himself was sent off on August 19 to Fort Hall to get provisions. Meanwhile, Frémont, beyond the scope of orders, decided to backtrack down the Bear River valley to visit the Great Salt Lake. "I reached the fort, was well received and [was] furnished all that I required," said Kit. He rejoined Frémont at the lake on September 4, having delivered "flour and a few other articles of light provision, sufficient for two or three days—a scanty but very acceptable supply."

After reaching the lake, paddling out to "Disappointment Island" (today's Fremont Island), and risking lives when an inflatable India rubber boat sprang a leak and nearly sank, Frémont decided to return to orders. These were to connect with Lieutenant Wilkes's survey of the Columbia River basin, a great distance yet to the west. It was by now late in the season, past time to move along. After releasing eleven members of the expedition who wanted to go back to St. Louis, Frémont finally set out for the Columbia. In Carson's words, the expedition at last "struck for the mouth of the Columbia River." It was September 22. Winter was coming on. Fresh snow lay on the mountains.

The expedition generally followed the Snake River across the Columbia River plateau toward Oregon. Always hungry, they were delighted by finding some new potatoes. "We ate [potatoes] twice," Preuss noted in his journal. "Kit put another potful on before we went to sleep." On November 4 they reached The Dalles, the narrows of the Columbia. Putting Carson in charge of base camp, Frémont drifted downriver to Fort Vancouver, where he bought provisions and visited with the six-foot-seven-inch Dr. John McLoughlin, chief factor from 1824 to 1845 of the Hudson's Bay Company's Columbia District, an area larger than Great Britain herself. That Frémont put Carson in charge of base camp speaks well for Kit's growing skill in handling men of an unusually independent nature.

Back at The Dalles by November 18, Frémont found Kit well in control of an orderly camp. "Carson had removed the camp up the river a little nearer to the hills, where the animals had better grass," he wrote. "We found everything in good order, and arrived just in time to partake of an excellent roast of California beef." Having connected with Lieutenant Wilkes's survey, Frémont now felt free to design his own route home, although Colonel Abert had ordered him to return by the trail over South Pass. Instead, as Frémont noted on November 18, "though homeward, [I] contemplated a new route, and a great circuit to the south and southeast, and the exploration of the Great Basin between the Rocky Mountains and the Sierra Nevada."

Thus began the epic journey south past Klamath Lake into northwestern Nevada, from there west in the dead of winter over the Sierra Nevada through "Carson's Pass" to Sutter's Fort at present-day Sacramento, then south down the center of California to near present-day Bakersfield, from there southeast to the Old Spanish Trail on the Mojave River near Oro Grande, then northeast across Nevada into Utah, and east again over the Rockies through Brown's Hole on the Green River to Bent's Fort and St. Louis. On Frémont's own initiative (unless, as is possible, he was operating on secret orders) the men would circumscribe the entire Great Basin and much of the mountain West, and along the way trespass far into Alta California, a territory that still belonged to Mexico. What man of energy and vision approaching madness would not take the opportunity? It was the sort of grand enterprise an independent spirit would admire, but an organizational soul like Colonel Abert would find appalling and inexcusable. Kit Carson, though without intending it, was to be a key player in the success of this mad venture.

The journey was grand of conception, sweep of landscape covered, survival skills proven and expended, and conclusions reached. Frémont with Carson as guide and companion, Preuss as cartographer, and a double handful of men, horses, and mules would circumscribe the "Great Basin," the name Frémont gave that vast, dry inland sea. They proved beyond any doubt that this immense, mostly alkaline basin had no outlet to the Pacific, as men had hoped. Someone had even named that imagined outlet to the Pacific the "Rio Buenaventura." In addition, in William H. Goetzmann's words, they became "acquainted with the Sierra Nevada, established their connection with the Cascade Range, and pointed up the existence of a separate coastal range."

Having planned, in his own words, "the exploration of the Great Basin between the Rocky Mountains and the Sierra Nevada," why did Frémont change course again in northern Nevada to cross the high California mountains in deep winter? Since war with Mexico was less than three years away, it is possible he was acting on secret orders to spy in California. Given his connections with Senator Benton, the seeming nationalism of an expedition towing a howitzer, and his later career as a military and political figure, that seems plausible, though the evidence is insubstantial. There remain the overwhelming facts of the deep snowfall, the great cold, and the high winds of the Sierra Nevada during the winter. Extreme conditions in this same area would shortly destroy the Donner party. What leader would risk his men's lives in such weather on such a bad gamble? He had already cut his chances by dallying at the Great Salt Lake while snow fell in the mountains to the west of him.

Consider other reasons for changing direction here. They make sense. Both Frémont and Carson daily examined the condition of their horses and mules, for the animals were the expedition's *only* means of transportation. Feed for them on Nevada's desert was extremely sparse. Rocky cliffs barred their path. The sandy, rocky footing dried out their hooves, causing the hoof walls to crack and split. This excessive wear made their feet sore, just as a split thumbnail makes the thumb sore. Several days before turning west toward Sutter's Fort, Frémont began to face his livestock's very poor condition, and therefore his expedition's plight. "In anticipation of coming hardship and to spare our horses," he wrote, "there was much walking done today; and Mr. Fitzpatrick and myself made the day's journey on foot."

A few days later he noted ominously, "I found [the animals'] feet so much cut up by the rocks, and so many of them lame, that it was evidently impossible that they could cross [to] the Rocky mountains," far to the east of their position at the time. Finally, he wrote, "Every piece of iron that could be used . . . had been converted into [horseshoe] nails, and we could make no further use of the [horse] shoes we had remaining. I therefore determined to abandon my eastern course, and to cross the Sierra Nevada into the valley of the Sacramento, wherever a practicable pass could be found."

The fact is that horses and mules, especially if burdened with packs or riders, *cannot* cross rocky desert country without sufficient feed and iron shoes (steel today) properly nailed on any more than an automobile can run down a gravel road without wheels and tires. Frémont had to choose the least bad of two very bad options, and Carson, knowledgeable as he was about animals and the conditions they required, would have agreed. The California option was increasingly the only choice they had. It may even have been Carson's choice before it was Frémont's. For Carson not only knew horses and mules, he had been to California with Ewing Young. He knew very well that Sutter's Fort was the nearest refitting point, and their only chance of getting out of this fix alive. The actual distance to Sutter's Fort was considerably less than that eastward to the Rockies. The footing would be somewhat better, if only because it was wetter. At least some feed might be found in the forested country along the way. A very daunting prospect, turning west into the Sierra Nevada's winter offered the only chance for life other than turning back, which Frémont would never have done.

Carson himself later stressed the desperate condition of the livestock and the plight of the men. "We struck for California," he told his clerk in 1856. "Our course was through a barren, desolate, and unexplored country till we reached the Sierra Nevada, which we found covered with snow. . . .

We were nearly out of provisions and cross the mountain we must, let the consequences be what they may." The pack stock, he said, "had, through hunger [,] eaten one another's tails and the leather of the pack saddles. . . . They were in a deplorable condition and we would frequently kill one to keep it from dying, then use the meat for food." At least one man froze his feet during the crossing. Two men lost their minds. Even the best horses "floundered in the snow," then refused to go forward. The American Indian guides deserted. One old Indian man, pointing ahead, kept saying: "Rock upon rock—rock upon rock—snow upon snow—snow upon snow . . . even if you get over the snow, you will not be able to get down from the mountains." No wonder that during this trial, the expedition finally abandoned the little howitzer.

From here on, Carson's knowledge, his skills, and his can-do spirit became indispensable to the expedition's survival. His confidence alone, suggested in this and other such dire circumstances by his repeated use of the words, "[we] must [succeed], let the consequences be what they may," carried the men through otherwise certain disaster. As days wore on, Frémont spent more time in his company, as if borrowing his confidence and feeling comforted by his presence. Little doubt the two talked of the country, the weather, the Indians, and of their own chances. Everyone depended upon Carson's knowledge, his unruffled temper, and his hopeful disposition. "I reminded [the men]," Frémont wrote, "of the beautiful valley of the Sacramento, with which they were familiar from the descriptions of Carson, who had been there some fifteen years ago, and who, in our late privations, had delighted us in speaking of its rich pastures and [its] abounding game." Frémont even relied upon Carson as a bodyguard, having him lie "across the door" of his tent one night when Indians stayed over in camp. If they met strangers, Carson could sometimes communicate verbally or in sign. In one instance, when they saw Native people watching them from a hilltop, he recognized their Shoshonean yell, which meant

"Whites!" He calmed a terrified Indian woman, who, with two children, was cut off from her group. "By dint of presents, and friendly demonstrations, she was brought to calmness," Frémont wrote, "and we found that [these people] belonged to the Snake nation, speaking the language of that people."

The Natives along the way were generally friendly, even helpful. Those near Klamath Lake had a bad reputation because a party of Umpqua River people had attacked Jedediah Smith's party near here and killed fourteen men in July 1828. But Frémont was able to buy grass mats from them, which he used as tablecloths and bedding. He bought a wolf-like pup his men named "Tlamath." Half-starved, the men later killed Tlamath for meat. All of these people valued horses very highly. They would steal a horse if they could, but no one would sell a good one. On December 26 someone stole Carson's own horse: "To-night a horse belonging to Carson, one of the best we had in the camp, was stolen by the Indians," Frémont wrote. An amusing domestic incident involved a fine horse. Wrote Frémont, "We found here a single Nez Perce family, who had a very handsome horse, which we endeavored to obtain in exchange for a good cow; but the man 'had two hearts,' or, rather, he had one [heart] and his wife had another: she wanted the cow but he loved the horse too much to part with it." There was no trade!

On February 6, 1844, in what reads like the climax of historical fiction, Frémont, Fitzgerald, and Carson with "a reconnoitering party" topped out on the Sierra Nevada to look off west. "Far below us, dimmed by the distance, was a large snowless valley, bounded on the western side, at the distance of about a hundred miles, by a low range of mountains, which Carson recognized with delight as the mountains bordering the coast," wrote Frémont.

While trapping with Ewing Young, Kit had traveled in central California years before. "There," said he, "is the little mountain—it is 15 years ago since I saw it; but I am just as sure as if I had seen it yesterday." His remarkable memory for features of the landscape brought back the image of Mt. Diablo sharply. He seemed to have a faculty for mental pictures, which, once imprinted, were never erased from his mind. The entire party took hope. "Between us, then, and this low coast range, was the valley of the Sacramento; and no one who had not accompanied us through the incidents of our life for the last few months could realize the delight with which at last we looked down upon it," Frémont wrote.

But the trip ahead into the valley remained just as difficult. Preuss got lost. Baptiste Derosier and Charles Town lost their minds. Town took a pleasure swim in a mountain torrent, "as if it were summer." Derosier went "deranged . . . hunger and fatigue, joined to weakness of body, and fear of perishing in the mountains, had crazed him." In this extremity Carson without fail kept up hope, strength, and good sense. On February 21 he roused Frémont "with an early fire, and we were all up long before day, in order to pass the snow fields before the sun should render the crust soft," Frémont wrote. On February 23, "our most difficult day," Frémont fell into a river. Kit leapt in, got a hold on him, pulled him out, and surely saved his life. On February 27 Kit found a patch of grass, feed for starving horses. "I heard a shout from Carson, who had gone ahead a few hundred yards," wrote Frémont. "'Life yet,' said he, as he came up, 'life yet'; I have found a hill side sprinkled with grass enough for the night."

On March 8 they reached Sutter's Fort in terrible condition, "each man, weak and emaciated, leading a horse or mule as weak and emaciated as themselves," wrote Frémont. Here they refitted. "When we arrived at the fort we were naked and in as poor a condition as men could possibly be," Carson recalled. "We were well received by Mr. Sutter and furnished in a princely manner." After resting, they began the journey south through central California to round the southern end of the Sierra Nevada. Near today's Oro Grande below Victorville in mid-April, they reached the Mojave River and headed for Utah on the Old Spanish Trail.

The caravan, truly an all-American composite, camped at a water hole on the Mojave River in late April. "Our cavalcade made a strange and grotesque appearance," Frémont wrote, "and it was impossible to avoid reflecting upon our position and composition in this remote solitude. . . . Guided by a civilized Indian, attended by two wild ones from the Sierra; a Chinook from the Columbia; and our own mixture of American, French, German—all armed; four or five languages heard at once; above a hundred horses and mules, half-wild; American, Spanish, and Indian dresses and equipments intermingled—such was our composition. Our march was a sort of procession." Here on the Mojave occurred an incident that tested all the men involved. It revealed several of Carson's traits, among them, besides his courage and determination, his readiness to punish, even to kill a man who broke the rules of the border code.

Two Mexicans, Andreas Fuentes and an eleven-year-old-boy named Pablo Hernandez, rode into camp with an appalling tale. Accompanied by Fuentes's wife, Pablo's parents, and a man named Santiago Giacome, they had been traveling east with a large caravan from Los Angeles. Since the caravan was slow, the small group of family and friends had gone ahead to Archilette Spring where they planned to rest and wait for the caravan. After they settled in at the spring, Indian warriors attacked them and drove off their horses. Fuentes and Pablo had escaped. Fuentes asked Frémont to help find his horses and, presumably, to learn the fate of the other members of the small party. Frémont gave permission to any of his men who wanted to go. Only Carson and Alexis Godey volunteered. Carson recalled years later: "Godey and myself volunteered with the expectation that some men of our party would join us. They did not."

After twenty miles hard riding, Fuentes's horse gave out. Carson and Godey rode on. They soon came upon the thieves, who had butchered five of the stolen horses and were by then feasting on the meat. Waiting out a miserable night, Carson and Godey crawled in among the horses at first light, hoping to gather them quietly, if possible. But the horses, being horses, spooked. "The Indians noticed the commotion among the animals [and] sprung for their arms," Carson recalled.

Now arose the imperative that border men who long survived learned early. *If outnumbered by an enemy, hesitate not. Attack with force, or die!* By Carson's account, "We now considered it time to charge. . . . They were about thirty in number. We charged. I fired, killed one. Godey fired, missed, but reloaded and fired, killing another. . . . The remainder run." Carson stood watch while Godey scalped both fallen warriors. One of these, still alive, shot an arrow through Godey's shirt collar. "He again fell," Carson recalled, "and Godey finished him." Godey and Carson then gathered the horses and ran them back to Frémont's camp. As they rode in, Godey waved the two scalps. He had tied them to the muzzle of his rifle.

Frémont's *Report* added detail and the usual simplistic interpretation: *civilization* had "triumphed over" *savagery.* As in the dime novels, when "civilized men" won, brutal punishment of "savages" was right. Preuss thought the whole affair disgusting. To him, Carson and Godey were more revolting than the warriors. To his clerk in 1856 Carson reported the details. "We then marched on to where [Fuentes and Pablo] had left the two men and women," he said. "The men we discovered dead, their bodies horribly mutilated. The women we supposed were carried into captivity [but] a party traveling in our rear found their bodies very much mutilated and staked to the ground." When the expedition came upon Pablo's father's body, Frémont noted, "A little lap-dog, which had belonged to Pablo's mother, remained with the dead bodies, and was frantic with joy at seeing Pablo, [who] poor child, was frantic with grief; and filled the air with lamentations for his father and mother—*Mi Padre! Mi Madre!*—was his incessant cry."

Shortly afterward, probably somewhere near present-day Glendale, Nevada, the killers of Fuentes's party reappeared. "They were the same people who had murdered the

Mexicans," wrote Frémont. In large numbers "they began to surround the horses," which "were immediately driven in and kept close to camp." They "insulted" the expedition from a nearby bluff by making rude gestures. Then one who seemed to be a chief and who was armed with weapons "forced" his way into camp in spite of Frémont's warning him to stay out. "When shown our weapons, he bored his ear with his fingers, and said he could not hear. There are so few of you and so many of us, he gestured, pointing around to the hills and mountains." Frémont wrote that he "had some difficulty restraining" his men, "particularly Carson, who felt an insult of this kind as much as if it had been given by a more responsible being." By the border sense of justice and code of male honor, a personal insult of this sort could not be let go. According to Frémont, Carson said, "Don't say that, old man. Don't you say that—your life's in danger." Carson was "speaking in good English; and probably the old man was nearer to his end than he will be before he meets it," Frémont wrote. Fortunately, Carson controlled his temper, and the old chief backed off.

After traveling northeasterly to Utah Lake, then turning east through Brown's Hole on the Green River, the expedition arrived back at Bent's Fort in early July 1844. On the fourth, William Bent served them up a big dinner. The fort undoubtedly displayed the nation's flag. No doubt there was drinking, target shooting, and fighting. Everyone joined in, all races, all tribes, all ages, all languages. Someone may have given a speech in the florid style of the day called "oratory," and there was surely much yelling of approval, clapping of hands, and swearing of allegiance. "The [fourth] was celebrated as well, if not better, than in many of the towns of the States," was all that Carson said later of the expedition's celebration and of its return from California. "Then," he said, "Frémont and party started for the States and I for Taos." So the expedition ended, and Kit returned home, where he resumed unemployment.

He stayed in Taos until March 1845. Restless and out of work, he and his friend Dick Owens now decided it was time to settle down. "[We] concluded," Kit recalled, "that, as we had rambled enough, it would be advisable for us to go and settle on some good stream and make us a farm. We went to Little Cimarron, about 45 miles east of Taos, built ourselves little huts, put in considerable grain, and commenced getting out timber to enlarge our improvements. Remained till August of same year." But he and Owens could not stay put. Though born of a rural people, these two could not follow the farmer's dream of settling, clearing trees, building a cabin, and planting corn. The skills they had learned in the mountains were not the farmer's skills. These two men were hunters. They wanted to see a new horizon each morning and to follow the wild game. When the first chance came along, Carson and Owens took up the long trail again. Now Kit heard that Frémont was already at Bent's Fort bound west on a third expedition.

"The year previous," he recalled, "I had given my word . . . that, in case he should return for the purpose of making any more exploration, that I would willingly join him. He reached Bent's fort about the 1st of August, made inquiries where I was [and] heard of my being on the Cimarron. [He] sent an express to me. Then Owens and I sold out, for about half [of what] it was worth, and we started to join Frémont and we both received employment." As for Owens, he too would serve Frémont well. Owens Valley in California is named for him. By the late 1850s, however, he reached a low point. In August 1858 John M. Kingsbury wrote his partner, James Josiah Webb, from Santa Fe: "[Owens] continues to drink all he can. . . . He totters . . . at a gait of an old man of 90. It is astonishing to all that he is still with the living."

At Bent's Fort, Carson and Owens rejoined Fremont. Again this was a well-equipped, well-manned expedition, made up of a very diverse group of men. The creoles and French Canadians were back, men like Auguste Archambeau, Alexis

Godey, and Basil Lajeunesse. Lucien Maxwell and Theodore Talbot were back too. Talbot would become a leader. The letters he wrote to his mother and sister in the East are rich in detail. Mountain man Joe Walker would join the expedition later as a guide. Charles Preuss stayed at home this time, but the young artist Edward N. "Ned" Kern of Philadelphia took his place as topographer. Lt. William G. Peck and Lt. James W. Abert, Col. John J. Abert's son, came along, at least for part of the way. Jacob Dodson, the Benton family slave, came as Frémont's servant.

Sagundai and Swanok led ten Delawares, all first-rate hunters, scouts, and hardened veterans of border combat. Chinook, the Indian boy who had come from the Columbia River with the second expedition because he wanted to learn about "white" people, was back. He had spent the winter with a Quaker family who gave him "such rudiments of practical knowledge as he might be able to put to good use," according to Frémont. But Chinook wanted to see his own people and his horses again. So here he was. And here again was Frémont's favorite saddle horse, Sacramento. The "Indian boys who had spent a happy winter in Kentucky met me at Saint Louis, bringing with them Sacramento, aggressively well," Frémont wrote. Sacramento later saved Carson's life in California by charging a Native warrior who was taking aim at Kit. This third expedition, the last upon which Carson would serve with Frémont, remains the most controversial and the most mysterious of the three.

"La Ciudad de Santa Fe." This lithograph shows Santa Fe about as it looked from the south in 1846–47. The road leading toward the center of town from the southeast is the Santa Fe Trail. Note the teams pulling covered wagons toward the plaza; also note the American flags. From *Report of Lieut. J. W. Abert, of His Examination of New Mexico in the Years 1846–'47*, 1848. Courtesy Western History Collections, University of Oklahoma Libraries.

"View of the Copper Mine." As a boy, Carson worked for Robert McKnight at Santa Rita, or the Copper Mine, shortly after running away from the saddle shop where he worked in Franklin, Missouri. This C. B. Graham lithograph depicts the area a few years after Kit first saw it. From Lieut. Col. W. H. Emory, *Notes of a Military Reconnoissance [sic] from Fort Leavenworth . . . to San Diego . . .*, 1848. Courtesy Western History Collections, University of Oklahoma Libraries.

View of the Copper Mine today, from approximately where the lithographer stood in 1846–47. Photograph by Elroy Limmer, 2009.

"Two huge and terribly angry grizzly bears were bounding towards him." Kit once admitted to being scared when two grizzly bears charged him. From *Kit Carson's Own Story of His Life; as Dictated to Col. and Mrs. D. C. Peters about 1856–57,* 1873. Courtesy Western History Collections, University of Oklahoma Libraries.

Reconstructed Bent's Fort. A close friend of the Bent brothers, Kit hunted for the fort and was briefly married to a Cheyenne woman who lived nearby. Marc Simmons collection.

Maria Josefa Jaramillo Carson, a few years after her marriage to Kit. Courtesy Kit Carson Historic Museums, Taos, New Mexico.

If this photograph is indeed of Carson, it is one of the earliest we know of, taken perhaps when he was an Indian agent, c. 1854. It is easy to imagine that he looked like this when he and Josefa were married. Courtesy Kit Carson Historic Museums, Taos, New Mexico.

The Taos home where Kit and Josefa lived for many years, as it looked in 1880. While Carson served as Indian agent, his office was also in this building. Today it is a museum operated by the Masonic Lodge (Kit became a Mason late in life). Courtesy Lee Burke.

An artist's rendering of the terrible winter weather that Carson, Frémont, and the men and mules with them suffered in crossing the Sierra Nevada to Sutter's Fort on Frémont's second expedition into the West. From *Kit Carson's Own Story of His Life*, 1873. Courtesy Western History Collections, University of Oklahoma Libraries.

Sutter's Fort. Built and operated by the German Swiss immigrant John Augustus Sutter, the fort was the capital and trading center of Sutter's Mexican grant of eleven square leagues called New Helvetia in the Sacramento Valley. Here arrived the half-frozen, nearly starved men of Frémont's second expedition. From Frémont, *Memoirs of My Life*, 1886. Courtesy Western History Collections, University of Oklahoma Libraries.

"Night Assault by the Indians." An artist's rendition of the Klamath man whom Carson praised for his bravery in taking rifle shots in the firelight on Frémont's third expedition. The Klamaths killed Basil Lajeunesse and two Delawares, Denny and Crane. Carson never again failed to set a night guard. From Charles Wentworth Upham, *Life, Explorations and Public Services of John Charles Frémont*, 1856. Courtesy Western History Collections, University of Oklahoma Libraries.

One of Frémont's favorite Delaware bodyguards on the third expedition, Sagundai scalped the brave Klamath man who stood in the firelight taking rifle shots on the night after the expedition met Gillespie and after Frémont and Carson failed to set a guard. From Frémont, *Memoirs of My Life,* 1886. Courtesy Western History Collections, University of Oklahoma Libraries.

Portrait of Carson, from a daguerreotype possibly taken in Washington, D.C., 1847. If so, this is about as he looked when carrying dispatches from California to Washington. Marc Simmons collection.

"Frémont's Army" marches into Monterey during the Bear Flag Revolt. This is the scene observed by Lt. Frederick Walpole, R.N., of the British flagship *Collingwood*, at anchor in the bay. Frémont, in the lead, is followed by his famous Delaware bodyguards, as well as by Carson, who may be mounted on the rearing white horse. From Upham, *Life, Explorations and Public Services of John Charles Fremont*, 1856. Courtesy Western History Collections, University of Oklahoma Libraries.

"Valley of the Mimbres." This C. B. Graham lithograph shows Lt. William H. Emory's men with General Kearny's Army of the West riding up the Mimbres Valley east of Santa Rita, or the Copper Mine, in New Mexico in 1846. In the background is Cooke's Peak, named for Lt. (later Gen.) Philip St. George Cooke, who led the Mormon Battalion with Kearny's Army. From Emory, *Notes of a ilitary Reconnoissance*, 1848. Courtesy Western History Collections, University of Oklahoma Libraries.

Cooke's Peak and the Mimbres Valley today, from approximately where the lithographer stood in 1846. Photograph by Elroy Limmer, 2009.

Carson's adobe home at Rayado, New Mexico, not far from Maxwell's mansion at Cimarron. Carson sometimes brought Josefa here when he felt the country was safe, but took her back to Taos when there was trouble with the Plains tribes. It must have been cold in winter if, as it would appear in this photograph, the large adobe building had only one corner fireplace. Courtesy Audrey Alpers. Marc Simmons collection.

Colonel Carson, 1865.
Courtesy State Historical
Society of Colorado, Denver.

General James H. Carleton, Carson's commanding officer during the Mescalero, Navajo, and Kiowa-Comanche campaigns, looking, as usual, as if he had chewed pickled horseshoes for breakfast. Courtesy Museum of New Mexico (negative no. 22938).

Colonel Carson in 1865. After more than three years of strenuous military service, he was looking "unwell and very much fatigued," as Capt. Asa B. Carey described his appearance late in the Navajo campaign. Mark Simmons collection.

A distant view of Fort Garland, Colorado, where Carson was stationed during his last military years. Today this is a National Historic Site. (After William Makepeace Thayer, *Marvels of the New West,* 1887). Marc Simmons collection.

A gathering of Masons in Santa Fe, 1865 (Carson at center). Nicholas Brown photograph, courtesy of the Palace of the Governors Photo Archives (NMHM/DCA) (negative no. 9826).

Carson with three members of the Ute delegation in 1868, when Kit was on his last trip for the government. D. C. Oakes, standing to Carson's right, accompanied him home to Colorado. Brady Studio, Washington, D.C. Courtesy of Kansas State Historical Society, Topeka.

Carson's eldest daughters, Teresina (left) and Stella (right). Teresina resembled her mother; Stella, it appears, her father. Courtesy Marc Simmons and family of Jess C. Carson.

7

"I Done So"

Unlike the two previous expeditions, largely scientific and literary excursions, this one had truly major political and military implications. Its inner workings are an important puzzle even yet. Colonel Abert's orders stressed the study of the eastern drainage of the Rocky Mountains and required Frémont to return by the end of 1845. He was to survey the Arkansas and "if practicable . . . the Red River without our boundary line" (i.e., the boundary line with Mexico), noting especially "the navigable properties of each" river and the location where "the boundary line of the U.S.[,] the 100th degree of longitude west of Greenwich[,] strikes the Arkansas, and the Red River." Exactly what Abert meant by "without our boundary line" remains unclear. William H. Goetzmann reads it as meaning "within." Frémont may just as well have read the word "without" as meaning beyond or outside of the U.S.–Mexico boundary, even all the way to the Pacific. In addition, Colonel Abert's orders were that he note "the geography of localities within reasonable distance of Bent's Fort, and of the streams which run east from the Rocky Mountains, and [to] so time" the "operations, that [your] party will come in during the present year."

And, Colonel Abert added, no doubt because he had experienced Frémont's tendency to wander off on his own: "Long journies [*sic*] to determine isolated geographical points are

scarcely worth the time and the expense." Immediately Frémont disregarded orders. Showing no sign of remaining
anywhere east of the Rockies, he set out directly across Mexican territory for California. "This project, like the previous
ones, represented a direct violation of official orders," wrote
Goetzmann. "Thanks to [Senator] Benton's powerful back-
ing, he seemed entirely immune from the rigors of military
discipline." Goetzmann finds evidence in letters Frémont
wrote to botanist John Torrey well before Colonel Abert issued his orders that Frémont's aim was California all along.
In addition, Frémont's *Memoirs of My Life*, written years later
with hindsight and with the intent to polish his reputation,
contains evidence that he intended to violate orders.

Why to California? It seems evident today that the United
States of America was headed in that direction. The sirens
of Manifest Destiny, like the scent of lilacs in April, wafted
on the winds, affecting men's souls and minds, as if some
powerful spirit had ordained that the continent belong to
the United States all the way to the Pacific, even beyond.
Emigrant wagons rolled by hundreds over South Pass into
California and Oregon. Texas had already broken away from
Mexico to form a new republic. Next she clamored for state-
hood, to be granted December 29, 1845, when President
Polk signed an act making her the twenty-eighth state. Even
before Frémont left St. Louis for the West on June 4, there
had been talk of war with Mexico. If it came, Alta California would be easy plunder. Her distance from the capital at
Mexico City made her people, already independent of attitude, hard to govern. Some of them could even see benefits
in becoming U.S. citizens. Besides, California lay unused,
her resources ready for exploitation. She could fulfill every
citizen's dream, could sate the farmer's, the gambler's, and
the miner's greed. She was the gateway to trade with the
Orient. However, Britain too was interested in California.
Best act soon. He who waits loses! James K. Polk, the new
president, was ready to lead westward. Polk was a model of

self-ordained western expansionism, a point man for Manifest Destiny.

Conveniently for Frémont, no other U.S. Army officer would be close enough to lead soldiers in, if and when the opportunity to grab California should come. But the U.S. Navy *was* already there, with ships, under the eye of U.S. Navy Secretary George Bancroft, "whose orders," Frémont wrote, "continuously evince comprehending foresight and insistence." What is more, Frémont had impressed Secretary Bancroft with his vigor and talent, and Bancroft was on very good terms with Frémont's father-in-law, Senator Benton. Both Benton and Bancroft saw eye to eye on westward expansion, and of course they backed Frémont. Curiously, however, Polk was unimpressed with the young officer.

Inconveniently for Frémont, therefore tangling his opportunities, was the fact that he was an officer of the U.S. Army's Topographical Engineers. He was a scientist, not an officer of the line. He had no training in battlefield tactics, no military training at all. Nor, of course, did Colonel Abert's orders permit him to take military action in California or anywhere near there. Had he been a U.S. naval officer, the situation would have been different, for Secretary Bancroft had written Commodore John Drake Sloat in the Pacific Ocean as early as June 1845, notifying him to seize California ports should he "ascertain" that Mexico had "declared war" on the United States. But Frémont was not navy. So matters stood when he, with Kit Carson and others, all well armed, rode westward from Bent's Fort toward California in 1845.

Frémont would claim some forty years later that he had foreknowledge of the direction events were headed, even that he had been given "the discretion" to act on his own. "California stood out as the chief subject in the impending war," he wrote in 1887, "and with Mr. Benton and other governing men at Washington it became a firm resolve to hold it for the United States. This was talked over fully during the time of preparation for the third expedition, and the contingencies anticipated and weighed. . . . For me, no distinct course or definite instruction could be laid down, but the probabilities were made known to me as well as what to do when they became facts. The distance was too great for timely communication; but failing this I was given discretion to act." Thus it would seem that Frémont may have been, or believed that he was, a man on a dual mission: under official orders on the one hand to perform scientific work east of the Rockies, and on the other hand, approved by the shadowy powers of Washington to take military action in California at his own "discretion."

After Carson and Dick Owens joined Frémont at Bent's Fort, the expedition rode up the Arkansas River, over the mountains through South Park, then northwesterly across the Colorado and the Green rivers to the Great Salt Lake by October 13. There the men camped for about two weeks while Frémont explored the country thereabout, collecting specimens. From Great Salt Lake, apparently unaware that Jedediah Smith and two others had crossed here traveling west to east in June 1827, he set out to pioneer a new route to Alta California. The route would run straight across the salty desert west of Great Salt Lake to Mary's River, which he renamed the Humboldt, and beyond there to the lake later named Walker Lake. This route was to be called the "Hastings Cutoff." Forever linked with the name of the promoter Lansford Hastings and his *Emigrants' Guide to Oregon and California*, this emigrants' "guide" and the cutoff would prove a death sentence for the Donner Party in 1846.

Now, however, Carson and three other old mountain hands went ahead to reconnoiter the first part of the route. "We kept around the south side of the [Salt] Lake to the last water[,] remained one day. [Then] Frémont started Maxwell, Archambeau, Lajeunesse, and myself to cross the desert," Kit told his clerk. "I [often heard] old trappers speak of the impossibility of crossing—that water could not be found, grass for animals, there was none. Frémont was bound to cross. Nothing was impossible for him to perform if required in his explorations." After traveling west for about sixty miles with "no water or grass, not a particle of vegetation," the scouts found grass and water. They sent up smoke signals telling the main party to come on. The entire party reassembled at the landmark Frémont named "Pilot Peak."

As he had done on the second expedition, Frémont sometimes divided his men into two parties with plans to reassemble at a chosen point ahead. Each party would explore different routes. The largest party packed the heavy baggage and took the easiest route. Possibly the men competed for the privilege of joining the smaller party, as they did for locating the best campsite. Probably the competition was meant as an incentive, for the campsite or a feature nearby would be named for the winner. There was no bias in this process. Three Delaware scouts won recognition: Sagundai, a campsite; Crane, a stream; and Connor, a spring-fed waterhole. When they came upon a lone Indian cooking squirrels to eat, the Delawares took away his beautifully made bow and arrows. Frémont made them give the weapons back because without them, he explained, the lone Indian might starve.

Somewhere west of Pilot Peak, the party divided into two groups with plans to reassemble at Walker Lake near the eastern slope of the Sierra Nevada. This part of the journey went well enough, one group under Theodore Talbot sticking to the Humboldt River, the other under Frémont taking the dry Hastings Cutoff. At Walker Lake they divided again. Mountain man Joe Walker and Talbot now took one group with the camp baggage south around the lower end of the Sierra Nevada. Eventually they would cross "Walker Pass" into California. The plan was that they would wait on a branch of King's River for the expedition to reassemble. Meanwhile, Frémont took his select group of fifteen with Carson over Truckee Pass to Sutter's Fort to refit. Fortunately, they got through the high mountain passes ahead of heavy snowfall. From Sutter's they headed south to rejoin Walker and Talbot.

Coming upon camping places littered with horse bones, they named the people "Horse-thief Indians." When Native warriors struck, Lucien Maxwell, on horseback, dueled with one of them and killed him.

The party reached King's River on December 22, but found no sign of Walker and Talbot, who, as it happened, were still on the way. They would arrive soon and go into camp on Kern's River nearby. There they would wait from December 27 to January 17. Always in a hurry, however, Frémont waited only two days, then headed back to Sutter's Fort with his party. "They were too strong to have met with any serious accident," he rationalized, as if forgetting that keeping the expedition together was *his* responsibility, not Walker's or Talbot's. Eventually the two parties got together again, almost by chance. Walker was mad at Frémont about this flap. After another unpleasant incident, he resigned the expedition in disgust.

After returning to Sutter's Fort, Frémont appears to have become increasingly irrational, his behavior ever more erratic. In her biography *Jessie Benton Frémont*, Pamela Herr suggests that Colonel Abert's phrase "your own efforts for more distant discoveries" in additional orders written to Frémont on May 14 opened the door for Frémont to depart from earlier orders and proceed to California. Be that as it may, after he returned to Sutter's Fort, leaving Walker and Talbot unaccounted for, he began to act ever more like a soldier at war, ever less like a biologist and topographer out collecting specimens and making maps.

Within days he took a boat from Sutter's Fort to Yerba Buena (today's San Francisco), then rode to Monterey where he met Mexican and American officials. He made little effort to treat the Mexicans diplomatically, and they soon ordered him out of California. After defying Mexican authority with a standoff of Gen. José Castro's army at Gavilan Peak, he made an embarrassing retreat on March 11, 1846. Finally, he and many of his men joined the Bear Flag Revolt to "free" California from Mexico. Later, he and his famous wife, Jessie, confused the issues further in statements and letters. Jessie at first insisted that both she and her husband had questioned the "justice" of this war. Later still, she became her husband's chief apologist. William H. Goetzmann wrote of Frémont, "[He] must always have had the subversion of California in mind. . . . He was a romantic, stormy figure . . . , a man of many moods and differing fortunes and attitudes, yet . . . attractive to many [people] in his time."

After the retreat from Castro's army at Gavilan Peak, Frémont led the expedition toward Oregon. They stopped for a few days' rest at Peter Lassen's ranch—Carson called it "Lawson's"—in the Sacramento Valley near present-day Corning, California. Here Frémont received "reports," perhaps little more than rumors, that local Indians planned to attack Americans and had already raided some settlers. Facts and dates remain unclear. According to Thomas S. Martin, who was there, after the settlers "asked Frémont to protect them," he gave his men permission to volunteer their service. A killing spree followed. His men's attack on the local Indians was in character with the most violent of border actions, although the ethnic diversity of the attack group in this tragedy should always be kept in mind. The brutal slaughter was not as simple as "the white guys killing the Indians."

Of later remarks by Martin, Carson, and Frémont, Carson's were the most forthright. About fifty men rode up the Sacramento River and attacked an Indian village near present-day Redding: "Found [the Indians] to be in great force," Carson recalled later. "They were attacked. The number killed I cannot say. It was a perfect butchery. Those not killed fled in all directions, and we returned to Lawson's. Had accomplished what we went for and given the Indians such a chastisement that [it] would be long before they ever again would feel like attacking the settlements." It was an example of retributive justice at its most violent and most primitive, a punishment based upon unconfirmed reports, then rationalized as a means of teaching a lesson. People of all sides made war for these reasons over the many years of American border conflict. Though the killing rituals themselves could be very elaborate, such warfare was, to put it mildly, not only crude, but ultimately ineffectual as a means of practicing "justice" or of "teaching" anyone "a lesson." Even in that day, many, especially in the East, were horrified by such actions.

Leaving Lassen's on April 24, the expedition wandered on in a leisurely manner into far northeastern California, then northerly to the eastern shore of Upper Klamath Lake. Here on May 6, already five months later than Colonel Abert's written orders permitted him to be in the field, Frémont met Klamath people, who, though surprised, seemed friendly. The expedition then crossed to the western shore of the lake and explored northerly along the eastern slope of the Cascades. Frémont dreamed of finding a pathway west through the coastal mountains to the Pacific, where he might discover "some safe harbor . . . where harbors were so few."

Generally he and his men wandered around like a troop of boy scouts looking for something of interest to do. On the evening of May 8, they found it. Out of the coming night, two tired horsemen, Sam Neal and Levi Sigler, rode into camp. They had covered nearly a hundred miles in two days to report that Lt. Archibald Gillespie of the U.S. Marines and three other men rode somewhere behind them carrying important letters for Frémont. Hostile warriors had trailed Sigler and Neal, who had outrun them with stronger, faster horses. By daylight, Frémont set out to rescue the dispatch carriers. He took a relief party that included Carson, Godey, Lajeunesse, Owens, and four of the Delawares. Carson estimated that they met Gillespie the next day "about 60 miles" south on the southern shore of Klamath Lake.

Posing as a retired businessman recovering his health, Gillespie and his African American servant, Benjamin Harrison, had left Washington with dispatches in October 1845. Gillespie represented Secretary of State James Buchanan and U.S. Navy Secretary Bancroft. He had met with President

Polk just before leaving the capital. After delivering private information and letters to U.S. emissary John Slidell in Mexico City, U.S. Navy Commodore Sloat in Mazatlán, and U.S. Consul Thomas O. Larkin in Monterey, he had set out to find Frémont. The letter to Sloat authorized him to seize California's ports when it became evident to him that the United States and Mexico were at war. Gillespie had memorized a letter from Secretary Buchanan to T. O. Larkin designating Larkin a "confidential agent" of the United States. Having memorized it, Gillespie had destroyed the letter.

Since little trace survives of any papers Gillespie carried to Frémont, the mystery remains over what "instructions" they may have contained. Frémont claimed forty years later that Gillespie delivered "a letter of introduction from . . . Mr. Buchanan, and letters and papers from Senator Benton and family." As to specifics, however, he was vague. Possibly Gillespie recited the memorized letter. Little doubt he passed along what he knew of the state of affairs with Mexico. He may have instructed Frémont, as he had Larkin, to report suspicious activities by either Mexican or British officials. Gillespie did *not* know, nor could Frémont have known, though he later claimed that he did, that the country was officially at war. Though hostilities had begun along the Rio Grande in April, Congress did not declare war on Mexico until May 13, 1846, four days after this meeting on Klamath Lake. Frémont's many remarks about the meeting are, in his biographer Tom Chaffin's words, "vague, largely unverified, and often contradictory." Frémont took it upon himself, as he would write later, "where uncertainties arose, to give my own country the benefit of any doubts by taking decided action." Carson would not have been privy to the information, nor would he have disagreed with his leader. He was bound to his sense of duty, and he too was one to take action.

In camp that night on Klamath Lake, Frémont believed he saw his way ahead clear as light. "The information through Gillespie had absolved me from my duty as an explorer," he wrote much later, "and I was left to my duty as an officer of the American Army with the further authoritative knowledge that the Government intended to take California." For the moment he was sure that he was authorized to lead the conquest. High on adrenaline, he failed to post guard as he rolled into his blankets for the night. Once he thought he heard a stir among the horses, but went back to sleep. Next thing he knew Carson was calling out. Then Kit and Dick Owens were on their feet yelling, "Indians!" There was a thunk as hatchet split bone. Arrows struck men climbing out of their blankets. A brave Klamath man stood in the firelight taking rifle balls.

Carson later gave the detail as he recalled it to his clerk. "We apprehended no danger that night, and the men being much fatigued, no guard was posted," he explained. "It was the first and last time that we failed in posting guard." The attacking warriors were soon driven out of camp. Then the Americans threw blankets over the bushes to protect themselves from the arrows. By morning's light they discovered Crane, one of the finest of the Delaware scouts, dead. Half-asleep, he had grabbed an empty rifle. "He was not aware of it and kept trying to fire," Carson said later. "Stood erect, received five arrows in the breast, four mortal, then fell." Another Delaware took a rifle ball. Basil Lajeunesse and Denny, the "half-breed," were both dead, their skulls split by hatchets.

The Klamaths lost the man who axed Lajeunesse in the head. The brave man died taking gunshots in the firelight. "He was the bravest Indian I ever saw," said Carson. "If his men had been as brave . . . , we surely would all have been killed." This man had given Lieutenant Gillespie a salmon a day or two before, feigning friendship. Basil Lajeunesse, the French-speaking voyageur Frémont had first hired in St. Louis for the 1842 expedition, was everybody's comrade and Frémont's favorite man. Carson said later he "particularly regretted" Lajeunesse's loss. "All of them were brave, good men." In the clutch of grief and rage, Carson grabbed the dead Klamath's hatchet and split the man's head as the

Klamath had done Basil's head. Sagundai, another very able Delaware, scalped the courageous Klamath.

A very black mood then settled in. "This event cast an angry gloom over the little camp," Frémont wrote. "For the moment I threw all other considerations aside and determined to square accounts with these people before I left them." Retributive justice. Getting even. The camp had just had friendly relations with these same people. Frémont had been generous. "It was only a few days back that some of these same Indians had come into our camp," he wrote, "and I divided with them what meat I had, and unpacked a mule to give them tobacco and knives."

Grieving the loss of their friends, feeling deceived, enraged, thus very dangerous, the members of the expedition packed their comrades' bodies on mules. They started back north along the west shore of Klamath Lake to rejoin the main party. The farther they went, the worse they felt. When they spotted canoes on the lake near the trailhead, they were convinced the Klamaths had set an ambush. Burying their comrades in a laurel thicket, they prepared to fight. Carson later added detail: "On account of the timber being so thick," he told his clerk in 1856, "the bodies knocked against the trees and, becoming much bruised, we concluded to bury them when we did." With their knives, they dug a shallow common grave. "Wrapping their blankets round them," Frémont wrote, "left them among the laurels. There are men above whom the laurels bloom who did not better deserve [flowers] than my brave Delaware [Crane] and Basil [Lajeunesse]. I left Denny's [the "half-breed's"] name on the creek where he died."

Of rejoining the main party that afternoon, Frémont later recalled: "All were deeply grieved by the loss of our companions. The Delawares were filled with grief and rage [by Crane's death] and went into mourning, blackening their faces. They were soothed somewhat when I told them that they should have an opportunity to . . . carry home scalps enough to satisfy the friends of Crane and the Delaware nation. With blackened faces, set and angry, they sat around brooding and waiting for revenge."

Severe grief at Crane's death increased everyone's fury. Seething for revenge, the men would soon go on another killing spree. A tightly knit little family, all of them "brothers of the trail," an ethnically and racially mixed group, would "pay back" these Klamaths who had caused them so much grief and rage. Moving his men around the northern end of the lake, Frémont sent Carson ahead in charge of ten "with orders," in Carson's words later, "that if I discovered any large village of Indians to send word, and in case I should be seen by them for me to act as I thought best."

Ten miles south along the eastern shore of the lake, Carson came upon what he estimated as "about 50 lodges" already astir. "I knew that they had seen us," he recalled, "and, considering it useless to send for reinforcements, I determined to attack them, charged on them, fought for some time, killed a number, and the balance fled." By his account, he and his men then set fire to the entire village, burning "some ten wagon loads of fish they had caught[,] All their fishing tackle, camp equipage, etc." Wishing "to do them as much damage as I could," he told his clerk later, "I directed their houses to be set on fire. The [cattails] being dry it was a beautiful sight. The Indians had commenced the war with us without cause and I thought they should be chastised in a summary manner. And they were severely punished." By border rules, "justice" had been done when "retribution" was ruthless and complete.

Frémont's account of this disaster differs substantially from Carson's in detail, as do the recollections of Thomas S. Martin. Martin claimed that the men wet their gunpowder crossing a creek. Both Martin and Frémont suggested that Carson overstated his own importance and was impetuous, that Frémont arrived in time to take an active part in what Carson called "the sport," a reprehensible term for the tragedy even

in that day. Reciting the conflicting details of the other accounts here does not change the fact that this was a disaster
of a type all too common on borders such as these men and
their ancestors had known in Missouri, Kentucky, and the
Ohio country. Driven by their darkest feelings of grief and
rage, men took quick action to do "justice," to "get even," and
to "teach a lesson" in ways their people and their cultures had
long practiced.

Other tragedies were to occur before the end of the expedition. The party's way south from Klamath Lake back to
Lassen's ranch, then down the Sacramento River toward Sutter's Fort was grim. Though the details are unclear, Carson
and two companions reportedly arrested and shot three un-
armed Californios, one of whom, according to nineteenth-
century western historian Hubert Howe Bancroft, may have
been guilty only of volunteering "to carry a message" between
Mexican officers. The three were shot after they came ashore
from a boat near San Rafael in San Francisco Bay. Theodore
Talbot's remarks in letters from California to his mother and
sister in the East do not mention Carson's part in the affair,
though Talbot must have known of it, for as a member of
the expedition he was nearby when it occurred. He wrote
to his mother from Monterey on July 24, 1846: "We killed
3 spies . . . from the main force across an arm of the bay at
San Pablo. I was left here to guard this post and keep a line
of communication open while Captain [Frémont] started off
with 100 men after La Torre."

The next day, in writing his sister, Talbot added detail that
may explain the shooting. "La Torre one of [Castro's] bra-
vos and best captains," he wrote, "killed two Americans going
express to rouse the settlers to arms. They butchered them
very cruelly cutting them to pieces limb by limb. . . . In the
[evening] our men shot 3 couriers who had just landed from
San Pablo a point of land on the other side of the bay opposite to the Mission of San Rafael." According to historian
Bancroft, the killing of the three Californios was payback for

the murder of the two Americans, Thomas Cowie and a man named Fowler. A gang of Californios had "mutilated [them] in a most horrible manner," Bancroft wrote. One report described the two as having been "tied to trees, stoned, and cut to pieces, one of them having his broken jaw dragged out with a reata." Carson said nothing of this entire matter to his clerk in 1856.

Years later, however, he described the affair to his friend William M. Boggs. He told Boggs that when he asked Frémont what to do with the three arrested men, Frémont told him, "Mr. Carson, I have no use for prisoners—do your duty." To Boggs's opinion that the execution was cold-blooded murder, Carson explained that he and the others were retaliating for the brutal murder of the Americans Cowie and Fowler. He added that Moses Carson, his older half brother, who by then was living in California, had discovered Cowie's and Fowler's mutilated bodies and had buried them. Bancroft described the shooting of the Californios as "a brutal murder . . . which was intended as a retaliation." Reconsidered today, the question as to whether Frémont actually gave the orders, or only approved the execution later, and the truth about the motives and the details, seem forever beyond reach. Both Carson and Frémont must bear responsibility for the bloody affair.

Frémont would now play an increasingly controversial part in the conquest of California. His reputation would ultimately suffer, his army career end in court-martial. The conquest was an epic struggle of egos, as well as a brutal war on the ground. On the Mexican side, the provincial capital had been moved from Monterey to Los Angeles, where Gov. Pío Pico was supposed to handle civil and legislative matters. Up north in Monterey, Gen. José Castro, refusing to take orders from the governor down south, continued operating as commandant for provincial defense. Neither man could agree on a course of action. Each acted as if he had the authority and the power to rule California. It is probably correct to say that Pico had the authority, but Castro held the power.

On the American side, Commodore Sloat, though he did not know that war would be declared on May 13, landed sailors peacefully at Monterey on July 7, as he had been authorized to do. Meanwhile, in mid-June Sonoma had fallen to local men who called themselves the "Bear Flaggers." Mimicking action in Texas earlier, they proclaimed California a "Republic," Sonoma its capital. Shortly afterward, some of the Bear Flaggers appeared in Yerba Buena to raise hell. After spiking the cannons at the old presidio, then celebrating Independence Day at Sonoma a few days later, the crowd chose Frémont as their leader. Conveniently on hand for the occasion, he was placed at the head of a 224-man "army" of locals and members of his expedition and was given the title "Oso 1." Marius Duvall, surgeon of the USS sloop *Portsmouth*, noted: "He and his party are very much sunburnt, and are the most ununiform [*sic*] and grotesque set of men I have ever seen. . . . Their buckskin dresses, with fringes at the seams, are something peculiar." Rounding up horses and cattle from the countryside, Frémont's little "army" then went into camp near Sutter's Fort.

There on July 10 arrived a messenger on horseback bearing word that Commodore Sloat had raised the American flag over Monterey. Meanwhile, Captain Montgomery of the *Portsmouth* had raised the flag at Yerba Buena and sent another to be raised on the plaza at Sonoma. Sloat's messenger brought Frémont orders to move to Monterey quickly in the event defensive action was needed. Happily obliging, Frémont departed camp on July 12. His ragtag army consisted of a dozen ethnic, racial, and national groups. Wrote James Marshall, who would soon find gold at Sutter's Mill, they included "Americans, French, English, Swiss, Poles, Russians, Chilians [*sic*], Germans, Greeks, Austrians, Pawnees, native Indians, etc." At the head of this rough mix, Frémont rode into Monterey. Lt. Fred Walpole, a young officer visiting from the Royal Navy's eighty-gun battleship HMS *Collingwood*, watched the colorful action from a hillside. It was drama in the style of a Douglas MacArthur "return."

"Here were true trappers, the class that produced the heroes of Fenimore Cooper's best works," wrote Lieutenant Walpole. "The men had passed years in the wilds, living upon their own resources; they were a curious set. A vast cloud of dust appeared first, and thence in long file emerged this wildest wild party. Frémont rode ahead, a spare, active-looking man. . . . He was dressed in a blouse and leggings, and wore a felt hat. After him came five Delaware Indians, who were his body-guard, and have been with him through all his wanderings; they had charge of two baggage horses. The rest, many of them blacker than the Indians, rode two and two, the rifle held by one hand across the pommel of the saddle. . . . The dress of these men was principally a long loose coat of deerskin, tied with thongs in front; trousers of the same, of their own manufacture." Frémont, Lieutenant Walpole added, "has one or two with him who enjoy a high reputation in the prairies. Kit Carson is as well known there as the duke is in Europe."

On July 15 U.S. Navy Capt. Robert F. Stockton arrived at Monterey to relieve the ailing Commodore Sloat, who wanted only to retire from naval service and go home. The two of them, "Fighting Bob" Stockton and "Oso 1" Frémont, working together, could stir up more trouble than five bobcats in a barrel. Of the two of these men, Richard White wrote, "Wherever Stockton's men or [Frémont's] California Battalion appeared, trouble erupted." In important ways, they were of a type: self-centered, risk loving, power hungry. An admiring Carson called Stockton "the bravest of the brave."

Assuming command of American military operations by land as well as by sea on his own authority, Stockton, a veteran of the War of 1812 and of hunting pirates in the Mediterranean, enlisted Frémont's cooperation by appointing him a major commanding his tiny "army," called "the California battalion of United States Troops" and, by one biographer, the "Navy Battalion of Mounted Riflemen." Frémont then named Carson, Maxwell, and Owens lieutenants in this loyal fighting unit. Wrote Neal Harlow, Frémont and his "California Battalion" would "volunteer [their] services . . . for as long as Stockton was in command and desired their support."

Bypassing T. O. Larkin, the U.S. consul in Monterey, who was hard at work on a *peaceful* transfer of California to the United States, Stockton ordered Frémont's battalion aboard the navy sloop *Cyane*, sailing for San Diego. Carson got so seasick on this journey that he vowed never again to board a ship. Landing in San Diego, the Americans took the city without a fight. Stockton then used sailors, marines, and Frémont's "Mounted Riflemen" in a pincers movement to take Los Angeles by mid-August. For the time being, the conquest appeared complete. Mexican soldiers had scattered. Governor Pico and General Castro had made a run for points south. San Diego's port captain, Santiago Arguello, welcomed Frémont's battalion. Citizens supplied them with food and horses. On his own authority, Stockton proclaimed California a U.S. territory, Frémont its "Military Governor." He even promised Frémont "the title of territorial governor."

In recognition of Carson's exceptional reliability and skill, Stockton and Frémont then chose Kit to lead a dispatch party to Washington carrying the news. Letters in hand, Carson with fifteen riflemen, including six of the indispensable Delaware scouts, and his old comrade of the trail, Lucien Maxwell, left Los Angeles for the East on September 5, 1846. Frémont later wrote: "[Kit] was to go direct to Senator Benton . . . who would personally introduce him to the President and Secretary of the Navy, and to whom he could give in fulness [*sic*] the incidental detail always so much more interesting than the restricted official report."

The dispatch party took the old trail across southern California to the Colorado River, then up the Gila River past the Santa Rita Copper Mine to the Rio Grande. Carson knew the route well from his time with Ewing Young. He believed he could make the transcontinental trip in sixty days, faster than any sail could round the Horn. Frémont recalled that

Kit was anxious to see his family in Taos, and he suggested how he must have felt about the journey. "It was a service of high trust and honor, but of great danger also," he wrote. "[Kit] went off, charged with personal messages and personal feelings. . . . Going off at the head of his own party with carte blanche for expenses and the prospect of novel pleasure and honor at the end was a culminating point in Carson's life." There can be no question why Carson all his later life appreciated Frémont's high regard.

The party traveled in a hurry, and at a cost. They packed short rations. Mules and horses were scarcely fed or watered. "At our departure from California we had only 25 lbs. of dried meat [and] a quantity of pinola [a mixture of wheat flour, cornmeal, and perhaps nuts]," Carson recalled. "We [traded for] some corn. We would dry the corn by the fire, parch the corn, then eat it. Not having other food during the trip, we suffered considerably." Kit mentioned only one stop, to trade worn-out mules for fresh ones, "within ten miles of the Copper Mines . . . at an Apache village." He counseled with Lucien Maxwell about the best way to approach this village. After seeing "frightened" at first sight, the Apaches "appeared friendly." Then, Kit recalled, "They visited us and we commenced trading and procured of them a remount, which was much required, our animals all having nearly given out." If Carson's mileage estimate is close—by then he had had plenty of experience estimating distances—the meeting would have been at San Vicente Spring (in present-day Silver City, New Mexico). Edwin R. Sweeney, author of *Mangas Coloradas*, believes "this was certainly [Mangas Coloradas's] camp, and he was likely present." Here Sweeney thinks Carson first learned, from talking with the Apaches, that an army under Gen. Stephen Watts Kearny had by then taken "possession" of New Mexico.

After passing the Copper Mine, today's vast Chino pit, where Robert McKnight had employed Kit, the party crossed the Mimbres Mountains, reached the Rio Grande, and turned north toward Santa Fe. A few miles south of Socorro they ran head-on into General Kearny and his "Army of the West" outbound from Fort Leavenworth via New Mexico to "conquer" California. William A. Keleher in *Turmoil in New Mexico, 1846–1868* places this meeting near the ruin of the old village of Valverde at the north end of Mesa del Contadero, or Black Mesa, about where the Civil War battle would later be fought. Enter General Kearny. Enter trouble for Frémont and Stockton.

War having been declared with Mexico on May 13, 1846, President Polk had immediately ordered General Kearny to Fort Leavenworth to organize an army to take the province of New Mexico. Orders were soon added to include Alta California to the grand plan of conquest. Kearny departed Fort Leavenworth on June 27, quickly took New Mexico, and set up a new government in Santa Fe. He then detached various units, including Col. Alexander Doniphan's famous "Missouri Mounted Volunteers," to the war in Chihuahua and left Santa Fe for California by September 25 via Albuquerque, Socorro, Santa Rita, and the Gila River route. The general too was in a hurry.

Meanwhile, Stockton and Frémont, who had already set up a provisional government in California, knew nothing of this Kearny business when Carson left Los Angeles on September 5. Polk, Bancroft, Benton, and the rest of the Washington crowd did not know of the California action when General Kearny organized his army at Fort Leavenworth, though possibly rumors had reached them. They received the news only after Kearny was well on the road from Leavenworth to Santa Fe. In a major snafu, one army was headed out to conquer for Manifest Destiny and the United States of America a territory already taken by another army and navy who believed they represented the U. S. of A. Neither one knew of the other. Washington was completely out of touch with action in the field, as were the officers on the Pacific coast. "Lieutenant" Carson of the "California Battalion" bore the news. "Came into camp late," noted Lt. William H. Emory of the army's Topographical Engineers, "and found Carson with an express from California, bearing intelligence that the country had surrendered without a blow, and that the American flag floated in every port."

Army from his campaign hat down to his bootheels, General Kearny had served as lieutenant colonel of the army's original cavalry unit, the Regiment of Dragoons, created by Congress in 1833. He had succeeded Col. Henry Dodge in command of the First U.S. Army Dragoons in 1837. That year he also had published the first *Manual of Rules* for the dragoons. He was, wrote historian Harwood Hinton, "an excellent disciplinarian, inflexible and stern." G. J. W. Urwin called him "a stickler for perfection" whose "two goals [were] efficiency and smartness." One shies at the mere thought of trying to imagine the general's stiff spine and his dark silence as "Lieutenant" Carson, on October 6, 1846, stood before him on a dusty New Mexico road near Socorro describing the California "victories" and Frémont's "successes."

Now, so far as the general could know, he was too late for the action. To make matters worse for him, the California business was commanded by an officer of the U.S. Navy, acting on his own authority, in league with a junior officer of the army's Topographical Engineers. The junior officer was not a West Point graduate and had no military training whatever. He had little more to offer the army than his ambition and a great deal of political pull in Washington. After this meeting on the Rio Grande, General Kearny appears to have nourished a feeling for Frémont that would eventually lead to Frémont's court-martial for mutiny and his resignation from the army.

To be correct as well as fair, it should be added that orders issued Kearny on June 3 "had anticipated that U.S. naval forces might be in possession of the coastal towns . . . and would cooperate in the conquest," as Neal Harlow put it. Secretary of War William Marcy had also written instructions to the general on June 18 that troops and equipment were being shipped round the Horn. "These troops, and such as may be organized in upper California," he addressed Kearny, "will be under your command." But, as Carson now told the general, Stockton and Frémont had already *taken* command. Commodore Stockton had appointed Frémont "Commandant of the Territory" and promised to appoint him "Governor and Commander-in-Chief of the Territory of California." In Senator Benton's words later, his own son-in-law "was fixed upon to be arrested for . . . mutiny of which the governorship [of California] was the point."

When the general had heard the lieutenant out, he told him that his services were required to guide the Army of the West to California. The lieutenant disagreed. He was committed to Stockton and to Frémont, and he wanted to visit his wife, Josefa, in Taos. The general then made it clear that he had the authority (whether or not he really did is another question) to *order* the lieutenant to guide the army to California. Tom Fitzpatrick, the famous mountain man and Carson's former employer in the fur trade, was traveling with Kearny. The general said that Fitzpatrick could just as well carry the lieutenant's dispatches on to Washington.

What he did not say, but everyone present surely recognized, was that Fitzgerald, given his long experience, was just as well qualified as Carson to guide the army to California. While Kearny's biographer Dwight L. Clarke believes that Kearny did not act vindictively, it is difficult to imagine credibly that the general was not only very disappointed but also mad as hell. Carson later said, in testimony dictated for Frémont's defense in the court-martial, "When [the general] could not persuade me to turn back, he then told me that he had a right to make me go with him, and insisted on his right; and I did not consent to turn back till he had made me believe that he had a right to order me. . . . I guided him through, but went with great hesitation."

Carson spent a long night after this meeting. It was another turning point in his life. Having promised Frémont that he would deliver the messages to Washington *in person*, he had to make a decision. Turning back here meant breaking a promise to his leader. It also meant missing a visit with Josefa. At first he decided to desert. Now, however, his loyal friend Lucien Maxwell intervened. In later testimony Kit said, "[I] had prepared everything to escape the night before they started [for California] and made known my intention to Maxwell who urged me not to do so." Fortunately for Carson's later career, Maxwell talked him out of deserting. Kit seldom spoke of this painful matter, then only tersely. All he said to his clerk in 1856 was, "On the 6th of October, '46, I met General Kearny on his march to California. He ordered me to join him as his guide. I done so, and Fitzpatrick continued on with the despatches [*sic*]." Kit's final decision and his later statements about it appear in line with his strong sense of duty. One cost not mentioned before was that his dispatch party had, by his own later testimony, "already worn out and killed thirty-four mules" on this express trip from California. Thus turning Carson around when Fitzpatrick could have done the job just as well was very costly indeed.

Assuming that California was under military control, General Kearny now decided to travel light, a decision he would soon regret. Keeping a third of his dragoons, 121 men with officers and aides, he sent the other two hundred back to Santa Fe with Maj. Edwin Vose Sumner. Because they slowed the troops down, he also sent the wagons back. He kept the two mountain howitzers. Always troublesome in rocky terrain, these often didn't get into camp at all. In at least one instance, according to Lieutenant Emory, they came in with "their shafts broken, and, indeed, everything that was possible to break about them." The odometer, attached to a wheel of a howitzer, soon got lost. After waiting a few days on the Rio Grande for packsaddles to arrive from Santa Fe, Kearny received them, then set out down the Rio Grande with mules packing his baggage. Lieutenant Emory complained to his journal, "My chronometers and barometer, which before rode so safely, were now in constant danger. The trip of a mule might destroy the whole."

Besides the soldiers and officers, a few experienced hunters came along. Carson and Antoine Robidoux served as guides. There were undoubtedly also hired *arrieros*, mule packers, for the army had learned by then that packing was a profession all its own. Packing the half-wild mules the Apaches stole down in Sonora, then traded off to the army and anyone else needing them, was an art akin to professional bull-riding today. The California-bound party, wrote Lieutenant Emory, at last "turned off from the Rio Grande and took final leave of it at a pretty little grove" (just below present-day Truth or Consequences, New Mexico). With a sadness known only to a soldier, he noted that when the two hundred dragoons were sent back to Santa Fe, "Many friends here parted that were never to meet again. Some fell in California, some in New Mexico, and some at Cerro Gordo."

Stopping briefly to trade mules with the Apaches west of the Santa Rita Copper Mine, General Kearny met Mangas Coloradas. Lieutenant Emory described the meeting, probably at Santa Lucia Spring, or "Night Creek" as Emory called it, now known simply as Mangas Springs. "[The Apaches] swore eternal friendship to the whites," Emory wrote, "and everlasting hatred to the Mexicans." The Apaches added that the road through their country "was open to the Americans now and forever." At that, Emory noted, "Carson, with a twinkle of his keen hazel eye, observed to me, 'I would not trust one of them.'" Although the Apaches "had mules, ropes, whips, and mescal" and the Americans had "red shirts, blankets, knives, needles, thread, handkerchiefs, &c.," trading was unsuccessful because "these people had such extravagant notions of our wealth," wrote Emory.

The meeting was the more interesting because of two mounted Apache women. When one of his pack mules ran off, Emory noted, "a large, elegant looking woman, mounted astraddle, more valiant than the rest, faced the brute and charged upon him at full speed." Bringing the mule back into line, she enabled Emory "through her intervention" to trade "two broken down mules for two good ones," plus "two yards of scarlet cloth in the bargain." For her services, Emory "rewarded her by half a dozen biscuit." The other woman was "deformed . . . with legs and arms no longer than an infant's. She was "well mounted" but "perfectly helpless when dismounted." She was treated "in a gallant manner" so that when "she asked for water . . . one or two were at her side; one handed it to her in a tin wash basin," clearly "her favorite drinking cup."

Leaving the Apache camp, the army crossed jagged mountains. One day's journey alone through mountains along the Gila River cost them "twelve or fifteen mules; one of mine fell headlong down a precipice" but "survived the fall," wrote Emory. In the California desert the animals suffered terribly from lack of water, which was usually salty. On one parched stretch they traveled "ninety miles from water to water," some going without water for sixty hours. On November 26 soldiers dug a hole in a dry channel, "15 or 20 feet below the surface," to bucket water up in camp kettles. When they found grass, dragoons cut it and tied it to their saddles to pack along for feed. "The lives of our animals were nearly as important as our own," Emory wrote. Expecting a feast, wolves hung around the exhausted mules day and night.

After crossing the desert, on December 2 the Army of the West reached a green oasis still called Warner's Ranch, or Warner's Springs, fifteen miles north of the present-day village of Santa Ysabel, California. A hot spring and a cold one flowed from the rocks nearby so that "without the aid of any mechanical instrument," Emory wrote, "the cold and warm water may be commingled to suit the temperature of the bather." Native people had long ago made bathing pools here. Jonathan Trumbull Warner's adobe house sat close by. Lieutenant Emory wrote with prescience: "A day will come, no doubt, when the invalid and pleasure seeking portion of the white race, will assemble here to drink and bathe in these waters, ramble over the hills . . . and sit under the shade of the great live oaks that grow in the valley." Later a station on the Butterfield Trail, today a spa for the wealthy, Warner's Ranch seemed to Kearny and his hungry army like heaven itself. Seven men sat down to eat a whole sheep in one meal.

But such comfort couldn't last. Someone captured a herd of horses being sent to a Mexican army officer. Another intercepted an express rider carrying mail. Thereby Kearny learned that California was again in rebellion. Upon arrival at Warner's, he had sent a message to Stockton in San Diego. Stockton dispatched the peripatetic marine, now "Captain" Archibald Gillespie, with a small force of U.S. and Californio volunteers. Joining forces, Kearny's men on their worn-out mules with the little howitzers in tow and Gillespie's volunteers charged full-on into a camp of well-mounted lancers led by don Andrés Pico. Contact occurred in heavy rainfall before daylight of December 6 near San Pasqual. One dauntless Californio lassoed a howitzer and towed it away, leaving its crew lanced or shot. While Carson was trying to gather loose horses, his own mount fell from under him. Other horses raced past, and probably over, him. He remembered seeing iron-shod hoofs striking rocks inches from his head. The fall broke his rifle, but he picked up another from a dead dragoon and fought the battle afoot. His luck continued. He broke no bones.

In official reports, Kearny later claimed victory because the lancers retired from the field. In fact, the U.S. soldiers got battered at San Pasqual and again a day or two later on the road to San Diego. This was not, however, for lack of grit. They were overmatched by the mounted lancers and their tactics of charge, impale, pull back, charge again, impale, and retire quickly. Some of Kearny's best officers died here: Capt. A. R. Johnston, Capt. Benjamin Moore, and Lt. Thomas C. Hammond. Others were badly wounded, including Captain Gillespie, Lt. William H. Warner, and General Kearny himself.

The general was so badly lanced that Capt. Henry Turner and Lt. John W. Davidson had to take field command. Assistant army surgeon Thomas Griffin tallied eighteen killed and seventeen wounded at San Pasqual. Today, a small California state park near Warner's Ranch marks the site.

A series of smaller fights occurred before the Americans reached San Diego and then retook Los Angeles on January 10, 1847. In one spell of fighting the Californios pinned down soldiers on a hilltop. Carson, navy Lt. Edward F. Beale, and his Indian servant, Che-muc-tah, volunteered to carry a message to Stockton requesting help. The three pulled their shoes off for silence, crawled between mounted sentries at night, and made their way barefoot to San Diego over rock and cactus. The courageous Che-muc-tah arrived first, then Beale, then Carson, who was in the best condition of the three. Beale had to be taken shipboard for medical care and did not fully recover for years.

Had moderate heads like those of Commodore Sloat and Consul Larkin prevailed from the beginning of the so-called conquest of California, much less bloody fighting would have occurred. General Kearny felt that he had missed his chance for glory. When he confronted Frémont, Frémont insisted that he was under Stockton's command, not Kearny's. He refused to take orders. As a result, the general would have him court-martialed for disobeying a superior officer.

8

"Burn the Damn Thing"

In late February 1847 Carson left California for Washington with dispatches. His small party included Lt. Edward F. Beale. Still weak from his desert ordeal, Beale needed continual care. "During the first 20 days, I had to lift him on and off his horse," Kit recalled. "I did not think he could live, but I took as good care and paid to him as much attention as could [be] given to anyone in the same circumstances." As a result of this intensive care, Beale always expressed warm feelings for Carson. He wrote that Kit had "tenderly as a woman would have laid her first born, laid me sore from wounds and fever on [his] only blanket" and "without a thought of ever seeing water again . . . poured upon my fevered lips, the last drop of water from [his] canteen." Carson was ever thoughtful and attentive with friends. He could grieve, especially over women. After the battle of San Pasqual, Lieutenant Beale remembered that Kit "mourned like a woman, and would not be comforted . . . not for those who had fallen, but for the sad hearts of [the] women at home."

The party survived a night attack by Indians on the Gila River by covering themselves with packsaddles to ward off arrows, then simply refusing to fight. They reached Santa Fe in early April, where they learned of the Taos massacre of Governor Bent the past February, and of the events that followed that disaster. When soldiers from Santa Fe arrived to quell the rebellion, the rebels blockaded themselves in the Taos Pueblo church. Soldiers then besieged the pueblo with artillery, killing an estimated 150 people, thus ending the fight. As a witness, Josefa testified in the trials. One can only imagine her emotional condition when Kit arrived home for the first time in twenty months. Undoubtedly he tried to comfort her, but he left home again on April 30, bound east with the dispatches. It must be remembered that, aside from his "duty," always so important to him, he was drawing government pay for services. That work was his family's source of income. As a wife of her day, Josefa would have agreed that going on with his task was the right thing to do. She must have found most of her comfort in her family and in her church.

In Washington, Jessie Frémont met Carson at the railroad station. She took him under her care, introducing him to "society" and to the politicians. Staying over for a few nights at the home of Lieutenant Beale's mother, he insisted upon sleeping outside on a porch. He had slept in the open air and on the ground for so many years that he couldn't rest indoors. He also stayed at Senator Benton's home, where Jessie entertained him by reading aloud from Lord Byron and Robert Burns. Kit enjoyed the poetry, especially the horse and rider in Byron's "Mazeppa." He visited President Polk twice about matters in California. Polk appointed him a second lieutenant of mounted riflemen in the regular army. In a pique over Frémont's actions, however, the Senate would refuse to confirm the appointment. Waiting for reassignment, the center of Washington's attention, written up in the newspaper, Kit was bored. Countryman to the bone, he was nervous with wealthy, urbane people, afraid, as he told his friend Lieutenant Beale, that the society ladies would find out that he had married an Arapaho girl. Jessie Frémont wrote down what he said of the elegant people: "With their big houses and easy living they think they are princes, but on the plains we are the princes—they could not live there without us." He was glad to leave Washington at last on June 15, bound for California with letters.

174

Dressed this time in a brand-new U.S. Army uniform, he traveled with Lieutenant Beale and Jessie Frémont to St. Louis. He stopped over in Howard County to visit his family. He must have been proud of Adaline, who by now could read and write. Then he was on his way again. From Howard County he went to Fort Leavenworth. From there he took the old trail past Bent's Fort to Santa Fe, where Josefa and Ignacia, who had come down from Taos, met him on the plaza.

After returning to Taos with Josefa, Kit took the Old Spanish Trail through Abiquiu across Utah. Besides military dispatches, he carried the news that Generals Zachary Taylor and Winfield Scott and Col. Alexander Doniphan had won major battles in the war with Mexico and that peace negotiations were underway. On a tributary of the Virgin River his party met about three hundred Indians, probably Paiutes, who insisted that they only wanted to come into camp. Carson warned them off: "I told them to retire, if not, I would fire on them," he recalled. Apparently they would not back off. "I was compelled to fire," he told his clerk later. "One Indian was killed and the balance went off." It was another instance of behavior by border rules. *Give fair warning.* If the warning goes unheeded, *punish*!

Back in Los Angeles by October, Carson heard the late news. General Kearny had charged Frémont with disobeying a superior officer and marched him off to Washington for court-martial. Col. Richard B. Mason, recently appointed governor, was serving in Monterey. Carson rode on to Monterey, where he delivered the letters. There he met young army Lt. William T. Sherman, who years later recalled their meeting in his own *Memoirs*. "[Carson's] fame was then at its height, from the publication of Frémont's books," Sherman wrote, "and I was very anxious to see a man who had achieved such feats of daring among the wild animals of the Rocky Mountains, and still wilder Indians of the Plains. I cannot express my surprise at beholding a small, stoop-shouldered man, with reddish hair, freckled face, soft blue eyes, and nothing to indicate extraordinary courage or daring. He spoke but little, and answered questions in monosyllables. . . . He spent some days in Monterey, during which time we extracted with difficulty some items of his personal history." Kit *would not play* the dime novel hero.

After spending the following winter with dragoons guarding a mountain pass, Carson left Los Angeles again on May 4, 1848, with letters for Washington. He also carried news of the discovery of gold at Coloma, although it isn't clear that he was the first to carry this news east. Traveling with a large party of twenty-seven, including young army Lt. George D. Brewerton, Carson again took the Old Spanish Trail. Brewerton soon discovered, as Sherman had, that Kit would not play the hero. He wrote later that he found the "real Kit to be a plain, simple unostentatious man; rather below the medium height, with brown, curling hair, little or no beard, and a voice as soft and gentle as a woman's . . . one of Dame Nature's gentlemen." He also noticed Carson's routine caution. Before bedding down for the night, Kit placed his saddle "as a barricade for his head," his pistols half-cocked above it, and his "trusty rifle . . . beneath the blanket by his side," where it was ready for immediate use, yet "perfectly protected from the damp." As late as two years before his death, Carson revealed his habitual caution to a visitor to his home in Taos. "He never turned in without examining his revolver and placing it under his pillow, and he awakened at the slightest noise," wrote Worthington Whittredge.

There were several interactions with Indians on this trip. In one instance, Carson, Brewerton, and two others fired at a lone Indian after they saw him watching their camp. A man named Lewis hit him in the arm as he ran. It was an ugly scene, even for that day. Four expert riflemen taking potshots at a running man who had not threatened them! No danger. No courage involved. Behavior at its worst.

In another instance Carson asked Brewerton whether he could see any Indians. Brewerton couldn't. "Well," said Carson,

"I saw an Indian's head there just now, and there are a party of at least a dozen more, or I am much mistaken." At that moment a man stood up from the rocks calling, "Tigabu! Tigabu!" Carson called back, "Tigabu! Tigabu! (Friend! Friend!)" The stranger led a small party of Indians into camp. Carson offered a gift. The visitors took some beef and coffee, then sat down for a friendly smoke.

Another time, Carson's party held a young Paiute overnight, supposing that his tribesmen were hostile because the Paiutes were nearly always hostile in this area. In the morning they turned him loose with a gift of a pair of old trousers. It was an example of border diplomacy at work. No harm to either side. The Paiute seemed happy with the gift. His friends held off. Near Little Utah Lake, the eastbound party met the friendly Ute chief Wakara and his band. Wakara came into camp for a meal, a smoke, and a talk. Still later on the trip came a standoff with an estimated 150 Utes and Apaches, well mounted and painted for war.

Kit's party finally got safely to Taos on June 14. As usual the stay was pleasant, but brief. Brewerton remarked that Carson put him up at his own home, where he was "hospitably entertained by Carson and his amiable wife, a Spanish lady, and a relative . . . of some former Governor of New Mexico." The relative could have been former governor Juan Bautista Vigil, Josefa's uncle, or Charles Bent, former governor and her former brother-in-law.

A few days later in Santa Fe, Col. Edward Newby, commanding Fort Marcy, informed Kit that the Senate had refused to confirm his presidential appointment as a second lieutenant in the regular army. Carson had been serving in uniform without the commission he had hoped for. Characteristically, he took the bad news in silence. Friends advised him to hand over the dispatches to Colonel Newby and be done with the job, but Carson considered it his "duty" to carry them on to Washington. "As I had been entrusted with the dispatches, chosen as the most competent person to take them through safely, I determined to fulfill the duty," he told his clerk in 1856. "I would on no account wish to forfeit the good opinion of a majority of my countrymen because the Senate . . . did not . . . confirm on me an appointment . . . that I never sought, and one . . . I would have resigned at the [end] of the war." But the blow had to hurt. Later he tried to toss the matter off: "[It] mattered not to me if, in the discharge of a duty of service beneficial to the public, whether I was of the rank of Lieutenant or holding the credit of an experienced mountaineer," he said in 1856. He did not mention the difference in income he would have received as an officer of the regular army.

Due to Comanche raids along the Santa Fe Trail, Kit now took a northern route over Sangre de Cristo Pass, across the Nebraska Plains down the Republican River, and into Fort Leavenworth. From there he took a steamboat, then a train to Washington. On this, his last trip as a dispatch carrier, he visited the Frémonts. They were distracted over Frémont's court-martial. Jessie asked Kit to be a sponsor for her first son's baptism on August 15. Then, done with the army job, out of work and short of cash as usual, Carson went home to Taos. He had gotten short pay for his years of government service. He did receive, as he put it, the "good opinion of a majority of my countrymen," but good opinion could not do what cash would. On the way home he stopped in Missouri, where he probably visited family. In 1856 he said little to his clerk about this trip. "Returned to St. Louis [from Washington]," he recalled. "Remained a few days and started back for New Mexico."

Home in Taos by October 1848, Kit needed to become acquainted with Josefa, and he needed to find work. Of their six years of marriage, husband and wife had spent just six months together. By habit always on the move, Kit was now restless as ever. During the winter he made at least two sorties with mounted soldiers against hostile Indians. He may also have made a trip to Adobe Walls, Bent's deserted trading post on the Canadian River. In *Bent's Fort*, David Lavender ascribed

178

the story to George Bent, who claimed he "had . . . it from both Carson and John Smith." Lavender said that when William Bent decided to reopen the abandoned post, he hired Kit to lead a small party to repair it. The party is supposed to have included Lucien Maxwell, Robert Fisher, "Blackfoot" John Smith, and a man everyone called Lucas "Goddamn" Murray because he couldn't utter a phrase without adding the expletive. At the ruined post Jicarillas killed the herder and ran off the livestock except for two mules that were tied inside the walls. Left afoot, Kit, Lucien, and the others hoofed it all the way back to Bent's Fort on the Arkansas, more than 150 miles, a very long walk for men who always rode. When Kiowas attacked them along the way, they killed three.

Kit took this hazardous job, according to Lavender, not only for the wages, but because "he wanted to settle down and build a home." Archaeological evidence suggests that Carson's Taos home had burned during the Taos uprising. If so, it would have called for very heavy repair. And he would soon add another home on Rayado Creek, across the mountains east of Taos. Both houses required money for building and repair. Steady work was hard to find now, especially for a man with Kit's skills.

He also made two forays during the winter of 1848–49 as a guide to Maj. Benjamin Lloyd Beall's detachment of dragoons stationed at Taos. The first was against Jicarillas, a difficult job other guides had refused. So Major Beall hired Kit. "I was employed as his guide, and we departed," was all he said of the matter. The other venture was to the Arkansas River country to attempt, unsuccessfully, to recover captives taken by Plains Indians. Hopefully this "employment" paid him something. But Kit often volunteered when it appeared that someone needed his help.

In the spring of 1849 he tried to settle down again. About then, he and Lucien Maxwell made some kind of business arrangement. Details of their agreements are unclear because the two concurred on the basis of mutual trust developed over many years, rather than by written contract. "In April [1849], Mr. Maxwell and I concluded to make a settlement on the Rayado," Carson recalled in 1856. "We had been leading a roving life long enough and now was the time, if ever, to make a home for ourselves and children. . . . Arrived at Rayado, commenced building and making improvements, and were in a way of becoming prosperous." Of course this statement was oversimplified, "a bit off target," in Marc Simmons's words. First, Carson was not a man who could ever stay put. He might run livestock on open range, but he simply was not a settler or a farmer, as his earlier attempts had shown. On one occasion, he and Dick Owens had sold their farm at a loss as soon as adventure called. Second, Kit never had a knack for handling money.

But Lucien did have the knack, and he developed it. He began by marrying Luz Beaubien. After her brother Narciso was murdered in 1847, her father turned to Lucien, by now his son-in-law. Home again from service with Frémont, Lucien was available. He was also bright, ambitious, and splendidly energetic. He had had plenty of border experience. Having worked for Bent–St. Vrain, he knew the trade practices of the day. He knew the tribes who hunted and raided in northeastern New Mexico. From early on, he appeared to have a talent for managing, and later for owning and developing, the Beaubien-Miranda or Maxwell Land Grant.

But Lucien had had a setback. He and an associate named James H. Quinn operated a store in Taos, and the two had received a contract to furnish beef for the army. For such purposes Lucien already ran cattle on the Rayado River on his father-in-law's grant. By February 1848 he had even put up buildings and corrals. Then Jicarillas ran off his livestock and stole six hundred tanned buckskins that were ready for market and had been stored in a shed. For a short while he saw hard times. Carson may have loaned him $1,000 just to get by.

By midsummer 1849, in spite of ongoing Plains Indian raids, the two had completed buildings on the Rayado. Capt.

Henry B. Judd, an 1839 West Point graduate commanding an army detachment at Las Vegas, New Mexico, reported on June 1 that Maxwell and Carson had "been twice driven from that place with the loss of all their stock, in efforts to obtain a foothold there." But by July 26 a traveler on his way to California could see signs of improvement. "The Ranch House was a two-story log affair, surrounded by adobe walls for . . . fortification," wrote Charles Pancoast. "Inside the walls were Adobe Houses, and outside a number more, as well as a large Corral . . . stables, Slaughter Houses, etc." Marc Simmons noted that Carson was building a flat-roofed adobe house for himself "about six hundred yards below Maxwell's." Kit also ran cattle, horses, and mules "on shares," branding them with a Cross J and a Double C on the left hip. The Rayado and Cimarron area was, as it remains today, as fine as any High Plains grazing land in the country, perhaps in the world. Speaking of the quality of the livestock on pasture there, Captain Judd noted on June 11, "The cattle on the Rayado are beyond comparison."

Then in October 1849 another life-changing incident occurred. A trader named James White, his wife, Ann, their daughter, Virginia, and an African American woman servant were traveling with a westbound caravan on the Cimarron Cutoff. Finding the freight wagons too slow, White took his family and five men ahead with a lighter vehicle. They reached a spring near Point of Rocks west of today's Clayton, New Mexico, where they stopped for the night. There Jicarillas attacked them, or they may have fired on the Jicarillas first. No one knows. When the news reached Indian agent James S. Calhoun in Santa Fe and Capt. William N. Grier in Taos, Grier mounted a detachment of dragoons with Antoine Leroux as guide to ride to Point of Rocks. On the road from Taos through Rayado, they picked up Carson as a scout. From there to Point of Rocks was less than a day's ride.

Kit was the first on the scene. All the men of White's party had been killed. Ann, Virginia, and their servant had been carried off. "Found trunks that were broken open, harness cut, etc., everything destroyed that the Indians could not carry with them," Carson told his clerk in 1856. Immediately he and Leroux picked up the trail. "It was the most difficult trail that I ever followed," Kit said later. "As they would leave the camps . . . in numbers from one to two [they] went in different directions, to meet at some appointed place. In nearly every camp we would find some of Mrs. White's clothing, which renewed energy on our part to continue the pursuit."

After ten or twelve days, the guides spotted crows circling ahead, a sign of a camp nearby, for crows feed on camp refuse. Discovering the Jicarillas at rest and certain that the soldiers would follow him, Carson immediately charged. But Captain Grier and Leroux hesitated. Then there were rifle shots. A ball struck Grier. The captain became "sick at the stomach," Carson recalled. Dick Wootton claimed that the ball "struck him in the breast," but "a suspender buckle changed its course and he was not seriously wounded." Another man thought a pair of heavy gauntlets tucked into Grier's coat pocket had stopped the ball. Grier was briefly stunned, and for moments the action stalled. The opportunity to save Ann White was lost.

It took minutes for the captain to recover enough to call the charge. By then the Jicarillas were putting up a running fight. Both sides were firing. Carson described the mess to his clerk in 1856: "In about 200 yards," he said, "pursuing the Indians, the body of Mrs. White was found, perfectly warm, had not been killed more than five minutes—shot through the heart with an arrow. She evidently knew that some one was coming to her rescue." He added, "She did not see us, but it was apparent that she was endeavoring to make her escape when she received the fatal shot."

In 1866 Kit repeated the story to Col. James F. Meline: "As God would have it, she was just dead when we reached her; and perhaps it was as well!" Meline then described Mrs. White's condition as Carson had described it to him: "The poor lady was wasted, emaciated, the victim of a foul disease, and bore the sorrows of a life-long agony on her face," Meline wrote. "For when a woman captive has not the signal good fortune of being made the mistress of one savage, she becomes the prostitute of the tribe." Apparently, several Indians had raped her. Another report had it that the woman servant had been killed because she could not keep up with the Jicarillas. Little Virginia was never found.

In sorting through what was left of the camp supplies, Carson picked up a copy of a dime novel that made him out to be a great Indian killer. It may have been Charles Averill's *Kit Carson, Prince of the Gold Hunters*, which appeared that year (1849). Carson put his feelings about such crude fictions sharply: "In camp was found a book," he said, "the first of the kind I had ever seen, in which I was made a great hero, slaying Indians by the hundred, and I have often thought that as Mrs. White would read the same, and knowing that I lived near[by], she would pray for my appearance and that she would be saved. I did come, but had not the power to convince those that were in command over me to pursue my plan for her rescue. They would not listen to me and they failed. . . . I suppose the consciences of those that were the cause of the failure have severely punished them ere this." Later he is supposed to have said that everything Averill wrote about him was a lie. Shown a copy of Averill's book, he announced that he would "burn the damn thing."

It might be said that after this tragedy, Carson was an older and a wiser man. Certainly he seems to have been a sadder man. His remark years later to his clerk about the "consciences" of Captain Grier and Antoine Leroux suggests the depth of his own regret over their hesitation at the critical moment when a charge might have saved Ann White's life. It also reveals Carson's feeling about the pain and hurt born by border women.

In all fairness, it must be added that the Jicarillas later claimed they approached Point of Rocks with peaceful intent, but that James White started the fight. Very likely he and his party fired first, thinking to defend the camp. Chief Chacon said that his men had taken care of Mrs. White, and would have returned her, if the soldiers hadn't attacked them. Whatever the circumstances of the disaster, the weather that day mirrored the darkness of the tragedy. "On the return we had the severest snow storm that I ever experienced," Carson recalled. "Had one man frozen to death. We were trying to make Barclay's Fort on the Mora [River] but, on account of the wind, we could not keep our course, but happily arrived at some timber near Las Vegas. I learned that in the same storm many of the Indians that we had been pursuing perished."

Fighting continued during the winter and into the spring of 1850. Far from Santa Fe and Fort Marcy, Rayado was a distant post in an area with a growing population. Tribal hunters and stock growers fought each other to control the big range, which was rich with nutritious grass and wild game. During that winter, to defend the settlers, the army stationed ten dragoons at Rayado under Sgt. William Holbrook. In March Indians attacked about two miles from Maxwell's and Carson's buildings. They ran off the stock and badly wounded two herders. Carson with the dragoons and four other men took the trail. One of these was old mountain man Bill New, who had recently taken up ranching on the Rayado. After a twenty-five-mile chase, the pursuers caught up with the cow thieves. Knowing well by now the power of surprise in border warfare, Carson charged. "Approached the Indians cautiously and, when close, charged them; killed five, the other four made their escape," he recalled. Most of the livestock was recovered. Though Carson says nothing of any scalping, Sergeant Holbrook reported that five scalps were taken as "a voucher." By whom, he did not say.

In May 1850 Carson teamed up with mountaineer friend Tim Goodale to drive forty or fifty horses and mules to Fort Laramie on the Oregon Trail. A fur trade post since 1834 near the Laramie River where it joined the North Platte, the fort was first named Fort William, for Bill Sublette. Its location put it directly on the Emigrant Road to Oregon and California. As the number of westbound wagons increased during the 1840s, the fort's business changed from buying furs to supplying emigrants, who always needed fresh horses, mules, and oxen. During the California gold rush, the refitting and supply business boomed.

After purchasing the fort from the American Fur Company in 1849, the army kept an emigrant register for each year. By using this and the notations in emigrant diaries, it can be calculated that the number of westbound wagons grew from 5,397 in 1845 to 18,847 in 1848. Thereafter the numbers mushroomed, from 45,797 in 1849 to more than double that, 98,297, in 1850 when Carson and Goodale drove the horses and mules up from Rayado. By 1853 the number had more than doubled again, to 209,997. Thus Carson and Goodale had a sure market for their stock. They traveled north along the east face of the Rockies on a line today followed by I-25 past Pueblo, Denver, and Cheyenne. They grazed the animals along slowly so as to keep the weight on them. "Disposed of our animals to good advantage," Kit told his clerk.

By now this stoop-shouldered, bowlegged little man discovered that his dime novel reputation had really caught up with him. People expected him to *look* the fictional part. At Fort Laramie, an old-timer walked up to him.

"I say, stranger," he said. "Are you Kit Carson?"

Taking that in, Kit answered, "Well, Sir. I reckon I am."

The old boy studied him up and down for a moment, then shook his head in disbelief.

"Lookie hyere, stranger," he said. "You cain't come that over me. You ain't the kinda Kit Carson I'm a lookin' fer!"

Back in Taos again by July, Carson spent a few days with Josefa, then returned to Rayado to discover that raiders, probably Jicarillas and Utes, had killed Bill New and run off all the livestock. Meanwhile, the army had increased the number of dragoons stationed there to two companies under Captain

Grier. In pursuing the thieves, Grier's dragoons had killed several and recovered most of the stock. There followed an unusually quiet summer.

Action picked up again when a man named Fox left Taos for Missouri with Elias Brevoort, a trader, and his two friends, Samuel Weatherhead and one Tully. It was rumored that Brevoort, Weatherhead, and Tully carried gold worth more than $40,000. It was soon discovered that Fox planned to murder the others, heft the gold, and run for Texas. Fox's accomplice in Taos had confessed the plan. Asked by Lt. Oliver Taylor to lead dragoons after Fox, Kit at first refused. Told of Fox's murderous intent, he agreed to go "immediately . . . when I knew their object," he said later. Pushing hard from Taos, Carson and ten dragoons, accompanied by Capt. Richard S. Ewell's twenty-five or so men they met along the trail, rode straight into Fox's camp and arrested the accused bad man. Told of his good fortune, Brevoort gratefully offered Carson anything he wished, but Carson turned his offer down. "I demanded nothing for my trouble," he said, "considering having done a good act, thereby saving the lives of two valuable citizens, was reward sufficient." A year later, however, Weatherhead and Brevoort sent him a pair of "splendid silver mounted pistols" made by Samuel Colt. As for Captain Ewell, he was to become the famous Gen. Richard Stoddert Ewell, a corps commander of the Confederacy, "dear, glorious, old, one-legged Ewell, with his bald head, & his big bright eyes, & his long nose like a wood cock's," as fellow Confederate officer Porter Alexander described him.

Now that a substantial number of dragoons was stationed at Rayado, the community seemed safer. In the fall Carson brought Josefa over from Taos to live with him for the winter. But in March 1851 he was off again, this time with Jesse Nelson on a buying trip to St. Louis for Lucien Maxwell. Kit had also decided it was time to bring Adaline out to New Mexico. After purchasing Maxwell's goods in Missouri, he visited his family and attended his niece Susan's wedding to

Nelson. Then he gathered up Adaline, Jesse, and Susan, supervised the loading of Maxwell's wagons at Westport, and set out again for Bent's Fort and home.

Near Chouteau's Island on the Arkansas River in Kansas his party ran into a band of very angry Cheyennes. To Carson this incident came as a complete surprise. He had known and lived among Northern Cheyennes for years. He had briefly married a Cheyenne woman. He spoke the Cheyenne language. Recently, however, they had had a run-in with an arrogant, probably drunken, army officer. The officer had insulted the entire tribe by flogging a Cheyenne man accused of stealing. Flogging a Cheyenne warrior for any reason whatever was an outrageous offense to the entire tribe. Accordingly, by Cheyenne rules, the first Americans to show up had to be punished. Quickly recognizing that the Indians intended to kill his whole party, Kit ordered them out of camp on threat of being shot. They went.

But the other members of his party were terrified. Adaline and Susan cried. While Kit reassured them, he sent a courier out with a request for help. After hanging around grumbling for a few days, the Cheyennes left, and Carson's party went its way. "We had two women traveling with us and their crying made me feel so bad that I was sartain ther was no fight in me," remembered Old Pete, one of Kit's party. "But Kit talked to them and then to the Indians, and put them both finally on the right trail. Wah! But them ware ticklish times."

Over the next two years Kit stayed a little closer to home and to Josefa. He and Lucien kept busy delivering beef on government contracts. In July 1851 the army established Fort Union about forty miles south of Rayado on the Santa Fe Trail to replace Fort Marcy as departmental headquarters. Besides protecting travelers, Fort Union served as the supply depot for the other forts and posts across New Mexico Territory. As part of the reorganization, the tiny post at Rayado was closed.

As for Kit's family, his and Josefa's first son, Carlos, had died in May 1851 while Kit was away in Missouri. Their second son,

Julian, called "Billy," was born in Taos on October 1, 1852. Though Kit stayed in Rayado most of the time, he shuttled Josefa back and forth to Taos as conditions changed. Life at the ranch was often believed to be too dangerous for women and children. Josefa's niece, Teresina Bent (not to be confused with Teresina Carson, Kit and Josefa's first daughter, born June 23, 1855) often stayed with Aunt Josefa when she was in Rayado. Teresina Bent later recalled two close calls.

In one of these, perhaps three hundred Comanches and Southern Cheyennes appeared while Carson, Josefa, and Teresina were all at home. After camping close by for a couple of nights, they rode off. As soon as they were gone, Kit packed Josefa and Teresina off to Taos for safety. In the other tighter scrape, Kit had left Tom Boggs in charge at the ranch while he went off, probably to Fort Union. Before breakfast one morning, a large war party of Cheyennes appeared, wanting to be fed. Tom told the women to cook up a feast while he sent a runner to Fort Union for help. When the Cheyenne chief spotted twelve-year-old Teresina, he demanded her for a wife and offered twenty horses in trade.

"Mr. Boggs said for us to act friendly . . . and not make the chief angry," recalled Teresina. "And while I carried platters of food from the kitchen the tears were running down my cheeks. That made the chief laugh." Then the Cheyenne told Tom he would wait until evening for a decision. If the answer wasn't "yes," he said he would take Teresina by force. During the afternoon, Tom had the women "run bullets, for if help did not come by sunset there might be a fight." Just at sunset, Carson came "galloping up the valley" with soldiers from Fort Union. Teresina recalled that she cried again when she saw the Cheyennes leave. "I was so glad," she said. "I did not want to go with the dirty chief."

In the spring of 1852 Carson apparently felt that matters were well enough in hand that he could take a vacation from ranch life. He and Maxwell "rigged up a party of eighteen" old mountaineers for a beaver trapping expedition. They rode north into Colorado's Bayou Salade, or South Park, then cut a huge circle up the High Plains into Wyoming, back south through the New Park and the Middle Park to the Bayou Salade, then down the Arkansas River to the Royal Gorge, and home to Rayado over Raton Mountain, "having made a very good hunt," as Carson put it in 1856. He and Lucien spent the next winter at Rayado planning another expedition, this one for profit rather than for fun. It would be Kit's last serious business risk, and this time it would pay off.

In February 1853 he borrowed money from merchants Henry Mercure and John Bernavette to go in with Maxwell and John L. Hatcher to purchase sixty-five hundred head of sheep to trail to California. He then rode down into the Rio Abajo, the "Lower River" country of New Mexico, below La Bajada, that great dividing east-west rim south of Santa Fe. This was sheep country. Here lived New Mexico's barons of wool, men with such names as Luna and Chavez. Here grazed the old Spanish churro (later nearly extinct as a breed, until recently recovered largely through the efforts of Dr. Lyle G. McNeal of Utah State University). The churro is a thin, leggy sheep. He has a long staple wool, ideal for the hand spinning and weaving done by Navajo as well as Hispano weavers of the upper Rio Grande.

Though the going price was probably a dollar or two a head, a story has it that Carson paid fifty cents apiece for the churros. Herders then gathered them and trailed the flock to Rayado, where the really big drive would begin in early spring. Needing to avoid the heavy snow in the Rockies, they trailed the great flocks north from Rayado along the east face of the Rockies to Fort Laramie. Morning sunshine melted winter snow and began to turn the grass green. Near Laramie, the sheepmen turned their flocks westerly to follow the Emigrant Road until they turned the woolies off again down the Humboldt River. Crossing the Sierra Nevada about where Kit had struggled through deep snow with Frémont, they finally trailed into Sacramento. Here and there they paused and turned the churros aside to better grass. The drive took about six months.

Carson, Maxwell, and Hatcher divided the drive three ways in order to make the best use of the grass. The first churros were started in March. The other two flocks followed behind, started at different times. The drive was also a social occasion. Besides the herders, Carson's companions included Mercure and Bernavette, his friend Tom Boggs, Missouri relative George Jackson, and Adaline with her new husband, Louis Simmons. This was the last, best visit Kit would ever have with Adaline, for Adaline and Simmons would remain in California. Of the three drovers, Hatcher reached California first, arriving in Placerville in June. Carson and Maxwell trailed in several weeks later. In Sacramento in August of 1853 they got $5.50 a head for the churros, of which about five thousand animals completed the trip.

After subtracting losses and expenses and sharing the profits, Carson believed he had done very well indeed. In truth he had, for in February 1855 came the big bust. That month the leading California bank of Page, Bacon, and Company closed its doors. That year there were 197 bankruptcies in San Francisco alone. The depression that followed lasted until the end of the decade. Sheepmen and speculators were ruined. Purely by luck, Kit had escaped financial disaster. How much money he received or how he spent his share is unknown. One story is that he set up Adaline and her husband on a farm in California. The story makes sense because Kit cared for Adaline. He felt responsible for her. More likely, however, he carried the cash back to New Mexico. Tom Boggs's brother, John Boggs, is supposed to have said that Carson and Maxwell got home with "so much money, they didn't know what to do with it." Another story is that he bought Josefa a new Singer treadle sewing machine for cash.

In California Kit discovered that he had become a real celebrity. He had had a role in the Bear Flag revolt, and he was the hero of dime novels. The *Sacramento Daily Union* carried a story on "the world-renowned mountaineer, Kit Carson" about the time he trailed his sheep into town. The *Alta California* and the *San Francisco Herald* also carried stories about him. All this attention made him nervous, especially in San Francisco, where people pestered him. One story carried later in the *Napa County Reporter* said, "Men sitting next to him at the table would speak of him and Kit would quietly eat his meal and walk off, shaking his head to his friends and talking with his eyes as much as to say 'don't you dare expose me.'"

After attending the Boggs and Carson family reunions and after saying good-bye to Adaline and Louis Simmons, Kit went back to San Francisco. He put up at the Niantic Hotel to wait for Lucien, who was to join him for the trip back to New Mexico. Kit hardly recognized the city. He had first known it as a little Mexican village called Yerba Buena. Now its port had a shipping tonnage just below that of New Orleans and New York. It had grown up to be a big city of forty thousand people. Celebrity seekers followed him everywhere. He is supposed to have bribed the hotel landlord to withhold all information about him. When Lucien at last showed up, the two quickly left for Los Angeles, Maxwell by steamer, Carson by land on a mule or a horse. He had never forgotten his seasickness on that journey years before. Maxwell reached Los Angeles in October, fifteen days ahead of Carson by land. "Made the necessary preparations, and then started for New Mexico," Kit recalled.

The two friends took the southern route home. Reaching the Gila River, they traveled easterly to its junction with the San Pedro, near today's Winkelman. Arizona. Then they rode up the San Pedro for three days in order to rest the livestock and give them a chance to fill up on good grass. From there "took a straight course for the copper mines, and then [to] the Del Norte, thence home through the settlements of the Rio Abajo," Carson recalled. All he said of getting home was, "Arrived at Taos Decr. 25th, 1853." Christmas day. He had just turned forty-four. His birthday was probably rich with memory as he swung along on a good saddle mule from Santa Fe to Taos on the very trail he had ridden as a boy fresh from Missouri in 1826.

While passing through Santa Fe, he met Jacob Bernhisel, Utah's congressional delegate. Bernhisel told him that the government had just appointed Kit the new U.S. Indian agent for the Moache Ute tribe. His office would be located in Taos. The new appointment was another turning point in Kit's life. With his office in a room in his own home, he could spend time with Josefa and their children. He was to be on a regular salary of $1,550 per year, paid quarterly in amounts of $387.50. He would receive $500 to hire an interpreter and have a "discretionary fund" for annuities and supplies to feed and care for the Ute agency's guests. He would deal with Indian people whose cultures and languages he understood. No evidence has been found that he ever applied for this job. One can only surmise how it came about. Someone with political sway recommended him, someone other than Frémont or Senator Benton, whose influence had by then declined. Tom Dunlay suggests that Kit's friend Lt. Edward F. Beale may have "brought up Kit's name in the right places." Well known in Washington society, Beale had recently been appointed superintendent for Indian affairs for California. He and his family would later develop California's great Tejon Ranch east of Bakersfield, a ranch that operates to this day.

Kit's appointment was dated March 1, 1853. As young George Brewerton said, it was "a highly responsible office, requiring great tact, much common sense, and a fair amount of judgment." By now Kit had proven his talent for dealing with Native people. Experience had educated him for the job. While he never spoke of moral laws and ethical principles, and would have had trouble defining the words, he seems to have had a strong intuitive sense that a kind of justice other than retribution ought to prevail. After a visit with him somewhat later, James Rusling noted that he was not only "very conscientious," but that he often puzzled about whether an action was right or wrong, "as if it was the habit of his mind to test everything by the moral law." Kit is once supposed to have told William Bent: "By dispossessing [the Indians] of their country, we assume their stewardship." Not to do so would be "a damning blot and reproach" upon the nation, he added. By the time he received the new job, he had also become one of America's early celebrities, well known everywhere he went, though not as the plain man he wished to be, but as a ten-cent hero. Most of the Utes he would work with already knew and respected him. He could speak their language. They could trust him to keep his word.

9

"I Do Not Wish to Incur Any Debts"

After taking a few days off to enjoy the holidays in Taos, Carson rode down to Santa Fe, where on January 9, 1854, he took the oath of office. He posted bond and got instructions from David Meriwether, governor of the territory and ex officio superintendent of Indian affairs. Being the agent to the Moache Utes (the Jicarillas and Taos Pueblo were to be added to his care) carried a great deal of responsibility. Few men at the time had any aptitude or experience for the job. Most agents were political appointees for a post that held a low priority in government circles. Most stayed on only until something better came along. John Greiner, an unusually honest man and something of a wit, wrote in 1852, "Left in charge of the superintendancy [sic] of Indian affairs by Governor Calhoun, without a dollar to pay expenses, without any means provided to meet any of the Indians, with only one Indian agent in the Territory, and he in the Navajo country, with a rumor that the Comanches are forming a league with the other wild tribes to pounce down upon New Mexico and Texas . . . you can judge of my condition." Greiner later testified before a congressional joint special committee: "The great difficulty in our Indian policy is in the selection of Indian agents, who are generally appointed for political services," he said. "Mr.

Wingfield came here as agent, because he was a friend of Mr. Dawson, of Georgia; Mr. Wolley, an old man of seventy years of age, because he was the friend of Mr. Clay . . . ; and myself, because I could sing a good political song. [None] of us was by habit or education better fitted to be Indian agent than to follow any other business."

If an earnest and qualified man did show up to work, he was soon moved up to another job, then replaced by an incompetent who let the work languish. In her book *The Jicarilla Apache Tribe*, Veronica E. Velarde Tiller tells of Agent W. F. N. Arny's replacement at the Cimarron Ute Agency. A bright, serious man, Arny in 1861 began a "civilization program" at the agency with hopes of creating a "model agricultural community." Besides an adobe headquarters with a council room and office, Arny built corrals and garden plots. Appointed secretary of the territory a year later, he was replaced by one Levi Keithly, who let the program at Cimarron go to pieces.

"The appointment of Kit Carson, through whatever influence at Washington, was one of those rare flashes of intelligence by Government," Kit's biographer Edwin L. Sabin wrote. Carson was different from most. From long experience he understood the people he was to work with. He was fluent in Spanish, which several of the southwestern tribes also spoke, and he had mastered "sign" and several Native languages. Otherwise, the situation was about as usual. The government was remote and stingy, the supply system corrupt. Governor Meriwether carped unceasingly. Because Kit was illiterate, he used his "interpreter" as a clerk to take dictation and to read orders to him. In one instance Meriwether complained over "charges for expenses for self and clerk at Santa Fe $13 when I am ignorant of any regulations which authorize an Agent to have a clerk."

Historian William A. Keleher wrote that Meriwether on one occasion even had Kit arrested and held until "apparent inconsistencies" in his agency "accounts could be reconciled." Since office space was not provided, Kit used a room in his home as the agency's office, gratis. His service to the government regularly included feeding his office guests and their assorted companions and families, also often gratis. On one occasion he reported, "Scarcely a day passes but I have five to twenty-five to feed and take care of." Albert D. Richardson, a guest at Carson's table in 1859, wrote, "his residence . . . in Taos is a popular place of resort for travelers passing through the country, and one often meets there a motley array of Americans, Mexicans, and Indians." All of this "array" expected to be fed.

Although the government was supposed to supply rations to the tribes, Carson often bought supplies on his own account to feed his many visitors. Not by habit a complainer, he wrote James Collins, the superintendent of Indian affairs, in November 1858: "I have nearly expended my available private funds [to operate the office] and as I do not wish to incur any debts is my reason for addressing you." The next spring he wrote Collins again to remark that he had spent "every dollar of my private money" paying for agency supplies "whether govt. money is in my hands or not." Meanwhile, Josefa must have ordered up the meals and directed the cooking, the serving, and the cleanup with a smile and with pleasant conversation as she did for Carson's many personal friends who often stayed over. Agent Carson, with her steady help, was expected to do wonders with little money and sparse resources in an area of ceaseless conflict between ever more desperate Indian people and growing numbers of settlers, miners, and fortune hunters.

One of the lasting problems of Carson's Utes was the distances they had to travel to consult with their agent. With distance went temptation to steal livestock, or to find alcohol, which always led to trouble, usually violent trouble. Another problem was the scarcity of wild game, being replaced by settlers' cattle and sheep. Since the tribes relied upon hunting for subsistence, they could hardly be *justly* criticized for killing livestock as their game disappeared, but they were always blamed. Carson's official correspondence throughout his years as Indian agent resonates to the point of tedium with this theme: the government *must* feed the tribes; they are starving and will kill livestock out of sheer need.

Another perpetual headache was the division of command between civilian and military officials and the very different systems of justice they represented. When there was Indian "trouble," or even when there was not, Carson had to try to coordinate his actions with the territorial governor and with the Indian supervisor in Santa Fe as well as with the army, for the soldiers were the enforcement arm of government. Soldiers acted as a sort of roving police force. The Utes—and other Native tribes—were trapped in what Clare V. McKanna calls an "ambivalent existence" between systems of military law, civil law, and their own tribal law.

Still another problem arose when treaties signed by one of-ficial were not approved by a higher office. This breaking of what the Indians considered promises occurred under both Governors William Carr Lane and David Meriwether. Gover-nor Lane (1852–53) settled the Jicarillas near Abiquiu and put them to farming in order to try to change their hunting-roving habits. He promised food supplies and instruction while the people tried to make the transition to farming. But a parsimonious Congress refused to ratify the treaty between Lane and the Jicarillas, and the succeeding governor, David Meriwether, found that this situation "caused much embar-rassment and difficulty." As a result of these broken promises, the Jicarillas took up "theft and robbery upon the citizens of this Territory for a subsistence," Meriwether reported in Sep-tember 1854. From his first day in office until his last at the end of May 1861, Carson was expected, on a severely limited budget, as one historian put it, "to prevent conflict as far as possible, to persuade the Indians to submit to the govern-ment's will, and to solve any problems arising from contact between Indians and whites." It was an imposing assignment and an impossible task.

Not a man of especially creative mind, Carson by now had a rather fixed vision from which he worked. This was probably fortunate, for it gave him a steadiness he would otherwise have lacked in a job in which *all* conditions at the touch point between Natives and intruders were in endless flux. His ideas roughly paralleled the beliefs about "the Indians" and the ways they should be managed held by most Americans of the day, by the Indian affairs office in Washington, and by the army. These were not fresh ideas in a society in which people on the left, mostly in the East, saw the Indians as victims of American aggression, while those on the right, mostly in the West, saw them as "good" only when they were dead. The argument continued throughout the nineteenth century "between those who believed that every effort should be made to save the [victimized] Indians by transforming them, and those who declared such an effort to be quixotic and futile," as one historian wrote. Such beliefs seldom matched reality until reality intruded painfully enough to force a change.

One of several widely held convictions of the nineteenth century was that American society was a Christian society, thus "civilized" and *superior* to other societies, which were generally considered "uncivilized" or "savage." A related supposition was that "Indians" as they were, "in the wild" so to speak, could not live among other Americans, for how could "savages" live among the "civilized"? The next conviction followed from that one. The Indians must be separated on reservations where they could be fed, housed, and trained, mainly in agricultural and mechanical skills, until they became "civilized" enough to become "good citizens" who did "honest labor." This process would presumably put them on the path toward "assimilation," though not everyone thought assimilation a workable or even a "moral" answer.

An important dichotomy in New Mexico was between the "settled" and the "unsettled" Native people. The Pueblo people, whose ancestors had moved to the Rio Grande beginning around the year 1200, produced most of their own food by farming, whereas the "wild tribes," people who had always hunted wild game wherever it took them, could hardly become settled farmers overnight. If they tried, they starved. Indian supervisor James Calhoun put the matter clearly in a recommendation to the government to support the Pueblo people in their traditional lifeways because they were already farmers, thus reasonably "civilized." In contrast, he believed, the Utes, Apaches, and Navajos "must be . . . confined within certain fixed limits and there compelled to remain . . . and cultivate the soil." Presumably, being forced to settle on a reservation and give up their traditional hunting-roaming lifestyle for farming would eventually "civilize" these "wild tribes."

The next conviction was a version of the notion so common at that time in education, that "sparing the rod spoils the child," that punishment, often severe, is a valid means of instruction. Somehow "civilizing" would result if American Indians were confined and punished if they became hostile, especially if they left the reservation to hunt or raid. Though he often recommended what he called "chastisement" to teach lessons, Carson quickly learned that the hunting tribes became sadly dependent people rather than "good citizens" when they were forced to give up their customary hunting habits or when punished for other traditional ways.

Carson was usually able to work his way through difficult circumstances with some success largely because of his broad practical experience on the borders. Unlike other citizens, he also often had to try to find solutions to dire problems *now*. After all, he had spent most of his earlier life doing just that, trying to find solutions quickly in one critical border situation or another. He could readily put suppositions aside in a moment to take required action, whereas government officials in Washington could only change slowly under long and continued pressure. This fact seemed to make Carson's actions and statements often appear disparate, as if he were an agent without a consistent theory of how to do his job. In one writer's words, "Kit's rhetoric was sometimes tougher than his actions, and his opinions, like other people's, varied with immediate circumstances." Thus at times he could say that "chastisement" would cause the Natives to make peace, even to "learn a lesson." In one instance he said, "The consequences of letting [the Tabeguache Utes] go unpunished will be injurious. Other bands of Indians, seeing that depredations are committed by these with impunity, will soon follow an example."

Frequently, however, he would act with leniency. Having reported to Superintendent James Collins that Utes had massacred five miners and two others in August 1859, he recommended chastisement. But after meeting with the Utes at Abiquiu, he reported, "They say they were not engaged in the massacre, and promising to act in good faith in the future[,] I accompanied them to Conejos, and there delivered them their presents." Carson was a man who could seize the moment. As Tom Dunlay put it: "Here he had seized an opportunity to pacify a group of Indians by hearing them out and, very likely, letting them know that they still had a chance to make peace and they had better take it." What mattered to him more than settling past accounts, especially as he matured, was creating an opportunity for a peaceful future.

Although he sometimes recommended chastisement, he didn't think of punishment as an end in itself, but as one way of getting out of a scrape, if temporarily. And while he also on occasion used a term in common use then, "extermination" ("genocide" was not in the language of that day), he did not consider it a way of handling what people called "the Indian problem." Carson was optimistic, he was a problem solver, and he tried to find a way that would work *for* people. He took his job seriously. As Indian agent, he noted the living conditions of the people who came to talk with him and for whom he was responsible. He reported upon these conditions weekly and annually. Often judge and policeman as well as negotiator and provider, he did not consider extermination to be an option. The reservation system itself he thought of as a means toward accommodation and survival for an

American Indian people who were dying off from the loss of their traditional ways of life, from warfare, disease, starvation, and alcoholism.

Of the Native people Carson dealt with between 1854 and 1861, the Utes and the Jicarillas were the most troubled. These were hunting people, thus by tradition roving and unsettled. Governor Meriwether reported in 1854 that the Utes were "probably the most difficult . . . to manage within the Territory," and that "whenever there is any mischief brewing, invariably [the Jicarillas] have a hand in it." Besides being their agent, Carson also sometimes served as guide and tracker for the army's expeditions against them. He was a tracker for Lt. Col. Philip St. George Cooke's winter campaign near Ojo Caliente west of Taos in 1854. Cooke surprised a band of Jicarillas who had been out raiding and killed several of them. (Tragically, a number of women and children also died here of exposure in the heavy snows.) An army captain by the name of Quinn reported later that Carson "charged hard on the left with the Mexicans and myself with my Pueblos," while Cooke "showed his well known activity and boldness."

Whether or not Carson had qualms of conscience after the fight is unknown. Within a few days of Cooke's battle, he reported to William Messervy, "In my opinion [the Jicarillas] were driven into the war, by the actions of the officers and troops. . . . Their Sufferings and privations are now very great." Being both the Ute agent and their tracker appears today to put him in a double position that no person of conscience could bear. One should be wary, however, of assigning guilt, or guilty feelings, to him, at least over the death of the hostile warriors, as one should be wary of generalizing from the occasional instance about his supposed pleasure in killing Indians. The moral bind that seems apparent today may not have occurred to him. Perhaps as he, and others of his day, saw it, he had performed a "duty." Perhaps in serving as agent for, and as tracker of, the Jicarilla people, he believed he was actively trying to manage "his" charges. If that could not be done one way, it might be done another. He had known personally and had heard stories of the terror and violence of all sides in border warfare since his earliest childhood. He may simply have accepted instances such as this as a part of daily life.

During this period Carson met then Capt. James H. Carleton. Stationed for a time in New Mexico, Carleton had been ordered into the San Luis Valley with the dragoons to pursue Jicarillas. Carson was enlisted as his "principal guide." Trailing their enemy into Colorado and eventually to just east of Fisher's Peak near present-day Durango, Carson told Carleton that they would come upon the Jicarillas by 2:00 P.M. that afternoon. Doubtful, Carleton announced that if Kit were correct, "he would present" him with "one of the finest hats that could be procured in New York." As skillful trailing and some luck would have it, the occurrence went off just at the time Carson had predicted. Surprised in camp, the Jicarillas lost several men, most of their horses, and the camp baggage. Later, the hat arrived direct from New York, "and a fine one it was," Kit recalled. On the inner hat band was lettered: "At 2 o'clock. KIT CARSON from MAJOR CARLETON."

If Carleton was grateful for Kit's skills, Kit admired Carleton's organizational ability. "It was entirely owing to the good management of Major Carleton that the Indians were discovered," he later said. These incidents, Carleton's gift of the hat, and Carson's giving all the credit to his commanding officer suggest the mutual respect that grew from the days of their first becoming acquainted with each other. The result was what might be called "a good working relationship."

Except for their mutual respect for each other's unique skills, however, the two could not have been more different. Carson was the Westerner, pragmatic, adaptable, nervous in high society, fearless in danger, child and man of borders. Carleton was the Easterner, oriented to social class, of fixed opinion, hard-nosed, moralistic, Yankee to the bone. Born in

Maine in 1814, he served in 1838 as a lieutenant in the Maine militia during a Canadian boundary dispute. In 1839 he entered the army, graduated from cavalry school at Carlisle Barracks, and received a commission as second lieutenant in the First Dragoons. He married Henrietta Loring, who died soon after at Fort Gibson. He fought in the Mexican War, earned a brevet at the Battle of Buena Vista, and served as aide de camp to Gen. John Wool. After the war he married Sophia Garland Wolfe, Gen. John Garland's niece. Later he worked his way up the ladder of command with various assignments in the East, the Southwest, and in California.

There he organized the so-called California Column of volunteers who marched to New Mexico in 1862 as the Civil War reached the West. On their way, his soldiers established Fort Bowie in Apache Pass, today a beautiful national historic site. In September 1862 he replaced Col. E. R. S. Canby in command of the army's Department of New Mexico, and, until relieved of duty April 30, 1866, he ruled the department as if he were God himself. Throughout his life, Carleton was a soldier first. C. L. Sonnichsen defined the type: "an extremely competent and aggressive officer . . . always driving himself and his men, a stickler for discipline, a man without weakness or mercy . . . spare and durable and ramrod straight in his army blues."

Even before the Civil War began, rumors of war between the states circulated in New Mexico. Still a people of strong regional attachment and clannish family loyalties, Americans and their soldiers usually identified with the state of their birth, North or South. Many of the officers were West Point graduates, a high percentage of these Southerners. Until the Civil War, every officer's devotion to honor and to country was taken for granted. Now, if and when war came, these same officers and their soldiers would have to face a crisis of decision: whether to remain loyal to the Union, or to the state from which they came. William A. Keleher put the matter well: "Officers and enlisted men at military posts in the

Territory talked and argued much about such things as slavery, the right of a state to secede from the Union; about allegiance to the state where [he] was born; about a man's duty when the time came to make a choice between North and South. Higher ranking officers . . . were obliged to consider seriously questions of vast importance to themselves, their careers, their families and their country. What course should they pursue?" Such decisions could be agonizing in the extreme. Families and old friends split forever. Among the officers stationed in New Mexico, several who resigned the Union were to have distinguished careers in the South. There were, for example, Richard Stoddert Ewell, James Longstreet, George Crittenden, William Loring, Thomas Fauntleroy, Henry Sibley, and others.

Carson appears not to have been torn by such pangs, although people of his culture, for whom individual rights and clan loyalty were paramount, had heavily stocked the border states and much of the upper South. That being their region, a large number of these men joined the Confederacy. Carson's Missouri family, who were Southern Democrats and "states' righters," as well as descendants of earlier border kin in Kentucky and the Carolinas, mostly went South. One of Kit's brothers was a Confederate soldier. His younger brother Lindsey, Jr., left California to settle in Texas in order to be in the South. After the war, Lindsey, Jr., is supposed to have vowed never to celebrate the fourth of July as long as the Republican party was in power.

Thus Kit's sympathies would seem to have been Southern, and indeed Marc Simmons in *Kit Carson and His Three Wives* cited some evidence that they were. Be that as it may, perhaps because of his strong sense of duty, the fact that he had long been on government payroll, and the probability that his immediate family would be threatened by war in New Mexico, he chose loyalty to the Union.

Two reported incidents suggest that if he gave the matter much thought at all, he made up his mind early. Smith H.

Simpson, a Taos friend of Carson's, recalled in 1911 that Kit was one of a few local men who, along with Simpson, had raised the Stars and Stripes over Taos plaza in defiance of local Southern sympathizers, though exactly when is not clear. Kit's biographer Sabin dates the occurrence at the time "the news of Lincoln's election was announced in Taos" in November 1860. Biographers Thelma S. Guild and Harvey L. Carter seem to think it happened after John Baylor's or Henry Sibley's invasion of the territory. Another suggestive detail is from the recollections of one Luther Wilmot, who spent part of the winter of 1860–61 at a ranch on the upper Arkansas near present-day Pueblo, Colorado. Everyone was talking rebellion. Since he was the only Northerner around, Wilmot thought it best to keep his mouth shut. He recalled Carson's stopping over for a few days, playing poker, and chatting with the ranch hands. He and Carson soon discovered what they had in common, but didn't talk about it. "Kit was Loyal," Wilmot said, "but he was like me and would not argue the point."

As threat of war intensified across the country throughout the winter, spring, and early summer, preparations increased in New Mexico, as elsewhere. U.S. Army officers stationed in the territory began resigning to depart for the South, three of them on May 13 alone, Loring, Fauntleroy, and Sibley. One estimate is that about one-third of the army's entire officer corps went south. Meanwhile, loyal officers and regulars prepared to move east where it was obvious that the major fighting would occur. Seven southern states seceded between December 20, 1860, and February 1, 1861. On February 4 representatives of these states met in Montgomery, Alabama, to form the Confederate States of America. Four more states went out in April and May, after President Lincoln announced the insurrection and called for seventy-five thousand three-month volunteers.

Learning of the call for volunteers to defend the territory, Carson resigned as Indian agent on May 24, 1861. By late

May or early June, presumably after discussions with his family, he volunteered his services. On June 21 in Santa Fe he was offered a commission and took the oath of allegiance before Judge Kirby Benedict, chief justice of the territorial supreme court. According to the record, on June 24, 1861, "the President . . . appointed Agent Carson Lieut. Colonel." Also according to record, he was mustered into service at Fort Union the next day, June 25. By now New Mexico's Native people realized that the territory's defenses were crumbling. Tribes took the opportunity to recover their land while Americans fought each other over issues that little mattered to Natives. Tribal raids increased after Baylor's Texans invaded New Mexico in July. Colonel Canby, New Mexico's departmental commanding officer, immediately ordered U.S. Army regulars still in the territory retained. Militia and volunteers were to organize and stand ready for action.

Carson mustered in as Lt. Col. Christopher Carson of the First New Mexico Volunteer Infantry Regiment. He was second in command under Col. Ceran St. Vrain, who had already recruited a substantial number of largely Hispano men, many from around Mora. It was almost an affair of family, friends, and neighbors. Kit and Ceran had known one another forever it seemed. Capt. José Valdez was the husband of Josefa's sister Manuela. Everyone in the territory knew Kit Carson, if not personally, by reputation. Like most other volunteer regiments who fought in the war, the First New Mexico was made up of neighborhood men and boys under officers from among local civil leaders, well known and usually financially well-off. Most such officers had no prior military training. Even Kit, with all his experience of border warfare, had no training in army discipline and battlefield tactics. The men themselves, like other volunteer soldiers across the country, were long on patriotic feeling, short on training.

During July and August 1861 the First Infantry recruited at Fort Union and Santa Fe. Still not up to full strength until well after the Confederates took Mesilla, the regiment was ordered to Albuquerque in October to recruit and to be ready to move down the Rio Grande if the Rebels threatened Fort Craig. By then Colonel St. Vrain had resigned for health reasons. Kit replaced him in command on September 20. On October 4 Gov. Henry Connelly promoted Carson to full colonel. By the nineteenth he was in Albuquerque with his regiment.

While Baylor's Texans remained near Mesilla, the First continued to recruit. Attempts were made to drill. Young men—innocent, energetic, and patriotic—had to be kept busy. Patrols were sent out regularly to the south, east, and west. Carson himself moved Josefa and the children to Albuquerque to be near him. By now four children were living: William, Teresina, Kit, Jr., and the baby, Charles, born while the regiment was still at Fort Union. Kit especially enjoyed his children. He had a rare talent for entering the child's world of play, teasing and toying, freed for the moment of adult responsibility, as if he were really just a child himself. Capt. Rafael Chacón recalled a scene when Kit and his children were at play: "He was very loving toward his family," Chacón wrote. "I remember that he used to lie down on an Indian blanket, in front of his quarters, with his pockets full of candy and lumps of sugar. His children would jump on top of him, and take the candy and sugar from his pockets and eat it. This made [him] very happy, and he derived great pleasure from these little episodes. His wife . . . was called by him by the pet name of 'Chepita,' and he was most kind to her."

Although John Ayers, a member of the regiment, recalled that Kit "had wonderful influence over the men," probably because of his long border experience and his being so widely known in New Mexico, he was also quick to act when necessary. Capt. Edward "Ned" Wynkoop of the Colorado volunteers recalled that though Carson had "a beautiful mild blue eye, [it] would become terrible under some circumstances and like the warning of the rattlesnake always sounded the alarm before the spring." Accordingly, Carson "could punish with the utmost vigor a culprit who was deserving." In one instance while Carson and Wynkoop were in Albuquerque, they watched "a rough looking Mexican Ranchero" harass a clutch of Hispanas in a boat attempting to cross the flooded Rio Grande to attend mass. The fellow jumped into the boat. The boatman ordered him out: he was endangering the lives of the "gaily dressed Señoritas." When he refused, Carson, by then at the water's edge, asked him "in a mild manner" to get out of the boat. He refused again. Carson "then spoke to him in a peremptory manner." Still no response. Quick as a cat Carson slapped the man on the side of the head with the flat of his cavalry saber, knocking him out of the boat. "The fellow sunk like lead," Wynkoop recalled, "when quicker than thought, Kit plunged headforemost after and dragged him out on the bank." Carson's endangering his own life, undoubtedly while he was in full uniform, to save the life of a crude fool whom he had correctly punished suggests that he did not hold grudges. There is no question that he acted responsibly here, toward the women and toward the fool as well.

Carson's troubles over matters of military etiquette could be amusing. His reactions in such instances, especially when someone had fun at his expense, suggest that he was not vindictive, but could chuckle at himself. In his day as in ours, as every young soldier very quickly learns, "There's the right way, the wrong way, and the army way!" Totally untaught in army rules and custom, Kit simply turned matters of etiquette over to the professionals. Or he acted in whatever practical way might come to mind that seemed like a fair solution. Captain Wynkoop recalled that Carson had a lieutenant he called "Mac," his drillmaster. Mac was a stickler for the rules. One Sunday he marched the men to mass. Of course they were armed. Since all the seats in church were taken, Mac marched the men right through the door down to the altar, where he ordered them to stand at "Peee Rade Rest!" When the priest arrived, Mac ordered them to "Purrreeeeee zzent Hharms!" to the padre. When the story got back to Carson as a criticism of Mac's "army way," Kit excused his overzealous lieutenant. "Mac is a Military man," Kit explained, "and if he did present arms to the Priest it must be according to Army Regulations."

On another occasion, a soldier came over to Colonel Carson's quarters one evening and asked him to sign an order on the commissary for a canteen of molasses. Since Kit was illiterate, he had the soldier write out the order on a sheet of paper. Kit then happily signed it, scrawling his hard-learned "C. Carson" on the paper. Soon other soldiers began to arrive wanting him to sign orders for molasses. After the matter began to get out of hand, Kit inquired of the commissary and was told that the orders were not for molasses, but for whiskey. It was said thereafter that Colonel Carson never again signed an order without having an adjutant read it to him first!

In spite of lacking any military training, Carson seems to have been a firm leader in the one fixed battle he took part in during the war. This battle centered on the left bank of the Rio Grande near the ruin of the old village of Valverde, about where Carson had met Kearny's Army of the West in 1846. Valverde lies a few miles south of Socorro, slightly north and east of the once bustling village of San Marcial but on the other side of the river. By late fall and early winter of 1861 Baylor's force of mounted Texans, with additional volunteers from Arizona and the Fort Bliss area, numbered roughly eight hundred men. From his headquarters at Mesilla, Baylor could threaten Fort Stanton, which the Texans were briefly to hold but abandon on September 9, 1861. Baylor also threatened the Santa Rita Copper Mine on the Gila River Trail, Cooke's Spring, and Pinos Altos, the placer gold camp in the mountains above present-day Silver City.

Panicked by Baylor's apparent threat on the night of July 26, 1861, Maj. Isaac Lynde abandoned Fort Fillmore, about five miles down the Rio Grande from today's Las Cruces. During a frantic retreat toward Fort Stanton, 154 miles northeast, Lynde surrendered to Baylor in San Augustine Pass, in the words of historian William A. Keleher, "his entire command of some seven hundred men, together with the women and children of the post, traveling on horseback, walking, riding in buggies, wagons, and ambulances." This circus included the officers and men of the Seventh Regular Infantry, many of them drunk, two companies of mounted rifles, and all those horses and assorted draft and pack stock! The disaster ended all hope of defending the Rio Grande below Fort Craig, which then became the key defense point in southern New Mexico.

Thus for a while it seemed that the Texans had secured southern New Mexico and Arizona. By August 1, 1861, Baylor proclaimed all that vast mountain and semi-desert area the "Confederate Territory of Arizona." Baylor himself was its governor, and Mesilla, a suburb of today's Las Cruces, its capital. Except for the Mexican citizens, local Americans around Mesilla, Tucson, and Franklin (today's El Paso) were mostly Southern in sympathy. Not only had the U.S. government largely ignored their interests but most of them had Southern or middle-border roots. So in March 1861 Mesilla and Tucson voters chose to join the Confederacy. For a time their only real threat came from Apaches, who increasingly attacked travelers between Cooke's Spring (north of present-day Deming) on the east and Tucson to the west.

Shortly, however, the situation changed again, dramatically. Col. Henry Hopkins Sibley, West Point class of 1838, had been stationed at Fort Union as second in command of the New Mexico Department of the Army. Resigning his commission on May 16, he left New Mexico for the Confederacy. Through his close connection with President Davis, he was sent right back to Fort Bliss as Brig. Gen. Henry Hopkins Sibley, C.S.A. Operating from Fort Bliss, Sibley would try to take *from* the U.S.A. the territory he had just been defending *for* her. In early February 1862 he left Fort Bliss with about 2,590 men. He marched this army directly up the Rio Grande toward Fort Craig.

As soon as this news got to Albuquerque and Santa Fe, all leisure ceased. Col. E. R. S. Canby ordered Fort Craig reinforced immediately. Dust rolled. Supplies were packed, horses shod, muskets and rifles cleaned, ammunition replenished, wagons repaired, harness mended, mules roped, those unwilling cussed out and kicked around. A jumble of regulars, volunteers, and militia, mounted and afoot, the troops took the road south down the Rio Grande. Colonel Carson said good-bye to Josefa at Albuquerque. A week later she and the children found safe passage home to Taos. This "army" started their march south on January 23. Colonel Carson got to Fort Craig on February 1.

The moment of contact soon came. Sibley's forces arrived about two weeks after Fort Craig was reinforced. Skirmishing began downriver from Fort Craig on February 16, each side feeling the other out. Having scouted ahead and done some hard fighting on the twentieth, the Rebels moved around the east side of Black Mesa on the twenty-first to avoid Fort Craig, which lay to their west across the Rio Grande on the right bank. Meanwhile, Colonel Canby, advised by sentinels watching the Rebels' movements from atop Black Mesa, ordered his forces north from Fort Craig early on the twenty-first. Their hope was to hold the fords of the Rio Grande near the ruin of Valverde. About daylight, elements of the two forces met just north of Black Mesa along the Rio Grande itself. First contact came on the left bank of the river among the cottonwoods. The firing began between the men of Charles Pyron's Texas Mounted Rifles, who were down watering their horses, and two companies of New Mexico mounted under Maj. Thomas Duncan. One of these companies was Capt. Rafael Chacón's Company K, detached from Carson's First New Mexico Volunteers.

As rifle and artillery fire increased, Union infantry and cavalry began crossing the fords trying to drive the Texans back. By midmorning, however, the steady firing of Rebel six- and twelve-pound guns and small arms had stalled Union forward motion in the cottonwoods east of the lower ford on the left bank of the river. Thus Capt. Henry Selden's Fifth U.S. Infantry, with Colorado volunteers, were ordered to the lower ford, adjacent to the north end of Black Mesa. Shortly they were joined by the additional seven companies of Carson's First New Mexico Volunteers, which totaled about 460 men. These had been ordered from near Fort Craig up to the lower ford to stand ready for action.

Now the flow of battle began to change as Union artillery destroyed one of the Rebel six-pound field pieces that had held Duncan's and Chacón's men to the protection of the cottonwoods east of the river during the morning. This luck briefly stabilized the Union position and permitted Lt. Col. Benjamin S. Roberts to move Selden's Fifth Infantry up to the middle ford where they crossed the river to the left bank and drove into the Rebel center and right. Capt. Alexander McRae's Union battery then followed Selden's Fifth across the river to take a position a little in front and to the left of Union center. Here they and the infantry stalled Rebel action until midafternoon, forcing mounted Texans to tie their horses and mules to trees while their riders bellied into sandbanks for cover. Tied hard and fast, the animals made perfect targets for canister and for Union riflemen, who took a ghastly toll on them. Sibley lost nearly a thousand horses and mules here. Meanwhile, after a report that Rebel cavalry were crossing the river farther north, intending to cut in behind the Union rear, Carson's volunteers were moved upstream along the river's right bank to prevent that catastrophe.

As the battle developed, Maj. Henry Raguet's Fourth Texas Mounted, sabers swinging, charged the Union right near the north end of Black Mesa where Union regulars and volunteers, backed by sustained fire from Lt. Robert H. Hall's battery, fought to repulse them. The volunteers here included Carson's First New Mexico, who by now had been ordered across the river to strengthen the Union center. From the center, however, they were soon pulled to the right to block Raguet's charge. For the moment, all seemed to be going well for the Union force. Raguet's charge had stalled. McRae's battery and Selden's Fifth Infantry firmly held the center. A known alcoholic, General Sibley had retired to his ambulance drunk. Col. Tom Green had taken command in his absence.

Around 4:00 P.M., however, the gods of battle changed their whims. Union Colonel Canby, who had by now taken charge in the field, and Rebel Colonel Green made fateful decisions that determined who was to win the day. Canby ordered units near the Union center, including Carson's First New Mexico and Capt. Benjamin Wingate's Fifth U.S. Infantry, to pull off to their right to hold up Raguet's charge. This movement, while it interfered with Raguet, weakened the Union center. It left McRae's battery all but unsupported, except for the untried Third New Mexico Volunteers to McRae's left. McRae's was the valiant little artillery battery that had blocked Rebel forces all afternoon.

At about this time, knowing nothing of Canby's orders, Colonel Green chose to throw everything he had at McRae, whose guns had held him up for hours. Screaming the maniacal Rebel yell, Green's men jumped forward into a dead run. Within seconds, they engulfed McRae's battery, killed the heroic captain himself, and charged straight ahead toward the river. A handful of them turned McRae's guns around to attempt firing upon retreating Union soldiers. Just as he fell, the dying McRae, his hand on a gun, artilleryman to the bone, is said to have shouted, "I shall never forsake my guns!"

Without any doubt, thirst motivated Green's men. They had gone without water all day and the night before that. But the charge also transfixed Union soldiers, particularly those who were untried. Many broke and ran. Although Capt. James Hubbell's Fifth New Mexico Volunteers rushed in to fill the hole on McRae's right, while elements of the Seventh and Tenth U.S. Infantries ran in to cover the left, it appeared to Colonel Canby that the day was lost. Green's charge nearly overran his command post itself. His favorite warhorse, "Old Chas," had been shot from under him that very day. Around 4:15 P.M., dispirited and defeated, he turned to his bugler and asked him to call "Retreat."

That ended the battle. Regulars and volunteers, including those on the Union right who believed they were winning the day, dutifully recrossed the Rio Grande and made their way toward Fort Craig and safety. As was the custom, an evening truce permitted soldiers of both sides, some carrying lanterns, to move over the ground, cluttered now with the bodies of horses and men, a field silent but for the everlasting calls of "water, water, water" from the maimed, the bleeding, the dying. (My own great-grandfather never got over having heard these pitiful cries in the night after the great battles at Chickamauga and Missionary Ridge.) After Valverde, wrote one Southern soldier, "The battlefield was a sad sight. So many poor fellows lieing [*sic*] cold in death and others biting the earth, horses dead and wounded. The whole seemed to be the abode of death itself." For those silent and caring soldiers who until daylight tried to relieve their wounded, and for those who sorted their dead, it was a task grim beyond all belief.

There was little criticism later of Carson's part in the battle. Colonel Canby, perhaps largely because he was lifelong regular army, blamed the volunteers. Regulars generally resented volunteers, who were more likely than battle-hardened regulars to panic and run during their first battle. The other side of the matter was given years later by Lt. Col. J. Francisco Chaves of the First New Mexico Volunteers. Colonel Chaves wrote that he and Carson were stunned when they heard the bugler call "Retreat." As it looked to them in the field, they were winning the battle! An eyewitness account by Capt. William Mills describes Carson's walking before his men, steady as rock, calling out, "*Firme, muchachos. Firme!*" Captain Wynkoop, who knew Carson well, recalled that "he knew how to lead men into battle and keep them there." An unconfirmed story

214

had it that Carson threatened to shoot anyone who cut and ran. Very possibly true, that practice was not uncommon.

Other volunteers and officers also differed with Canby's opinions. One wrote that Carson's "regiment . . . fought bravely . . . and they would have retaken the guns that the enemy had captured if the retreat had not sounded." It was "the strong opinion of some of Carson's fiery fighters," wrote another, "that victory was within their grasp at Valverde and lost by mismanagement."

Instead of resuming the fight next day, both sides rested. The Rebels camped on the battlefield. They rifled the bodies and equipment of the Union dead, picking through everything they could use. Sgt. Albert Peticolas noted in his diary that he got a good blanket and found a stray horse to replace his dead mule. "Light bread, coffee, sugar and bacon for three days were all snugly stored away in haversacks," he noted. General Sibley demanded that Colonel Canby surrender Fort Craig, hoping that Union soldiers would come out to fight. Protected by the fort's walls with plenty of supplies in store, however, Canby refused both options. His position impregnable, he had everything to lose. Sibley, on the other hand, was in a bad way without the provisions that a surrender, or a victory, would have given him. As it was, very short of everything, especially of horses and mules, he was going to have to travel much afoot and live off the country, his soldiers pushing and pulling half-broken wagons along the road north to Socorro.

"The command was badly torn up," recalled one Texas veteran. "The batteries [were] shot to pieces and things in general in a dilapidated condition." Struggling north to Socorro, Sibley's men took the local military depot from its militia guards. They got a much needed haul of U.S. property, including rifles, carbines, and muskets; barrels of flour; and three hundred horses and mules, all of them branded "U.S." The long-range accuracy of weapons with rifled barrels made such weapons a valuable acquisition, for the

Texans were armed with whatever they had brought from home. Many carried only shotguns and old muskets, all with smooth bores. Because they lacked rifled barrels, these pieces were nearly useless at seventy-five yards and beyond, though they did terrible damage at fifteen to forty.

Albuquerque and Santa Fe were easy pickings. The citizens put up little fight, although retreating Union guards did succeed in keeping federal property out of Sibley's hands by torching the Albuquerque warehouse. Grease from tallow and salt pork ran afire out into the street. While a few wealthy sympathizers helped the Texans out, most of what the Rebels took they foraged from farms, ranches, mercantile stores, and family stocks. Such foraging did not win them any friends. They got a haul of supplies from an army depot at Cubero and waylaid a train of U.S. wagons bound from Fort Union to Fort Craig. Taking Santa Fe with little more than a song, they started to Fort Union, now well stocked but lightly guarded. Sibley himself remained in Santa Fe, drinking and congratulating himself. Canby and his army were still down south at Fort Craig. For a short time it seemed the invaders had everything in hand. Heading northeast toward Fort Union, they got as far as Glorieta Pass.

There on March 28 the gods of battle changed their whims again. While the Texans fought Col. John P. Slough's Colorado volunteers in the rocks and cactus of Glorieta Pass near Pigeon's Ranch, Col. John M. Chivington with more than four hundred volunteers circled around behind the Texans. Near the mouth of Apache Canyon (that narrow throat through which all traffic headed east from Santa Fe on I-25 must pass through today), Chivington came upon the Rebel supply wagons and livestock left lightly guarded by the Texans as they advanced up the pass itself.

Chivington's men piled and burned the wagons and all the supplies, then shot the horses and mules. With everything gone up in fire and smoke, the Texans broke off and turned toward Santa Fe, Albuquerque, and home down the

Rio Grande. By May they were out of New Mexico altogether and back in Franklin, where they had started this ruined campaign. Starved and wounded, the survivors were diseased and lice ridden. Though Sibley reported a victory to President Davis, the South would not threaten New Mexico again.

With the Confederacy out of his way, Colonel Canby could again focus on his troubles with Indians. These troubles had increased over the months during the war. For Carson himself, two important factors now came into play. One was the arrival in August 1862 of Gen. James H. Carleton with his California Column, a brigade of volunteers organized to drive the Texans out of New Mexico and prevent any possible invasion of the West Coast across Arizona. Two was the fact that Carson was the man Carleton would turn to for dealing with the Apaches and Navajos. In his various lives as mountain man, guide, husband of Indian women, scout, interpreter, and Indian agent, Carson probably had more experience dealing with Indian people than any other prominent westerner had. He had acquired all the complex skills of borderland living. He could think clearly and take action under great pressure. He had few enemies. Nearly everyone liked him. Others respected him. For Carson, these factors, especially the return of Carleton, would become, for better and for worse, aside from his family, the major matters of importance for the rest of his life.

10

"My Duty as Well as Happiness"

After the Texans left New Mexico, the U.S. Army focused on the Mescaleros and the Navajos. Still in command of the Department of New Mexico, Colonel Canby had been making plans for the Navajos when he was reassigned to the East. Before leaving, he ordered Colonel Carson from Fort Craig to Albuquerque to recruit a new regiment, the First New Mexico Volunteer Cavalry. Things would change again after August 1862, when Brigadier General Carleton arrived with his California Column. Carleton was to replace Canby in departmental command. Meanwhile, Josefa and the children had rejoined Kit in quarters that summer. Husband and wife had missed each other. By dictation, Kit had written Josefa from Fort Craig in April to say that he was well. She had responded warmly, also by dictation: "The receipt of your letter has been a source of great relief to Mrs. Carson, and indeed to all your friends," her acquaintance wrote for her. "[She] and the children send their best love and prayers to you."

By late summer Carson had moved two companies of his new volunteer cavalry to Los Pinos south of Albuquerque to defend the community from Indian raiders. By September 21 he responded to Canby, still in command, about the Navajo operation already planned. He asked permission to come to Santa Fe for "a full and explicit conference with [you] as regards my duty [in this campaign]." He may have had suggestions for the plan, or he may have wanted to offer his resignation, for he would soon request that in writing. Unfortunately, he never had the chance to talk with Canby, for shortly after dictating the letter, he learned that Carleton was now in command of the department.

An intensely aggressive officer, Carleton at once put *his* signature on all departmental plans. Howard R. Lamar suggests the man's motivating demon: "Since he could not seek glory on the eastern front [in the Civil War, he] . . . assumed the role of deliverer of the Southwest." Having also missed the chance to defeat Sibley, he undertook "the . . . subjection of the wild Indians, and the opening of the country to prospectors." He immediately changed the department's focus from conquering the Navajos to crushing the Mescaleros. Subjection of the Navajos could come later. For Carson, as for the Mescalero and Navajo people, the general's plans would prove fateful.

Carleton soon ordered Carson to reopen Fort Stanton. Built in 1855 to guard a reservation set aside for the Mescaleros, the fort had been deserted ahead of Baylor's advancing Texans in 1861. Carleton, who himself held substantial investments in mining properties, intended to use the fort to defend the increasing numbers of settlers and miners in the Sacramento Mountains and along the Rio Grande. He also reactivated Canby's earlier plan for a reservation at the Bosque Redondo far to the east on the Pecos River. Recalling the well-watered bosque from having visited it during a survey in 1852, having then recognized its cavalry potential, he now decided to build a post there named Fort Sumner. The Mescaleros, and later the Navajos, could be "relocated" to the new fort for the safety of New Mexico's settlers.

In August 1862 Carleton's action against the Mescaleros was hastened by reports from their agent, Lorenzo Labadie, that the people "during the year have been in a continuous state of hostility." During late August alone, Labadie wrote, "they killed some forty men and six children, and carried a

219

number of children into captivity," besides taking "horses, mules, donkeys, and cattle [and] large numbers of sheep." Carleton quickly activated his new plans. With the look of a commanding officer who chewed horseshoes pickled in lime juice for breakfast, he started in, as Howard R. Lamar put it, "at a breathless pace." He set up a pincers movement by ordering Colonel Carson and his cavalry south to Fort Stanton, Capt. William McCleave with two companies of California soldiers northeast from Mesilla, and Capt. Thomas L. Roberts with two companies north from Franklin. In order to shut down the Mescaleros in the Sacramento Mountains and beyond, the three military groups swept over a vast piece of country. Carleton's orders to Carson read, "All Indian men of that tribe are to be killed whenever and wherever you can find them. The women and children will not be harmed, but you will take them prisoners and feed them at Fort Stanton." Carson ignored the part about killing the men. It is doubtful that Carleton, ideologue that he was, really intended that either, for he offered an alternative: "If they beg for peace," he told Carson, "their chiefs and twenty of their principal men must come to Santa Fe to have a talk."

So the matter actually worked out. Though some fled, others, outnumbered by the soldiers, came in to Fort Stanton where Carson took them in. Tragically, soldiers under Capt. James Graydon fired into a band of Mescaleros under José Largo and Manuelito, even though, reportedly, this band was making peace gestures. A woman, several men, and the two chiefs were killed. According to Lawrence Kelly, Carson immediately opened an investigation, and Carleton later ordered a formal one. Meanwhile, army surgeon J. W. Whitlock accused Graydon in the *Santa Fe Gazette* of cold-blooded murder. Upon Whitlock's arrival at Fort Stanton, Graydon challenged him to a duel but was himself shot. In an act of sheer retaliation, Graydon's soldiers then killed Dr. Whitlock, reportedly threw his body in a ditch, and riddled it with bullets. Thus ended the chance to court-martial Graydon, or to question Dr. Whitlock. "Carleton wanted Graydon tried," Tom Dunlay wrote, "but it was too late for that." Carson himself reportedly disarmed Graydon's company, publicly denounced them, and even threatened to have every fourth man shot.

With a sizable number of men and women under his care at Fort Stanton by late 1862, Carson "had once again seized an opportunity to end the fighting, whatever he [or Carleton] had said before," wrote one historian. Carson also sent Cadete, Estrella, and Chato to Santa Fe to talk with Carleton, and he sent a military escort along to protect them. "We have fought you so long as we had rifles and powder," Cadete told the general, "but your weapons are better than ours. Give us weapons and turn us loose, and we will fight you again; but we are worn out; we have no more heart; we have no food; no means to live; your soldiers are everywhere. . . . Do with us as may seem good to you."

Carleton's terms: Every Mescalero and his family who wanted peace must go to the Bosque Redondo and stay there. The army at Fort Sumner would feed and protect them they were told. Those who did not go would be hunted down and killed without further talk. As soon as all those behaving were settled in the Bosque Redondo, terms of peace could be discussed. According to C. L. Sonnichsen, by March 1863 about four hundred people "were drawing rations at the new post." By midsummer, even more had come in. "Fields had been laid out, crops had been planted [and] housing of a sort had been set up." At the time, Carleton intended to return the people to the Fort Stanton reservation after they had signed a treaty in which *all* of them were represented. "Eventually," he wrote, "we shall have the whole tribe at the Bosque Redondo, and then we can conclude a definite treaty, and let them all return again to inhabit their proper country."

Thinking he had now resettled the Mescaleros, Carleton turned to the Navajos. If he had shown any hint of compromise before, he now became obdurate—the martinet, the tyrant. Howard R. Lamar outlines the process by which he acquired influence within the territory. Upon arrival in Santa Fe he courted the friendship of Gov. Henry Connelly, a Democrat whom Lincoln had appointed to the governorship in 1861 and would reappoint in 1864. He next courted Kirby Benedict, who was at once chief justice of the territorial supreme court *and* Republican party boss. He wooed such important New Mexican families as the Chavezes. "The General's most remarkable conversion, however," Lamar wrote, "was that of James L. Collins, editor of the Santa Fe *Gazette* and Indian Superintendent." Carleton purchased an interest in the *Gazette*, which thereafter became his trumpet. "By the summer of 1863 Carleton was being hailed as the deliverer of New Mexico," wrote Lamar. "Santa Fe was at his feet, and the Collins press . . . had difficulty finding new adjectives to praise [him]." Meanwhile, the opposition newspaper, the *Santa Fe New Mexican*, over the years ahead would pillory the general.

Now Carleton picked up on the Navajos where Canby had left off. Since Spanish colonial times, Navajos and New Mexicans along the Rio Grande had developed a lethal routine in which raid and retaliation had become habit. *Ladrones* (thieves) from both sides stole from *ricos* (the rich) of both sides literally everything of value that could be moved—corn, melons, sheep, horses, mules, women, children. A thriving slave trade had grown up. Women and children of both sides were traded to families of both sides as laborers and servants, concubines and wives. In the avenger's eye, revenge for these outrages justified every kind of meanness: more thievery, and more killing, which then must be "made right" by further retaliation in cultures of retributive justice.

Lt. William H. Emory described the situation in the Rio Abajo along the Rio Grande in 1846. "As we marched down the river," he reported, "[the Navajos] attacked the settlements three miles in our rear, killed one man, crippled another, and carried off a large supply of sheep and cattle." On October 4 he noted that "about one hundred Indians, well mounted, [had] charged upon" the town of Polvadera and "drove off all the horses and cattle." As the people of Lemitar, attempting to relieve their neighbors in Polvadera, blocked the way out, "the Indians seeing their retreat with the cattle and goats cut off, fell to work . . . killing as many of these as they could, and scampered off over the mountains . . . with the horses and mules." Emory continued, "Women, when captured, are treated by the Indian wives of the capturers as slaves, and . . . if they chance to be pretty, or receive too much attention from their lords and masters, they are, in the absence of the latter, unmercifully beaten and otherwise mal-treated. The most unfortunate thing which can befal [*sic*] a captive woman is to be claimed by two persons. In this case, she is either shot or delivered up for indiscriminate violence."

That Carson fully understood this dark and violent pattern is clear in testimony he gave in 1865 to a congressional com-mittee looking into Indian matters. "I know that even before the acquisition of New Mexico there had about always existed an hereditary warfare between the Navajoes [*sic*] and the Mexicans," he testified. "Forays were made into each others' country, and stock, women, and children stolen. Since the ac-quisition [by the United States], the same state [has] existed; we would hardly get back from fighting and making peace with them before they would be at war again . . . there is a part of the Navajoes, the wealthy, who wish to live in peace; the poorer classes are in the majority, and they have no chiefs who can control them." This pattern, Robert M. Utley wrote, "had to be broken." Canby didn't get the chance. Carleton took up the job as his personal mission.

He began in October 1862 by establishing Fort Wingate in the Navajo country at present-day San Rafael. The next April at Cubero he met with peace chiefs Barboncito and Delgadito, both ricos, to announce his plan to isolate the peace party from the war party. Presumably this would put him in a position to defeat the war party. Those Navajos who wanted peace must go to the Bosque Redondo where, under protection of the army at Fort Sumner, they would learn to support themselves by farming, or so he may have believed. The offer was refused. In June 1863 he tried again. This time he ordered Col. J. Francisco Chaves at Fort Wingate to warn the ricos that they had until July 20 "to come in—they and all those who belong to . . . the peace party; that after that day every Navajo that is seen will be considered as hostile and treated accordingly . . . the door now open will be closed."

By June Carleton prepared to enforce his ultimatum. He ordered Carson's cavalry regiment from Los Pinos to Fort Wingate. Under pressure of the general's orders, the colonel would comply. It cannot be argued convincingly, however, that he was happy about the orders, that he enjoyed subduing the Navajos, or that he took any pleasure in destroying their fields and killing their people. It should by now be clear that, having lived among Indian people of different tribes, languages, and cultures on borders all his life, and having married an Arapaho wife and treated their daughters responsibly, Carson was not a man who believed that "the only good Indian is a dead Indian." Now that the Confederates had been thrown out of the territory, he would soon submit a letter of resignation from military service. As he would put it in this written request, "My duty as well as happiness directs me to home & family." He had done his duty to his country. He had served the Union cause. He had defended New Mexico from invaders. He had protected the land of home and family. Now he was tired. He was ill. A bad fall from a horse or a mule while on a hunting trip with Lucien Maxwell to Colorado earlier had seriously injured him. Afterward, he was always in pain.

By this time Carson also suffered from enlarged veins and soreness in his legs, a condition he believed was caused by a footrace to escape Blackfeet years before. As early as 1859 a visitor noted that Carson had decided "thenceforward to avoid horseback riding and travel only in carriages" because of his continual pain. In any event, being at home was now more important to him than anything else, although he was soon going to have to decide, as he had done before, between duty to family and to his personal health, and duty to country. Unfortunately for Carson and for everyone else concerned, especially for the Navajos, this time "duty to country" meant carrying out the orders of a self-centered, compulsive general officer on a mission of destruction.

As early as February 3, 1863, while he was still stationed at Fort Stanton, Carson surprised Carleton with a letter of resignation. In stilted phrasing, the letter gave his reasons. He explained that he had resolved "long since" to resign from service, but had "delayed" on the "supposition" that there might yet be "another opportunity of proving my devotion to that Government which was established by our Ancestors." It had now become clear, however, [presumably with Sibley's defeat] that "there is no probability that we shall be again called upon to defend our Territory against hostile invasion." Should he be wrong, it would be his "pride and pleasure" to serve again "in any capacity in which I can best serve my country." But, he continued, "at present I feel that my duty as well as happiness, directs me to my home & family and trust that the General will accept my resignation."

Having asked once before to come to Santa Fe to discuss with Colonel Canby the terms of his "duty," he was now called before Carleton to discuss, not *his*, but General Carleton's terms. Unfortunately, notes of this discussion, if any, have not been found. Since Carson remained in service, apparently Carleton refused his request. Probably the general tried to convince him of his indispensability, his "duty," and so on, all the principles that would have seemed important to Carson. Interestingly, for whatever it may suggest about Carleton's view of Carson's worth, resignations for personal reasons by citizen soldiers were at that time generally accepted as a matter of course. While apparently refusing the resignation, Carleton did offer Carson two months' leave of absence to spend time at home with his family. Marc Simmons noted that this was only "the first in a string of unsuccessful resignations

[Carson] would tender to Gen. Carleton, before finally leaving service in 1867." Time after time Carleton refused him.

Notwithstanding Carson's physical pain and his worry over family and personal matters, he remained in service until the end of the Navajo campaign, performing his "duty" to the letter of the law. In the spring of 1863 Carleton ordered him to recruit Ute scouts from the post at Abiquiu. "The Utes," noted Lawrence Kelly, "were excellent trackers and fierce foes of the Navajos, and in the early phases of the campaign" proved "their usefulness on more than one occasion," although they would later leave because of disputes with Carleton over "the spoils of war—women, children, sheep, and horses." Carson thought the Utes should be permitted to keep the Navajo women and children they captured. The Utes traded many of these captives to New Mexican ricos as servants. Carson believed this new status improved their living conditions and general well-being. But Carleton disagreed altogether. In the summer of 1863, under Carleton's orders to build "a defensible Depot" at Red Town Wash, near today's Hubbell Trading Post at Ganado, Arizona, Carson departed Los Pinos with only four companies of his volunteers fitted out and ready for action. Since the Arizona site was found to lack water and forage, however, previously abandoned Fort Defiance thirty miles north and east was refitted for service and renamed Fort Canby.

From here during late summer, fall, and winter Carson's forces carried out separate expeditions called "scouts." At Carleton's insistence, Carson led most of these himself. David Lavender called them "long, corkscrewing rides through a dry, wind-scoured land." Sgt. George Campbell remembered Carson as "reeling in his saddle from fatigue and loss of sleep . . . still pushing forward." The volunteers breached the remote Navajo country, mainly west of Fort Canby. Carson and the Utes scouted ahead, while the volunteers by companies, mostly afoot, followed along behind. Over the course of the campaign, battle casualties for the New Mexicans were few but eventually very heavy for the Navajos, who were masters of a style of warfare that had to be learned from them and from other Native warriors. This style was to ambush, fade away, and live to fight again. The Native people knew the country as no one else did. They knew where to hide, where to rest, where to find water, and where to attack. It was a style foreign to European and American battle tacticians of the time, theirs being a style in which armies of uniformed men fought in ranks and died by thousands on great bloody fields.

Unable to get the Navajos to stand and fight in their own vast country, Carson and his volunteers took the responsibility for practicing Carleton's program of total warfare. It was not easy, and it was not a task Carson enjoyed. Carleton himself could avoid the reality of the awful operation by remaining in the office away from the field of battle. He was, as Frank McNitt put it, "intensely involved in the operation[,] but far removed from the scene." Carson and his volunteer soldiers were the people who had to follow their foe day after day, summer and winter, never allowing him to rest, burning his hogans, his fields and grain, destroying his livestock, and indeed everything he needed to subsist. By razing everything of use to them, Carleton hoped the Navajos' will to fight could be broken. On a much smaller scale, it was Sherman's "march to the sea," the modern warfare of its day. Robert M. Utley described it tersely: "This meant warring on a whole enemy population, combatant and noncombatant alike." In Tom Dunlay's words, "The point was to deny them three vital things: subsistence, security, and sanctuary. Battle casualties might be few but the toll of suffering on the whole population would ultimately force surrender."

Not only New Mexico volunteer soldiers but also traditional enemies were active in this assault. The Utes and even people from Jemez, Zuni, and Hopi Pueblos took part. In the fall of 1863 three hundred Pueblos reportedly attacked a party under a Navajo named Barboncito (at least two leaders used this name). They killed him and sixteen of his men, captured the women and children, and took their sheep. Plunderers from the Hispano villages along the routes of the Long Walk also ranged the land, bent on getting even for old ruin and insult, intent on using that as an excuse for pillage now. Lawrence Kelly wrote of "the continued invasion of the Navajo country by armed bands of New Mexicans," even "disturbing reports" of "Navajo children . . . being kidnapped and sold into slavery by the citizens of the Territory [of New Mexico] as the Navajos made their way through the towns and villages," headed to Bosque Redondo. "The Ute[s] had declared themselves long since, and were happily applying the Carleton policy to their traditional enemies," wrote Charles Avery Amsden.

The march through Canyon de Chelly was the last step in the open warfare. Considered by the Navajos their haven, to the soldiers the canyon was essentially a vast, menacing enemy stronghold where the Navajos found both protection and food supplies. Red sandstone walls stab straight upward into light blue sky for hundreds of feet from the sandy bottom of this awesome canyon in the Arizona desert. Now, Carleton insisted, it must be taken. Carson himself hung back. Though he had asked for a leave of absence to go home in December and January, Carleton ordered him to Santa Fe to consult, making it clear, however, that "it is desirable that you go through the Canyon de Chelly before you come." But Carson did not. Between January 6 and 12, 1864, through the worst of weather, he led nearly four hundred officers and men from Fort Canby to the western end of the canyon, while Capt. Albert H. Pfeiffer led two companies to the eastern entrance. Carson's soldiers then scouted along the high walls of the western end while Pfeiffer's men came through the canyon from the east. The Navajos gave Pfeiffer little serious trouble even though they showered arrows and rocks down upon the soldiers from the forbidding canyon walls.

On the morning of January 15, 1864, sixty Navajos surrendered to Carson near the mouth of the canyon because, as reported to Carleton, "they are in a complete state of starvation, and . . . many of their women and children have already died from this cause." In an article entitled "The Destruction of Navajo Orchards in 1864," Stephen C. Jett wrote that about five hundred Navajos actually surrendered to Carson's forces at Fort Canby during January. There followed a lull in the action partly because, wrote Jett, Carleton wanted to give the Navajos a "grace period." In March Capt. Asa B. Carey replaced Carson in command of Fort Canby, and Carson was transferred. Carey then spent two days in the canyon, apparently urging the people to surrender. His official report makes no mention of destroying anything.

Under orders of Capt. P. W. L. Plympton, by then in command at Fort Canby, Capt. John Thompson marched through the canyon in late summer 1864, several months after Carson's departure. According to Thompson's report, his men destroyed "3,200 mature peach trees" and "eleven acres of maize and beans." Although orders given at Fort Canby and remarks Carson made later suggest that he had intended having the trees cut down while he was still in command, it was Capt. Thompson's soldiers under Plympton's orders who actually did the massive damage so offensive to the Diné. Considering that the peaches were one of several food sources the canyon provided the Navajos, along with their maize and beans, it seems likely that the army wanted the trees destroyed for the same reason that they had destroyed other food sources during the campaign. Understandably, the unfortunate destruction of these revered trees became a point of deepest bitterness in Navajo memory, to this day a rallying point in their identification as a people.

As a result of all the devastation, especially during late winter of 1863–64, the Navajos came in by hundreds to Fort Canby and Fort Wingate. There they surrendered and were gathered up for the Long Walk east, many with their horses, sheep, and goats. Fed short rations of meat and flour, weak from dysentery, dressed in rags that became ribbons on the way to Fort Sumner, men, women, and children walked, the oldest and sickest riding in wagons, through summer's heat and winter's snow. The ordeal of the Long Walk itself continued from the summer of 1863 until 1867. Groups of every size were gathered and started. Several routes were taken: via Albuquerque, via Santa Fe, even via Fort Union; and there were still others, ranging in distance traveled from 375 miles at the shortest to 436 miles through Santa Fe and 498 through Fort Union. The favored "Mountain Route" was 424 miles in length.

A count was made of the groups as they started at Fort Canby or Fort Wingate, and again as they arrived at Fort Sumner. By December of 1866 a total of 11,468 people had by report been started on the journey. Nearly a year later in November 1867 a count revealed 8,570 Navajos confined at the Bosque, the highest number reportedly held in confinement during the entire sorry episode. What happened to those of all ages who were missing can never be known. Many died on the way. Some were stolen and sold into peonage. Others escaped into the mountains. The ordeal of death and confinement did not end until the summer of 1868.

When Carson arrived in Santa Fe for "consultation" in January 1864 he looked so sick that Carleton placed him on detached duty and sent him home to Taos for what Kit called only "some private business of importance." Josefa was expecting her sixth child, to be named Rebecca, to be born April 13. By then, however, Carson was back at Fort Canby, where he arrived March 19, appearing, according to Captain Carey, "unwell and very much fatigued." A month later, reporting that "so far as active operations are concerned" the Navajo war was over, Carson requested reassignment to a post where his family could be with him, or, as the alternative, "that I may tender my resignation." He added, "My children are small" and "need my presence to look after their education . . . and [they] have the next claims on my time and attention." Again, Carleton refused him.

Calling Carson briefly back to Santa Fe, Carleton reassigned him on May 30 to Fort Sumner to be a supervisor.

There Carson found living conditions appalling. The Navajos and Mescaleros, both hunting-roving people, were trying to grub life out in the sand of the Pecos River bottoms in brush hovels or under worn-out blankets and old pieces of canvas supported by sticks. All were starving, and many lived out in the open without any shelter at all. Firewood was increasingly hard to find. Over the next months and years, flood, drought, and insects destroyed the crops people planted. Horses and sheep were lost to poor grass, alkaline water, and thieves who always hovered about. Comanches and other Plains tribes attacked them, while the Navajos feuded with the Mescaleros, who simply left one night and disappeared into their mountain hideaways. They never came back.

By now the civil and military departments of the U.S. government argued continually over "Indian policy." Dr. Michael Steck of the Department of the Interior regularly went head-to-head with Carleton. Never having favored Navajo "removal," Steck disagreed with the general on every point. By 1868, after a congressional investigation, the entire operation at Fort Sumner was shut down and a treaty was signed with the Navajos. At last the Diné could return to their homeland. "The effects of this violent and complete disruption of Navajo life are beyond calculation," wrote Charles Avery Amsden. "As long as a Navajo remains upon earth the epilogue of Bosque Redondo will be still in the playing, for this episode of five years duration turned the stream of tribal history into a new channel for all time to come."

Carson remained at Fort Sumner for only a few months. Lonely for his family, miserable about the filth, hunger, and disease—angry—he argued with the fort's commanding officer, Capt. Henry Bristol. Again he submitted his resignation. Again Carleton refused, but he offered a field assignment. On October 22, 1864, he ordered Carson out on a campaign to the plains east of Fort Bascom against Kiowas and Comanches, who had increased their raiding on the Santa Fe Trail. As elsewhere across the Great Plains, the tribes had taken the opportunity the Civil War offered to attack settlers and travelers. Kiowas and Comanches had killed five men near Lower Cimarron Spring in August 1864, saying that "they would kill every white man that came on the road." At Walnut Creek, Indians killed ten men. They scalped two boys, then went off and left them alive. Others ran off livestock from wagon trains and even from army posts. Houses and barns were set afire. In October 1864 Col. J. C. McFerran reported that matters could not be worse. He predicted that the army's supply lines would even be cut, "not to mention the complete stoppage of our mails to and from the east." Not surprisingly, Indians threatened to slaughter Carleton himself.

Carleton now called on Carson to recruit Ute and Jicarilla scouts, promising them "all the plunder that they might acquire," wrote Lt. George H. Pettis. The general also hoped that "200 Apaches and Navajoes" from Fort Sumner would pitch in to attack the warring Plains tribes. The Navajos declined, but a party of Jicarillas and Utes were ready for a raid, *if* plunder were to be their reward. On November 10 Carson with seventy-five of these scouts arrived at Fort Bascom on the Canadian River, a little north of today's Tucumcari, where the soldiers he would lead were posted.

These consisted of about 325 California and New Mexico volunteer infantry and cavalry with two mountain howitzers, the little cannons-on-wheels like the one Frémont had abandoned in the Sierra Nevada in January 1844. Carleton's orders were to kill only men, to spare all the women and children. Carson would march east from Fort Bascom along the Canadian River to Adobe Walls, the ruin of Bent's abandoned trading post. Near here ten years later on June 27, 1874, perhaps five hundred Southern Cheyennes, Southern Arapahos, and Kiowas would battle twenty-eight men and one woman of a buffalo hunting party led by Dodge City merchants J. Wright Mooar, Robert M. Wright, and Charlie Rath. Now, however, Carson planned to use the ruined walls as a base from which to scout the surrounding country, hoping that he could surprise his enemy in winter camps. The weather could not have been worse. Snowstorms held the soldiers up for two days. The Ute scouts danced a war dance every night, keeping the soldiers awake until all hours.

The action that developed had grim results for both sides. After Carson's little army of infantry, cavalry, and Lieutenant Pettis's howitzers marched all night long on November 24, the cavalry under Capt. William McCleave surprised three Kiowas who were out gathering horses early in the morning. McCleave immediately charged into the big Kiowa village nearby and set it afire.

The day's fight was on. Comanches, Kiowas, and Plains Apaches from nearby camps rushed in to defend their neighbors. Determined to win on their own ground, the mounted warriors rushed the soldiers, who corralled their own spent horses in the ruin of the walls and took up fighting afoot. The battle went on until about half past three on the afternoon of the 25th, the warriors armed mostly with lances and bows and arrows and mounted on good horses. Pettis's howitzers prevented them from massing for a charge, which, had it come, would little doubt have overrun the soldiers. As it was, they just held on, fighting from the ground near the ruin of the walls while the Kiowa village with all its supplies went up in a wall of smoke.

One officer later testified that they "made it hot for . . . us by their excellent marksmanship . . . mounted and covered with their war-dresses [they] charged continually across our front from left to right . . . about two hundred yards from our line of skirmishers, yelling like demons and firing from [under] the necks of their horses." From somewhere behind the main action, a warrior blew a bugle in reverse of the army's bugle calls. "When our bugler sounded the advance, he would blow retreat and when ours sounded retreat, he would blow advance," said one soldier. The Indian bugler kept this up all day, "blowing as shrill and clear as our very best bugler." Carson himself estimated that his men fought "at least 1,000 Indian warriors, mounted on first-class horses." He reported that Lieutenant Pettis's two mountain howitzers "did good service, and finally drove the enemy out of range."

By midafternoon Carson took counsel of his Ute scouts, but did not ask the advice of his own officers. The scouts thought it was time to pull back. When they learned of it, the officers, younger and less experienced than Carson and the Utes, objected to what they considered retreat. Ignoring their opinion, having succeeded in burning a village with all its baggage, Carson, however, ordered withdrawal. Though some later accused him of cowardice, he had had enough experience by then to know better than to risk a disaster two hundred or more miles east of his supply base at Fort Bascom. During the withdrawal, the Ute warriors set fire to the grass to drive the soldiers toward the bluffs along the Canadian River. Lieutenant Pettis, ably commanding the howitzers, protected the rear. Carson effectively held the command together, avoiding a rout and the piecemeal killing that would have marked it. Heroic actions, as well as the usual outrages, occurred. Two Indians raced in horseback under fire to sweep up a wounded comrade by his elbows and carry him from the field. Among the outrages, according to Lieutenant Pettis, two Ute women "searching for plunder" killed "two old, decrepit, blind Kiowas and two cripples" in a tepee "by cleaving their heads with axes."

The soldiers made their way back to Fort Bascom very slowly on account of the poor condition of their horses. These had had little if any feed. There had been no time to graze. Leading their mounts, the soldiers limped back to the fort by December 10. They had had quite enough by then, although Carleton, in the manner of office-bound commanders, declared a victory. He complimented Carson and the command "for the handsome manner in which you all met so formidable an enemy and defeated him." Carson biographer and historian Harvey L. Carter also pronounced the day a victory. In fact, the Plains warriors, certainly in the sense of having driven the enemy from the field, won the day. But they were also alerted that they no longer had a sanctuary. In terms of the losses to both sides, the reports vary substantially. Probably the soldiers suffered fewer losses than the Plains warriors, but no one really knows.

Adobe Walls was Carson's last pitched battle with Indian people. Later, as an old soldier going over memories of past fights, he admitted to his friend George Bent that he'd gotten "whipped" that day. Bent complimented him and the Ute scouts, however, for effective action in a bad situation. "But for the coolness and skill of Carson and his Indian scouts the retreat would have become a rout and few would have escaped," said Bent. Others appreciated Carson's experience and his sense of responsibility to his command. "He was responsible for the lives of some four hundred men," Dunlay wrote, "and he had no intention of being a 'damned fool,' whatever younger, less experienced men might think of him." One interesting opinion was that of Senator James Doolittle, chair of the congressional joint special committee that investigated "Indian affairs" in the West in the summer of 1865. Talking of "these wars that some general gets up on his own hook," he mentioned Carson at Adobe Walls. Kit Carson, Doolittle said, "was beaten last winter in his expedition gotten up by Carleton against the Comanches."

What came afterward for Carson, insofar as his public life is concerned, were chiefly administrative and diplomatic duties. After the battle at Adobe Walls, he remained in military service until the New Mexico volunteers were disbanded in the fall of 1867. Carleton apparently had asked him to stay on as long as he himself commanded the army's Department of New Mexico, and Kit had agreed. "It gratifies me to learn that you will not leave the service while I remain here," Carleton had written him on January 30, 1864. "A great deal of my good fortune in Indian matters here—in fact nearly all with reference to Navajoes, Mescalero Apaches, and Kiowas—is due to you." Carleton's regard was so high that he recommended Carson for a brevet brigadier general-ship of volunteers. Carson received the rank in March 1865. Though their backgrounds, personalities, and training were altogether different, he and Carleton had worked fairly well together as a kind of an "odd couple." Now continually in pain, Carson had tried to leave military service several times, but Carleton time after time had refused his request to re-sign. And there is another very important factor in Carson's staying in service. He had to make a living for a large and growing family. He was supporting a wife and six children. He could not go back to trapping and hunting. Those were a young man's jobs. Besides, the market was dead. The beaver were long gone, and soon the buffalo, in their great herds, would be very nearly extinct.

After his return to Fort Bascom in December 1864, Carson spent time at home in Taos. He and Josefa enjoyed the holi-days with their children and friends. By the next May, how-ever, Carleton called him out again. Kiowas and Comanches, seeking revenge for what had happened at Adobe Walls and encouraged by having driven the soldiers off, were raiding along the Cimarron Cutoff. The army had been running bi-weekly military escorts between Fort Union and Fort Larned, Kansas, to protect travelers and to keep the Santa Fe Trail open. "Sometimes wagon trains were forced to wait several weeks at the forts for military escort," recalled Marian Rus-sell, the wife of Lt. Richard D. Russell. Costly of manpower, horseflesh, and everyone's time, these long-distance escorts did nothing to solve the larger problem. The better solution might be a post located between Fort Union and Fort Larned on the cutoff. To be named Camp Nichols, it would be lo-cated about 130 miles east of Fort Union. Carleton put Car-son in charge of the new post. "Upon duty at that point you will be able to have a talk with [the] chiefs of the [Southern] Cheyennes, Kiowas, and Comanches, and impress them with the folly of continuing their bad course," he wrote Carson on May 4, 1865.

Lieutenant Russell and his wife, Marian, were stationed at Camp Nichols during the summer of 1865. Marian's *Land of Enchantment: Memoirs of Marian Russell along the Santa Fe Trail* opens a window onto daily events at the camp, a typical outlying border post of the day. Toward women, the officers and soldiers were courtly. While she and her husband were stationed at Fort Union, the soldier boys had given Marian their pay to keep for them. Colonel Carson himself had ridden over from Camp Nichols to Fort Union with a military escort to accompany her back to Nichols when the new post was considered safe enough that wives could be present. Although already quite a horsewoman, Marian took riding lessons from that hard-nosed old line officer, Maj. Albert H. Pfeiffer, who was also stationed at Nichols. Besides the soldiers, the camp "boasted ten Indian scouts, two Indian squaws, and two Mexican laundresses," Marian recalled. Each soldier paid a dollar a month for his laundry. On hot summer afternoons she watched Carson lying on his cot in his tent with the sides rolled up to gather the prairie breeze while he studied the horizons through field glasses. The scouts, mostly Carson's friendly Utes or Jicarillas, left camp every morning and returned in the evening. Laundresses, the wives of Hispano soldiers, "pound dirt out of the soldiers clothing on the bank of the little Carrizo" while "the squaws tan buckskin," Marian wrote.

When Carson was called in again, this time to testify to the congressional joint special committee (called the "Doolittle Commission"), he came over to Marian's tent to say good-bye. He had once told her, "I promised your mother I would look out for you, Marian." Now, "leading his big black horse by the bridle," she wrote, he mounted and rode away to the west, saying, "Now remember the Injuns will git ye if you don't watch out." Marian had recently noticed a "frown" about his face and a suggestion of what she called an "infinite capacity for tenderness" in his eyes. This may well have been the result of the pain he increasingly felt. He had recently written, "The state of my health warns me that I can no longer render my country efficient service."

Years before, Marian Russell and her mother had known Carson when they lived in Santa Fe. Marian was a schoolgirl then. She had occasionally seen him on the street while she walked home from Catholic school. He had called her, she remembered, "Little Maid Marian." One evening when she met him on the street, "he shifted his hat to the back of his head and tried to engage me in conversation," she wrote. "I exchanged a few, simple, shy words with him. I remember that he said, with a glance at my books and my uniform, 'Them nuns do a heap sight of good in this god-forsaken country.'" Marian also knew Carson's "girl wife" Josefa. She described her as "a lovely Mexican girl with heavy braids of dark hair." According to Marian, Carson called Josefa "Little Jo."

Carson regularly wrote home to Josefa while he was away on army duty. Though most of these letters are lost, one of them is noteworthy by way of suggesting the language he used with his wife and children. Dated October 10, 1862, from Mora near Fort Union, the letter addresses Josefa by the term of endearment, "Chepita." Carson dictated: "*Adorada Esposa . . .* Chepita do not worry about me because with God's help we shall see each other [again]. I charge you above all not to get weary of caring for my children and to give each one a little kiss in my name . . . begging God that I may return in good health to be with you until death . . . your husband who loves you and who wishes to see you more than to write to you. Christobal Carson."

Carson's affection for Josefa and their children did not mean, however, that he could not enjoy the company of other women. Those who mentioned him in writing seem to have found him quite charming. Eveline Alexander, the wife of Capt. A. J. Alexander, rode out with him to visit a Ute camp one day from Fort Garland while he was stationed there. She found him, she wrote, "a most interesting, original old fellow." Another army wife, Lydia Spencer Lane, recalled riding from Santa Fe to Fort Union with Colonel Carson and others. "To see the quiet, reticent man, you never would dream that he was the hero of so many romances," she wrote. "I believe he would rather have faced a whole tribe of hostile Indians than one woman, he was so diffident."

11

Just Another Call to Duty

After Carson said good-bye to Marian Russell at Camp Nichols, he rode back to Santa Fe, then home to Taos. There, in July 1865, he testified to members of the Doolittle Commission, who were in the West investigating tribal conditions and treatment of Indians by military and civil authorities. In traveling from Santa Fe to Denver, the members of this special congressional committee stayed over in Taos with Josefa and Kit. "Knowing him as a bear-hunter and Indian fighter," Senator Doolittle later said, "you can hardly imagine the impression which this most modest and unassuming man[,] with a voice almost feminine in accent and expression[,] made upon us." Carson entertained his guests with hunting stories until late one evening, then testified the next morning.

Now that the Civil War was over, the government could turn to the struggle with the western tribes. Matters had accelerated greatly during the war. Doolittle's committee had come to Colorado and New Mexico especially to get the facts regarding the Sand Creek Massacre: the murder of 160 or more men, women, and children of Black Kettle's band of Southern Cheyennes with Arapahos by Col. John M. Chivington and his Colorado volunteers in the winter of 1864 at Sand Creek on Colorado's eastern plains. Carson knew well several of the people involved in this slaughter. George Bent, his friend of many years, was staying in the Cheyenne camp

240

with his brother Charlie Bent and other family members at the time.

Both Carson and William Bent testified at length. Bent's testimony, given several weeks earlier, was read aloud to Carson before he answered questions. Both men offered practical advice based on years of personal experience with Plains people. Remaining generally consistent with his views on tribal conditions and treatment of Indians expressed earlier, Carson said he believed that tribes should be held to reservations "to protect" them from such "evils" of society as the liquor traders, and "from the reckless injustice of those outlaws of society thronging upon the border." The old way of life of the hunting tribes was simply out of the question because the West was so rapidly settling up. Allowed to go free, he thought, these hunting people would only "carry . . . fire and desolation to many a homestead in the West." He was sure, however, that the Jicarillas would object to any reservation whatever, "as they know nothing of planting, and when spoken to on the subject have invariably objected."

Both he and William Bent criticized Indian agents for their inexperience and for their general low quality. Both men understood that long familiarity with Indian people was a requirement to be an effective agent. Both agreed that reservations were essential. Carson would have these located with attention to the customs of their people so that tribes with incompatible ways of life or traditional conflicts were not placed close together. Both men believed, as Carson put it, that as for the present conflicts on the plains, "I think, as a general thing, the difficulties arise from aggressions on the part of the whites." Finally, when asked, both very strongly condemned Chivington's murderous actions at Sand Creek.

Greatly impressed with Carson's and Bent's comments, the committee quoted both men at length as expert witnesses in their final report. To their credit, they also condemned Chivington's massacre, widely considered an outrage in its own day. In the words of one staff member, the committee took enough testimony in Colorado to convince them that Chivington broke "the plighted faith of the government," that he was "a monster that should be loathed and shunned by every Christian man and woman." Even before taking testimony, Senator Doolittle had written Secretary of the Interior James Harlan on May 31 about "the treacherous, brutal, and cowardly butchery of the Cheyennes . . . in which the blame is on our side." Though the committee would recommend court-martial for him, Chivington had by then resigned from service and was beyond the reach of military courts. Most officers of the regular army, federal officials, and thoughtful Americans considered the Sand Creek massacre a disgrace to the entire nation.

Carson and William Bent also said they believed the army was better qualified to handle the tribes than was the Interior Department's Office of Indian Affairs. After serving through months of standoff between General Carleton and Dr. Michael Steck over this very point, Carson remained loyal to the army. It was the only major point of difference he had with Senator Doolittle's commission, which finally recommended Interior in its report. Interior eventually won this bureaucratic battle with the army, but the differences of opinion remained. As one writer put it, "Soldiers believed that military control would ensure honesty and consistency," while "humanitarian reformers and, of course, [Interior] believed that the Army only wanted control of the Indians so that its use of violence could be unrestrained."

In any event, severe reduction of troops at the end of the Civil War caused hardship in the army's operations with the tribes. The government sliced its troop numbers back as if officials weren't aware that another kind of war was being fought on the plains. Meanwhile, greatly increased traffic by settlers, cowmen, farmers, and miners raised more trouble, especially along east-west trails like the Smoky Hill River route across Kansas to Denver. By interfering with buffalo migrations, this traffic upset the hunting needs of the Plains people. And, as the influence of federal civil officials began to outweigh that of the army's generals, thoughtful Americans, especially in the East, more and more sympathized with the plight of the Plains tribes. Senator Doolittle himself, especially after hearing Bent and Carson out, supported the efforts of civil officials like Indian agent Jesse Leavenworth, who was trying to arrange a general peace council with the Southern Plains tribes. The senator was all the more supportive of Leavenworth's plan after he learned that Bent and Carson believed they could make peace with the tribes south of the Arkansas River. Meanwhile, military operations south of the Arkansas were scaled back and then canceled altogether.

Jesse Leavenworth was an 1830 West Point graduate and the son of Gen. Henry Leavenworth. Working with other civil officials, he planned an October council on the Little Arkansas River not far from its junction with the Arkansas at the site of present-day Wichita, Kansas. Using the newly installed telegraph line, Senator Doolittle wired the secretaries of war and state from Denver to recommend that Bent and Carson be sent, without military interference, to try to make a general peace at this council. Gen. John H. Pope, who knew Carson's work from having served in New Mexico from 1851 until 1853 and who was currently chief of the army's Division of the Missouri, himself requested that Carson and Bent appear at the council. In his report to Gen. Ulysses S. Grant from St. Louis on August 1, 1865, General Pope explained the reasons for the wars with the tribes as he understood these reasons, and he described the hard conditions under which the Plains people were living. He then suggested to Grant what he called a reversal of "Indian policy." Thus a way was opened for the shift of control of "Indian affairs" from the army to the Department of the Interior.

And so the grand council came about. In August Leavenworth and others arranged a truce so that plans could be made. General Carleton placed Carson on detached service:

"Special service upon the Plains for the purpose of seeing if the Comanches, Kioways [*sic*], and other Indians living on, and south of the Arkansas River, cannot be induced to stop their acts of hostility," as Carleton described it. Though disagreeing personally with the peace plan, Carleton believed that Carson and William Bent were ideally suited to "smoke with Indians." Carson then went to Fort Lyon to confer with Bent, who lived close by. Brought together again by these events, these two key figures throughout several eras in the mountains and on the plains must have had a rich visit talking over old times. Asa F. Middaugh, interviewed in Denver in 1903, recalled being present when Carson and his Indian companions rode up to Bent's ranch on the Purgatory near its junction with the Arkansas River across from Fort Lyon. "Bill Bent pulled Kit off his horse and they hugged and kissed like a couple of children," Middaugh said.

From Fort Lyon, Carson traveled to Fort Riley, Kansas, by army ambulance with an escort of six soldiers, wagons, teamsters, and a cook. There he talked with Gen. John B. Sanborn, head of the peace commission, who had met with the chiefs earlier at a truce arranged by Leavenworth. Besides Sanborn, Carson, and William Bent, the commissioners included Jesse Leavenworth, Thomas Murphy, and James Steele, of Indian Affairs. The other commissioner was Gen. William S. Harney, an old plains hand, an athlete with "luxuriant" snow-white hair, who stood six feet four "in his moccasins." Some wag remarked of Harney, "His temperament was revealed in a large vocabulary of expletives upon which he drew liberally at the slightest provocation."

Lasting from October 14 to 18, the council resulted in the signing of the Treaty of the Little Arkansas. Chiefs present included the great names of the Southern Plains: Satanta, Lone Wolf, and Satank of the Kiowas; Ten Bears, Buffalo Hump, and Horse Back of the Comanches; Heap of Bears and Little Raven of the Southern Arapahos; and Seven Bulls and Black Kettle of the Cheyennes. Most of Black Kettle's people, suffering from the Sand Creek atrocity, stayed north of the Platte and refused to participate. Present as interpreter for the Kiowas was Jesse Chisholm, the famous southern plains trader for whom the Chisholm Trail was named.

Although all sides seemed to want peace, little came of the work of this august and colorful gathering for two reasons. First, the chiefs who signed the treaties could not speak for tribal members not present. Second, the government men wanted to locate the reservations where land, as it would turn out, had become unavailable because settlers and profiteers had already rushed in. Thus plans were doomed even before the smoking and talking began. Except for the talking itself, which may in fact be the best that can result from such meetings, "peace was restored to the plains [only] for the time being," as James Mead put it. If it is true that talking together has value in itself, then much of value did occur, for there was indeed much talking over, and "smoking through," of old hunts and old battles, of buffalo killed, ponies stolen, and scalps taken. Thus old enemies became friends, and old friendships were renewed.

James Mead, a hunter and trader in that part of the country, attended the talks to represent the Wichita Indians, whose agent was ill at the time. Years later Mead recalled the scenes and participants. "At that time the most dreaded warrior on the plains, Satanta[,] was a perfect specimen of manhood, both mentally and physically," he recalled. "His brawny breast was covered with scars, mementos of many a battle and adventure." Mead sketched in the look of the place: "At that treaty about three thousand Indians camped along the river on either side, as did the one or two companies of soldiers who were present," he wrote. "The Wichita, Waco, Caddo, Ioni, Tawakoni, Kechi, and other Indians, some 1500 in number, were living here at the time and were scattered along down the river to the junction where Wichita now stands. They had cultivated extensive gardens and had scaffolds covered with sliced pumpkins, beans, and corn drying for winter use, with plenty of melons in their gardens, which were a feast to visiting brethren."

Mead also left a detailed portrait of Carson at this point in his life. "I found him to be quite a different man from what he is depicted in dime novels," Mead said. "He was short-legged, standing . . . about five feet five or six, stoutly built, with short arms, a round body, ruddy face, and red eyes with rays running from the pupils like the spokes in a wheel. His silky, flaxen hair reached almost to his shoulders. He was a man of fierce, determined countenance. With a kind, reticent, and unassuming disposition, he combined the courage and tenacity of a bulldog. He had nothing to say about himself, though occasionally he might be drawn out by some question. He was bluff, but very gentlemanly in his conversation and manner, with nothing of the border bravado about him. His prominent characteristics seemed to be utter fearlessness, infallible judgment, and instant decision and action."

Perhaps a more telling point is how little Carson seemed to rest. He and Mead bunked in the same tent "and occasionally took a nip from the same bottle, though neither of us drank habitually," Mead wrote. "[Carson] seemed to be awake at all times of the night; if a horse got loose or anything occurred during the night he seemed to know all about it as though he had been standing guard." When Mead asked him "about some of his adventures of former years, of which I had read in the papers," Carson replied, "Some of these newspaper fellows know a damn sight more about my affairs than I do." Then, as ever self-effacing, he told the story of the night when he was a young man first headed out to Santa Fe in 1826, when his party was camped at Pawnee Rock. He took a shot in the direction of the "Indians" who "rode over us in the dark, yelling to stampede our stock," but discovered the next morning that all he had done was shoot his best mule.

Leaving the treaty grounds early, Carson and Bent went on to St. Louis to report the proceedings to General Pope. When he returned to New Mexico, Carson was briefly placed in command at Fort Union. While there, he received good news. In March 1865 President Lincoln had ordered him breveted a brigadier general for exceptional service with the New Mexico volunteers. The brevet, awarded in recognition of an officer's distinguished service, was, unfortunately, honorary only. There was no extra pay, no "benefits." Kit was now a "general" in name only. He even went on wearing a colonel's uniform and insignia. But of course he was pleased. On January 2, 1866, he dictated stiffly a letter to the secretary of war: "[Though] unsolicited by me, I accept [the brevet] with grateful pleasure." And he added that he considered this an acknowledgement of "the exertions of the New Mexico Volunteers." Thereafter, strangers felt compelled to call him "General, Sir." Or, if they were old compadres of camp and trail, they spoke of him within his hearing as "the Jinral," largely to make fun at his expense. One time when someone forgot and called him "Colonel," then apologized, Kit said, "Oh call me Kit at once, and be done with it!"

From Fort Union, General Carleton soon transferred Carson to Fort Garland, an assignment that truly seemed to utilize his experience. Built in 1858 near the mouth of La Veta Pass along the eastern edge of the San Luis Valley in Colorado, Fort Garland stood in the heart of Ute country. After the Civil War, rapid growth of settling, mining, and ranching in south-central Colorado and northern New Mexico pushed the Utes off their land. Cattle and sheep replaced game animals. Short of deer, antelope, and buffalo, Ute hunters killed cattle, drove off flocks of sheep, and raided settlements. Settlers, believing them "mere savages," always retaliated. It was a situation ready-made for Carson's long experience of such things, and for his diplomatic skills. Carleton thought him indispensable, although in truth Carson could do little more than try to plug the dam against a tide of change, in the end without success. Kit knew this as a fact, and he was not happy about it. It may seem easy to look at these last duty years at Fort Garland as Carson's years of ease. They were not!

At last, however, Josefa and the children could live with him. He could visit daily with the Ute people, who were his friends. They called him "Kitty" or just plain "Kit." Colonel Alexander's wife, Evy, and others who saw him at work here left that kind of picture in letters and diaries. Mrs. Alexander, evidently a superb horsewoman who undoubtedly rode sidesaddle, a mastership as well as a very dangerous seat on even the most quiet horse, often accompanied him on his rides. She recalled a day when, "instead of the sullen, stolid appearance I had always noticed . . . before, the [Utes'] faces brightened with smiles as they held out their hands to him with . . . 'Como le va?' or the Indian 'Hough!' He shook hands with one old squaw who seemed right pleased. . . . He told me that . . . on his last campaign against the Navajos . . . he was accompanied by fifty Utes, and this old squaw went with them all the way." Army surgeon George Gwyther wrote, "At [Fort] Garland, Carson kept open house, exercising the most unbounded hospitality to all visitors and passers-by, who were often sufficiently numerous, and these . . . included the Ute Indians."

By now General Sherman had replaced Pope in charge of the army's Division of the Missouri. At Fort Garland on an inspection tour with Gen. James F. Rusling in September 1866, Sherman watched Kit's children play happily about the fort. Years later he wrote to Carson's early biographer Edward S. Ellis that Kit's "half a dozen children, boys and girls [were] as wild and untrained as a brood of Mexican mustangs. One day these children ran through the room . . . half clad and boisterous." Thereupon Sherman asked Kit whether he planned to educate them, and Kit revealed a worry heavy on his heart. "That is a source of great anxiety," he said. "I have never had the advantage of schools, and now that I am getting old and infirm, I fear that I have not done right by my children." This question was to worry him until his last day. Sherman and Rusling both noticed what people who knew Kit called his "integrity." Sherman exclaimed to Rusling one day: "His integrity is simply perfect. The redskins know it, and would trust Kit any day before they would us, or the President either!"

General Rusling wrote biographer Ellis that Carson had explained to him the Ute side of their miserable situation: losing their hunting grounds and being forced to live on a reservation. Carson told Rusling more than once that white aggression against the Indians caused all the trouble, even that "Indians never commit outrages unless they are first provoked to them by the borderers, and that many of the peculiar and special atrocities with which they are charged are only their imitation of the bad acts of wicked white men." Rusling did not repeat in writing Carson's special words for Chivington and the Sand Creek massacre. Without any doubt they were much too raw for an eastern audience.

Rusling could see that Carson was aging. "From what I had read about him, I had expected to see a small, wiry man, weather-beaten and reticent," he said. "But [I] found him to be a medium-sized, rather stoutish, and quite talkative person instead. His hair was already well-silvered, . . . his face full and florid." Though he told Rusling that he had given up drinking, Carson smoked continually. In his book *Across America*, Rusling later described two councils with the Utes. At both of these Carson interpreted, translating into Spanish "with profuse pantomime, after the Indian fashion." So fluent was he that, "in talking, I observed, . . . he frequently hesitated for the right English word; but when speaking" Spanish or "Indian" he was "as fluent as a native." Both chiefs Ouray and Ancotash rode in for one of these councils. Ouray rode "a bright little bay, that would have taken a first-class premium almost anywhere." The "poor squaws . . . freighted with their papooses" were there too.

After the commissioners and the head chiefs sat down on blankets spread "on a sloping lawn on the banks of the Rio Grande," the warriors and "young chiefs" sat in a circle around them. "Beyond these still were the women and children." At the first council, Sherman appeared. Speaking with the language of children, both Sherman and the commissioner himself tried to get the Utes to accept a reservation. Both chiefs declined the offer. Ouray, a Tabeguache, and Ancotash, a Moache, argued that, one, they couldn't control their young men, and two, if they took up reservation life while their longtime enemies the Cheyennes and Comanches continued roaming the plains, they themselves would simply become targets. "[If] Utes settle down; then Comanches come and kill," said Ouray. "Tell Great Father [that] Cheyennes and Comanches go on Reservation *first*; then Utes will. But Comanches first." Rusling had to admit, "There was a deal of good common sense in it, too—the instinct of self preservation—and the governor [A. A. Cummings of Colorado] could not help admitting this, much as he desired to enforce the views of the Government." That was that. "Ouray has spoken!" said the chief when he was done. "And there the matter ended," wrote the general.

Carson's reports and letters during the fall of 1866 reveal his fear that war with the mountain tribes was imminent. One incident suggests good reason for fear. It also reveals the tension that afflicted Kit at the time. Years later, his son, Kit, Jr., told an interviewer that his father once gave a banquet at Fort Garland for a band of Moaches who had raided and killed some settlers, perhaps near Trinidad, or near the mouth of the Purgatory. Evidently Kit wanted to feast and parley with the Moaches rather than punish them. They would have taken punishment as retribution. Then they'd have had to get *theirs*, and ongoing warfare would have been the result.

Kit, Jr.'s story involved his sister Teresina. About twelve years old at the time, she had come up from Taos to Fort Garland to visit. Making herself useful serving food to the Moache guests, she noticed a Moache man wearing a pair of woman's shoes. When she asked him where he had gotten them, he told her he had pulled them off a white woman he'd killed. Horrified, Teresina refused to feed him. He slapped her with his quirt. Instantly, Carson "rushed at the fellow and would . . . perhaps have killed him . . . but mother seemed to realize what the result would be and begged father to let it go," Kit, Jr., recalled.

A letter of about this time explains Kit's situation, as well as his thinking and feeling. Men and supplies were short because of the severe cutbacks after the Civil War. "Yesterday all the hostile Indians came in under the guidance of [Ouray] and I made a treaty with them," Kit reported on October 11, 1866. "My action . . . has been influenced solely by a desire for the public good; we were totally unprepared for a campaign. Citizens . . . would be surprised and massacred and I could afford them no assistance." Furthermore, "anxiety and dread prevailed everywhere," he said. "Without sufficient troops or means of effecting successful war, I was forced into making terms with them, this may be only temporary, but it was the best I could do under the circumstances." Having long ago learned about the explosive probabilities of starting a fight without sufficient forces to support him, Kit had become very cautious. He had learned to know when compromise *might* avoid bloodshed and even defeat. By this point in his life, he understood that almost any way of solving a problem was better than shedding blood and losing lives.

Carson had been practicing a pragmatic style in explosive human situations for much of his later life. More recently he had even been thinking about another way of "justice" as it *might have been practiced,* but mostly *was not* on the borders he had known. What he had seen from other men and sometimes exercised himself was not true justice, but justice as quick and violent retribution. For him, the new way of thinking probably began during his years as the Ute agent in Taos, very likely even earlier. He had suggested several new ideas in a rambling letter to Capt. Benjamin C. Cutler from Fort Riley in September 1865 as he stopped over there on his way to the Treaty of the Little Arkansas. It is as if the man of action was becoming an abstract thinker, a man questioning old assumptions. He was growing intellectually. While, as always, the clerk turned Kit's mountains and plains vernacular into the acceptable English of the day, the thoughts are Carson's.

"It has long been the practice to hold whole nations responsible for the bad actions of a single Indian, or a small party," he said. "The wrong[,] if not criminality of this, must be apparent." All sides had practiced such injustices on the borders Kit had known. Now he was suggesting, and willing, if possible, to follow a better way, to practice a different principle of human justice: hold the *individual, not the whole nation* responsible for a man's violent acts. During the gold rush to California, Kit added, "ruthless outlaws" without doubt had "shot down" many Indian people "in cold blood." Such outlaws, he hints in this letter, should have been tried in court for their acts, and might have been had it not been for what he called "the lawless state of society." That is, the absence of a legal system and courts had put trial of the outlaw out of the question.

And he continued, generalizing the principle further. "The Indians are entitled to at least the same consideration . . . [as] their more civilized neighbors in determining the responsibility to be attached to the nation for the criminal acts of an irresponsible savage." Having at times in the past argued for and even performed "chastisement" of entire tribes for the acts of one or of a few, Carson could now understand and admit that such treatment was not only wrong, but very limited in producing peaceful solutions to conflict. By now he understood that punishing the whole tribe for one man's crime was hardly the practice of true justice, and that getting revenge perpetuated the same. He had learned, as many in his time and place had not, that settling scores with an entire tribe for what one, or even a few Indians had done, only promised that old scores would be "settled" by violence time after time after time.

This new mode of thinking was a long way from the dangerous notion of "the only good Indian is a dead one" that Kit's Scots-Irish border culture had approved in Missouri and in Kentucky, and that he had seen so often practiced in the mountains and on the plains. It may be added that the fervent sense of duty that had driven him all his life, that was so strong in his ancestors' devotion to family and to clan, was now asserting itself in new ways. Kit's idea of *his* community, the one to which *he* was responsible, had been greatly broadened to include a sense of responsibility to people of other cultures, and other ethnic groups—very clearly to American Indian people.

He could also understand the opposite, the possible wrong, when, for example, the government held *one* particular chief responsible for the violent actions of *all* or a number of the individuals of a tribe. This kind of situation often resulted because the Plains cultures had such "open" structures of authority. Who was actually in charge, who was truly responsible, was often a very real question in the Plains understanding of things. The English system of civil justice with its written laws and its established structure of judges and juries was in sharp contrast, as was the army's system of military justice. You could find the particular person responsible by trying him within the system, then sentence him to punishment if he were found guilty, and set him free if he were not. As Kit put the matter in the letter to Cutler, "How absurd to presume, that the nominal Chieftain of a band of wild nomads, should possess more power to seize and punish, or turn over to us for punishment [thus be responsible for] all [the] turbulent spirits of his tribe, who . . . commit some act of depredation along the road." Carson understood, as few did, that very often a chief lacked the authority or the power to control, thus to answer for, young men who were trying to earn their manhood in a war culture, or who were pushed to violent acts in order to feed themselves and their families. Was it right to hold an individual chief responsible for the violent acts of men belonging to his tribe who were not under his authority or control?

By early 1867, because the New Mexico volunteers were soon to be disbanded, Carson had to think about his future.

Probably his last official army duty was a trip to Lucien Maxwell's home at Cimarron to recruit Indian scouts for army service. In August Col. George Getty, who had now replaced Carleton, ordered Carson out on this assignment. Hiring scouts was partly a way to keep young Indians busy in what was, for them, an especially difficult time. Paying the young men for a kind of work they could do well and supplying their families with rations might hopefully reduce their need to kill livestock. In spite of his constant physical pain, this trip must have been a pleasure for Kit. Not only was he doing what he did best—working with Plains people in languages they both understood—it was also the chance to visit his old friend Lucien. The two had traveled and worked together since they were hardly more than boys.

Col. Henry Inman, who visited Maxwell's ranch about this time, described the scene with Carson, Maxwell, and several Ute chiefs caught up in conversation. "I have sat there," he wrote, "when the great room was lighted only by the cheerful blaze of the crackling logs roaring up the huge throats of its two fireplaces . . . watching Maxwell, Kit Carson, and half a dozen chiefs silently [share] ideas in the . . . sign language. . . . But not a sound had been uttered during the . . . hours, save an occasional grunt of satisfaction . . . [from] the Indians, or when we white men exchanged a sentence."

That fall, the fall of 1867, Kit's job came to its end. With his old "First Regiment" of volunteers he had seen heavy service in the field since 1861 when the Civil War began. He now had to stare at his financial situation and the plight of his large family. Without army pay, he had no dependable earnings, for an officer of volunteers received no retirement income. Josefa, who had already had seven children, would soon have another. And Kit would have to provide somehow. He was in bad health, had complained of chest pain as well as the pain in his legs for several years. He had always literally soldiered on. For him, soldiering on would soon be out of the question.

In November he went down to Santa Fe to receive his formal separation from service. Almost for the first time since March 1854, when he first became the Ute agent, Kit was out of a job.

He went looking for work. There seemed to be several possibilities. There was talk of separating the office of the superintendent of Indian affairs from the governor's office in Colorado. Kit applied for the job, but Colorado's Gov. Alexander C. Hunt already held the job ex officio. He also wrote Senator Lafayette Foster, a former member of the Doolittle Commission, a man who had enjoyed his hospitality in Taos. He asked Foster to recommend him as the sutler, the post trader, at Fort Garland. By then, however, a sutlership was out of the question because of a recent law that sutlers must have no military connections. Kit also experimented with mining. Marc Simmons points out that while at Fort Union on May 23, 1866, he threw in with nine others to register the "Kit Carson Mining Company" to prospect "a copper deposit not far from the garrison." Nothing more is known of this venture. A territorial survey by the U.S.G.S. in 1867 states that Carson with others in 1865 and 1866 prospected and took up claims in the San Juan Mountains. But that venture apparently came to nothing either. Finally, Kit hoped for reappointment as U.S. Indian agent at Taos, his old job. By then, however, another man held it and had no intention of quitting.

Kit did make one last trip at the government's request. It was another of those jobs with many thanks, but no pay. In November 1867, Indian Affairs planned to send a delegation of Ute chiefs to Washington. The hope was that the Utes could be induced to sign a treaty ceding most of their land to the government and accepting in return a reservation on the western slope of Colorado. Kit's services were needed.

He was sick, though, and had already seen a doctor. After receiving his discharge from the volunteers, he and Josefa had moved their family from Taos over to a new settlement called Boggsville on the Purgatory River southwest of Fort

Lyon, Colorado. Here they could live close to where Kit's friend Tom Boggs was building a place of his own on land he and his wife, Rumalda (Josefa's niece and close friend), had acquired from Ceran St. Vrain. Apparently Kit hoped to build his own house on a river plot he had bought from St. Vrain earlier. Until he got that going, he and Josefa were welcome to live in a small apartment Tom owned in Boggsville.

Every true countryman recognizes Kit and Josefa's dream. Tend a house garden. Keep a couple dozen hens, good layers. Milk a cow. Plant a few apple and apricot trees. Feed out a steer. Fatten a sow and pigs. Ride a good horse down to the post office once a week. Stop at the neighbor's to visit. Take life easy.

Having arrived at the Purgatory, the Carsons temporarily put up in Tom Boggs's little building. They also went to visit William Bent, who now spent his days at his ranch nearby. By good fortune, Dr. Henry R. Tilton, the army's post surgeon at Fort Lyon, happened to be visiting Bent at the time Kit showed up. He and Carson immediately struck up a friendship. Dr. Tilton was an amateur trapper. He needed Kit's expert knowledge of fur bearing animals. Carson needed medical attention. The two made a trade good for both of them.

The friendship grew. Dr. Tilton recalled, "As I was a successful amateur trapper, he threw off all reserve, and greeted me with more than usual warmth, saying, 'the happiest days of my life were spent in trapping.' He gave me many practical hints on trapping and hunting." Then, however, came the hitch. "He was then complaining of a pain in his chest, the origin of which he attributed to a fall received in 1860," Dr. Tilton remembered.

Carson often went to Fort Lyon that winter for diversion and for medical attention. All the officers and men enjoyed his company. Dr. Tilton gave him a thorough medical exam. The diagnosis brought bad news. Kit had an aneurism of the aorta—it was enlarging, and it could burst at any time. He might be kept comfortable, but nothing whatever could be done to change the condition. He didn't have long to live. Dr. Tilton knew that much. He undoubtedly told Kit. Whether or not Kit told Josefa is unknown. Probably he kept quiet about it in order to ease the stress for her.

About this time came the government's call to go to Washington with the Ute delegation. The Carsons had just moved from their old home in Taos to Colorado. Josefa was expecting a baby. Kit was sick. A neighbor on the Purgatory later wrote biographer Edwin L. Sabin, "Carson's health at that time was very bad. Not being able to ride about, he spent most of his time keeping me company, my trading store being only a few feet away from our quarters." Josefa at thirty-nine years was showing the strain of a woman's life of that day. Dr. Tilton described her as "evidently having been a very handsome woman." In spite of all this, Kit chose to make the trip. His reasons are a mystery. Did he want one last trip across the plains? Did he want to visit the Frémonts and see old Missouri once more? Was he afraid of being stuck at home after a lifetime on the open road? Did he want to consult a doctor in the East? Or was it really, as Kit, Jr., said many years later, "just another call to duty"?

Whatever his reasons, he went. Good wife that she was, Josefa probably agreed. A visit to old haunts might help his health. Seeing an eastern doctor for his heart condition was a good idea. At least his expenses would be paid. In January 1868 Kit took the stage from Fort Lyon to Fort Hays, Kansas, where he boarded the Kansas Pacific Railroad to Kansas City, then went on to St. Louis. By February 2 he was in Washington to join the Ute delegation and the officials who shepherded them about. The chiefs and the officials had traveled as a party from Denver to Cheyenne by stage. From there they took the new train service through Omaha to Chicago. During the time the treaty was being talked about and "smoked through," Carson took time to visit other dignitaries and friends, including Generals Sheridan and Sherman. The Utes and the officials with them, twenty-one in all, got a special invitation to the White House where all of them, along with Carson, met President Johnson.

John C. Frémont came down from New York to Washington to see Kit. He was astonished at how much Kit's health had failed since their years together in California. Because the Utes were to go on to New York City to see the sights after they signed the treaty, Frémont probably suggested that Carson see Dr. Lewis Sayre, a famous surgeon in New York. Kit did visit Dr. Sayre after arriving in the city on March 15. The surgeon gave him no hope. Simply by resting, by avoiding excitement, and by staying off alcohol, he might put off death for a time. Hearing that bad news, Kit was very anxious to start for home.

One brief meeting in New York, seeing Jessie Frémont again, must have meant worlds to Carson. Jessie arranged their meeting at the home of a friend of hers who lived on Madison Square. She and Kit had last said good-bye in Washington twenty years before. Now she was appalled to see how much Kit had aged since then, how bad he looked. He was sick enough that he insisted there be no show of emotion between them. To prevent that, he cut the visit short. Jessie later wrote, "He was already stricken with death." She ordered flowers sent to him at the Metropolitan Hotel, where he and the Ute delegation were staying.

From New York, the delegation went on to Boston. They visited Bunker Hill and the State House, where they sat in on a legislative session. The governor greeted them. Asked to say a word before the legislature, Carson "was obliged to decline on account of his feeble health," the *Daily Journal* reported the next day. Before he left Boston, a local photographer, J. W. Black, took his photograph. This and the group photo made by Mathew Brady's studio in Washington were the last photographs taken of Carson.

Then he boarded the train for home. Daniel C. Oakes, one of the officials with the Utes, traveled with him. Their route took them to Chicago, Omaha, and Cheyenne. There they caught the stage to Denver. Having come down with a bad cold in Washington, Kit checked into a Denver hotel to rest. Each day respectful citizens gathered to wait outside. Just before leaving, Kit felt well enough to speak a few words to the crowd.

Then he and Oakes got into a wagon behind a team. With Kit lying down on a pad of blankets in the wagon bed, Oakes drove the team south to Pueblo. In an interview years later, Mrs. W. A. Bennett, Oakes's daughter, said that the two stopped over the first night south of Denver at the Bennett Ranch, eight miles out. "Carson was much distressed by severe coughing spells," she said, "and declined to sleep in the house, saying he would only keep everybody awake."

At Pueblo the two men stopped at a hotel for lunch, but Kit felt so bad by then that someone went for the doctor. When he got the call, Dr. Michael Beshoar hurried to the office. Carson and Oakes met him there within minutes. Kit said, "I can hardly breathe." The exam revealed the bulging aneurism. Dr. Beshoar told Kit that his heart was beating too rapidly, that the aneurism could burst at any time. He advised him to stay over at the hotel to rest, but Kit said no. By now he just wanted to make it home.

As he left the office, Dr. Beshoar gave Kit a bottle of cherry syrup that contained opium to ease his cough and tincture of veratrium to slow his heart rate. Kit paid the bill: three silver dollars. Then he and Oakes were off. Home was eighty-five miles from Pueblo down the Arkansas River. As they did these days wherever Kit Carson was known to be, a crowd of citizens gathered. He was already the most famous American in the West. He must have seemed much more real to the curious people who saw him in Pueblo than even Boone and Crockett did. After all, those two had belonged to an earlier West, the West of the Ohio Valley, and of the Upper South. To Colorado people, Kit Carson belonged to *their* West.

Before leaving Denver or Pueblo, Kit sent word to Josefa, either by express rider or possibly by landline telegraph, that he was on the way. When she received the message, she asked Tom Boggs to drive her up the Arkansas River to meet her husband on the road. On April 11, perhaps seven or eight miles west of Bent's Old Fort on the Arkansas, on the Santa Fe Trail near present day La Junta, husband and wife came together. No record has been found of their meeting, but it must have been intense, Josefa near childbirth, Kit near death. There were so many memories to share by then, years upon years of good days, and bad, spent together, and spent apart. Riding down the Arkansas in a buggy behind a familiar team, quiet horses with names like Maude and Old Baldy, going at an easy trot, harness leather creaking, Kit and Josefa in better times would have sat in front, Kit driving from the right side, as was the custom, Josefa beside him to his left. Tom Boggs drove now, alone in front, while Kit and Josefa sat in back, going home together. None of them would be together long.

Two days later on April 13, Josefa gave birth to a daughter they named Josefita, "Little Josefa." Though being home revived Kit's spirits and briefly seemed to improve his health, Josefa had trouble after the baby's birth. She lived on for a few days, growing thinner, weaker, her fever ever higher. On April 27 at 8 o'clock in the evening, she sat on a blanket on the dirt floor of their sleeping room, quietly combing thirteen-year-old Teresina's hair. She stopped. Caught her breath. Called out. "Cristóbal! *Ven acá!*"

Kit came to her from the next room. Took her in his arms. She spoke. "Cristóbal. *Estoy muy enferma.*" They were her last words. She was forty years old. Kit was fifty-eight years and four months.

The little community of friends and loved ones buried her the next day in a house garden nearby. Kit stood. Silent. Numb. Beside her grave. They had been married twenty-five years.

Kit's old friend George Bent was one of the first to talk to him. George and Judge R. M. Moore drove down the next day just to visit. Neither knew Josefa had died. "He was one of my father's best men in the good old days of prosperity,"

George recalled. "We talked with him for an hour about the good old days. Owing to bad health and the shock[,] he was in poor spirits. He had a fine race horse, which he asked me to buy as we were leaving. After paying for the horse, Judge Moore and I left for home."

Kit's youngest son, Charles, remembered much later, "That was a terrible time. Father was sick[,] and we children didn't know what would become of us. He just seemed to pine away after Mother died." Of Kit's condition, Dr. Tilton wrote, "Her sudden death had a very depressing effect upon him."

The very best that can be said for Kit afterward is that, for him, events moved fast. A week after Josefa's burial, he dictated a letter to Aloys Scheurich in Taos. Aloys was the husband of Teresina Bent, Ignacia Bent's daughter. Ignacia was Josefa's older sister and her closest friend. The two had experienced Charles Bent's murder together. Kit wanted Aloys to ask Ignacia to look after his children. "Please tell [her]," he said, "that there is nobody in the world who can take care of my children but her, and she must know that it would be the greatest of favors to me, if she would come and stay until I am healthier."

Within three days of receiving the request, Ignacia, Aloys, and Teresina had packed up and were on the road to Colorado. By the time they arrived at Carson's place on May 15, however, Dr. Tilton had moved him to Fort Lyon in an army ambulance. Hurry was essential because the spring rise of the Purgatory and the Arkansas rivers would soon make them too deep to cross. Leaving the two women with Kit's children at Carson's house, Aloys went on to Fort Lyon, where Kit asked him to stay over.

Dr. Tilton had moved Kit into his own house by then, a small stone building at one end of Fort Lyon's parade ground. There the doctor could keep watch of him. As he later described it, Kit's being there "enabled me to make his condition much more comfortable." Kit insisted on lying on a pile of buffalo robes and blankets on the floor. It seemed to him, he said, the only way he could relieve his continual

261

spasms of coughing. Dr. Tilton administered chloroform whenever Kit asked. He described Carson's condition thus: "His disease, aneurysm of the aorta, had progressed rapidly; and the tumor pressing on the pneumo-gastric nerves and trachea caused frequent spasms of the bronchial tubes which were exceedingly distressing."

The doctor read to Kit from the first biography, *The Life of Kit Carson: The Nestor of the Rocky Mountains.* Kit would have recognized the exaggerations in the book, and might have been amused, or angry, except that he was too sick to care. Meanwhile, Aloys Scheurich stayed nearby, while Tom Boggs, who had also come up to Fort Lyon, returned home. There he told Ignacia and Teresina that Kit had said he was too sick to see either them or his children. He was too distressed to think about what the children were going to do after he was gone.

Nonetheless, he soon sent word that he would like to see his oldest son, Billy, and his youngest boy, Charles. When they arrived for a short visit, Kit sent someone out to buy each boy a new hat. On the way home, little Charlie's hat blew off and spun away with the wind on the surface of the flooded Purgatory. Charlie remembered that lost hat, and his dad, all the rest of his life.

Late on an afternoon in May, Aloys and Dr. Tilton were resting near Kit in the sickroom. It would have been warm outside by then, the songbirds come back, the smell of prairie wildflowers in the wind, the windows open to catch the breeze, the linen curtains waving lightly. Aloys, whom Kit called "Compadre," was talking to him about something that hardly mattered.

Kit called out.

"I sprang to him," Dr. Tilton said later. "Seeing a gush of blood from his mouth [I] remarked, 'This is the last of the general.' I supported his forehead on my hand, while death speedily closed the scene."

Kit spoke one more time. His last words seem fitting. To both his companions, he said, "Doctor. Compadre. Adios!" It was exactly 4:25 in the afternoon, May 23, 1868.

Bibliographical Essay

Two essential biographical studies of Carson are recent: Marc Simmons, *Kit Carson and His Three Wives: A Family History* (Albuquerque: University of New Mexico Press, 2003); and Tom Dunlay, *Kit Carson and the Indians* (Lincoln: University of Nebraska Press, 2000). Harvey Lewis Carter, *"Dear Old Kit": The Historical Christopher Carson* (Norman: University of Oklahoma Press, 1968), is the best edition of Carson's 1856 biographical dictation to his clerk, John Mostin. Every student uses Edwin L. Sabin, *Kit Carson Days, 1808–1868*, rev. ed., 2 vols. (Lincoln: University of Nebraska Press, 1995), because it contains so much information and because Sabin interviewed many people who knew Kit. Thelma S. Guild and Harvey L. Carter, *Kit Carson: A Pattern for Heroes* (Lincoln: University of Nebraska Press, 1984), is probably the best of the older biographies, though the authors tend to romanticize Kit's life. M. Morgan Estergreen, *Kit Carson: A Portrait in Courage* (Norman: University of Oklahoma Press, 1962); and Bernice Blackwelder, *Great Westerner: The Story of Kit Carson* (Caldwell, Idaho: Caxton Printers, 1962), are readable but must be used with care for the authors admired Kit and perpetuated errors. A short book presenting opposing views of Kit's reputation is R. C. Gordon-McCutchan, ed., *Kit Carson: Indian Fighter or Indian Killer?* (Niwot: University Press of Colorado, 1996). Carson biographies by Noel Gerson and Stanley Vestal, a pseudonym for Walter S. Campbell, should be avoided.

To understand the culture of Kit's ancestors and other Britons in early America, see especially David Hackett Fischer, *Albion's Seed: Four British Folkways in America* (New York: Oxford University Press, 1989). Of Scots-Irish values in particular, most useful are Charles Knowles Bolton, *Scotch-Irish Pioneers in Ulster and America* (Baltimore: Genealogical Publishing Company, 1972); James G. Leyburn, *The Scotch-Irish: A Social History* (Chapel Hill: University of North Carolina Press, 1962); R. J. Dickson, *Ulster Emigration to Colonial America, 1718–1775*, repr. (Belfast: Ulster Historical Foundation, 1976); and the recent James Webb, *Born Fighting: How the Scots-Irish Shaped America* (New York: Broadway Books, 2004). Two other useful books are Bernard Bailyn, *Voyagers to the West: A Passage in the Peopling of America on the Eve of the Revolution* (New York: Alfred A. Knopf, 1986); and Alan Taylor, *American Colonies: The Settling of North America* (New York: Penguin Books, 2001). To understand the stern Protestantism that shaped Scots-Irish belief, see Edwin S. Gaustad and Leigh E. Schmidt, *The Religious History of America: The Heart of the American Story from Colonial Times to Today*, rev. ed. (San Francisco: Harper-Collins, 2002). Richard White, *The Middle Ground: Indians, Empires, and Republics in the Great Lakes Region, 1650–1815* (New York: Cambridge University Press, 1991), offers a seminal view of Indian-white relations.

For border history in the Ohio Valley, see Malcolm J. Rohrbough, *The Trans-Appalachian Frontier: People, Societies, and Institutions, 1775–1850* (New York: Oxford University Press, 1978); R. Douglas Hurt, *The Ohio Frontier: Crucible of the Old Northwest, 1720–1830* (Bloomington: Indiana University Press, 1996); Andrew R. L. Cayton, *Frontier Indiana* (Bloomington: Indiana University Press, 1996); and Thomas D.

Clark, *A History of Kentucky* (New York: Prentice-Hall, 1937). R. Carlisle Buley, *The Old Northwest Pioneer Period, 1815–1840*, 2 vols. (Indianapolis: Indiana Historical Society, 1950), for which Buley won the Pulitzer Prize, is encyclopedic. No single study contains more detail of daily life on the borders in the Ohio Valley.

A recent book that goes inside the troubled minds of border people is Elizabeth A. Perkins, *Border Life: Experience and Memory in the Revolutionary Ohio Valley* (Chapel Hill: University of North Carolina Press, 1998). Perkins's border people are flawed, thus real; they struggle to make sense of their lives; they are not the "conquerors" of the West as in the earlier triumphalist histories. Other important studies with fresh views of border life are Stephen Aron, *How the West Was Lost: The Transformation of Kentucky from Daniel Boone to Henry Clay* (Baltimore: Johns Hopkins University Press, 1996); John Mack Faragher, *Daniel Boone: The Life and Legend of an American Pioneer* (New York: Henry Holt and Company, 1992); R. Douglas Hurt, *Nathan Boone and the American Frontier* (Columbia: University of Missouri Press, 1998); and Stephen Aron, *American Confluence: The Missouri Frontier from Borderland to Border State* (Bloomington: Indiana University Press, 2006). For the early history of Missouri, the standard is William E. Foley, *A History of Missouri: Vol. I, 1673–1820* (Columbia: University of Missouri Press, 1971).

Editions of western journals, diaries, and letters are innumerable, and rich in detail. I have used Timothy Flint, *Recollections of the Last Ten Years* (Boston: Cummings, Hilliard, and Company, 1826); Henry Marie Brackenridge, *Views of Louisiana Together with a Journal of a Voyage Up the Missouri River, in 1811* (Pittsburgh: Cramer, Spear, and Eichbaum, 1814); Rufus Babcock, ed., *Forty Years of Pioneer Life: Memoir of John Mason Peck* (Carbondale: Southern Illinois University Press, 1965); and a gem of a book, John Francis McDermott, ed., *Travelers on the Western Frontier* (Urbana: University of Illinois Press, 1970). For the experience of children, see Elliott

West, *Growing Up with the Country: Childhood on the Far Western Frontier* (Albuquerque: University of New Mexico Press, 1989). For nineteenth-century scientists and explorers of the West, see William H. Goetzmann's, *Exploration and Empire: The Explorer and the Scientist in the Winning of the American West* (New York: Alfred A. Knopf, 1966), and *Army Exploration in the American West, 1803–1863* (New Haven: Yale University Press, 1959).

Essential for learning about the Santa Fe Trail are Stephen G. Hyslop, *Bound for Santa Fe: The Road to New Mexico and the American Conquest, 1806–1848* (Norman: University of Oklahoma Press, 2002); and David Dary, *The Santa Fe Trail: Its History, Legends, and Lore* (New York: Alfred A. Knopf, 2000). Other books used for understanding trade and travel on the Santa Fe Trail are Kate L. Gregg, ed., *The Road to Santa Fe: The Journal and Diaries of George Champlin Sibley* (Albuquerque: University of New Mexico Press, 1952); Josiah Gregg, *Commerce of the Prairies*, ed. by Max L. Moorhead, repr. (Norman: University of Oklahoma Press, 1954); Marian Russell, *Land of Enchantment: Memoirs of Marian Russell along the Santa Fe Trail* (Albuquerque: University of New Mexico Press, 1981); Jane Lenz Elder and David J. Weber, eds., *Trading in Santa Fe: John M. Kingsbury's Correspondence with James Josiah Webb, 1853–1861* (Dallas: Southern Methodist University Press, 1996); David Lavender, *Bent's Fort*, repr. (Lincoln: University of Nebraska Press, 1972); and Marc L. Gardner, *Wagons for the Santa Fe Trade: Wheeled Vehicles and their Makers, 1822–1880* (Albuquerque: University of New Mexico Press, 2000).

The literature of the fur trade is enormous, if somewhat outdated. I have used Hiram Martin Chittenden, *The American Fur Trade of the Far West*, 2 vols., repr. (Fairfield, N.J.: Augustus M. Kelley, 1976); appropriate chapters in LeRoy R. Hafen, *The Mountain Men and the Fur Trade of the Far West*, 10 vols. (Glendale, Calif.: Arthur H. Clark Co., 1965–72); Robert Glass Cleland, *This Reckless Breed of Men: The Trappers and Fur Traders of the Southwest* (New York: Alfred A. Knopf, 1963);

Richard Edward Oglesby, *Manuel Lisa and the Opening of the Missouri Fur Trade* (Norman: University of Oklahoma Press, 1963); David J. Weber, *The Taos Trappers: The Fur Trade in the Far Southwest, 1540–1846* (Norman: University of Oklahoma Press, 1971); John C. Ewers, *The Blackfeet: Raiders on the Northwestern Plains* (Norman: University of Oklahoma Press, 1958); and *Plains Indian History and Culture: Essays on Continuity and Change* (Norman: University of Oklahoma Press, 1997). William E. Foley and C. David Rice, *The First Chouteaus: River Barons of Early St. Louis* (Urbana: University of Illinois Press, 1983), covers the early days of this great fur trade family.

Biographies of mountain men, reports by travelers, and trappers' accounts depict the trapper's life, his views, and his language. See J. Cecil Alter, *Jim Bridger* (Norman: University of Oklahoma Press, 1962); Burton Harris, *John Colter: His Years in the Rockies*, repr. (Lincoln: University of Nebraska Press, 1993); and in my opinion the best biography of a mountain man to date, Bil Gilbert, *Westering Man: The Life of Joseph Walker* (New York: Atheneum, 1983). Two classic travelers' accounts are George F. Ruxton, *Life in the Far West Among the Indians and the Mountain Men, 1846–1847*, repr. (Glorieta, N.Mex.: Rio Grande Press, 1972); and Lewis H. Garrard, *Wah-To-Yah and the Taos Trail*, repr. (Palo Alto, Calif.: American West Publishing Co., 1968). Garrard offers details of the Taos massacre and the later trial. Also used were George R. Brooks, ed., *The Southwest Expedition of Jedediah S. Smith . . . 1826–1827* (Glendale, Calif.: Arthur H. Clark Co., 1977); and Reuben Gold Thwaites, ed., *The Personal Narrative of James Ohio Pattie of Kentucky* (Cleveland, Ohio: Arthur H. Clark Co., 1905). A recently published, very useful account is William R. Goulding, *California Odyssey: An Overland Journey on the Southern Trail*, ed. by Patricia A. Etter (Norman, Okla.: Arthur H. Clark Co., 2009).

For Bent's view of Carson's part in the battle with Crow horse thieves, the source is George E. Hyde, *Life of George Bent: Written from His Letters* (Norman: University of Oklahoma

Press, 1968). Henry Inman and William F. Cody, in *The Great Salt Lake Trail* (New York: Macmillan, 1898), describe Carson leading trappers in battles with the Blackfeet. James Hobbs, *Wild Life in the Far West, Personal Adventures as a Border Mountain Man*, repr. (Glorieta, N.Mex.: Rio Grande Press, 1969), offers information, though perhaps fabricated, on Adaline.

For Manifest Destiny, Frémont's explorations, and the "conquest" of New Mexico and California, as well as for understanding Carson himself, very useful are Robert M. Utley, *A Life Wild and Perilous: Mountain Men and the Paths to the Pacific* (New York: Henry Holt and Co., 1997); and David Roberts, *A Newer World: Kit Carson, John C. Frémont, and the Claiming of the West* (New York: Simon and Schuster, 2000). See also Daniel Walker Howe, *What Hath God Wrought: The Transformation of America, 1815–1848* (Oxford: Oxford University Press, 2007). For the Apaches Carson knew, see especially Edwin R. Sweeney, *Mangas Coloradas: Chief of the Chiricahua Apaches* (Norman: University of Oklahoma Press, 1998).

Much about the "conquest" of California remains unexplained. The best single book on the subject is Neal Harlow, *California Conquered: War and Peace on the Pacific, 1846–1850* (Berkeley: University of California Press, 1982). Hubert Howe Bancroft, *The Works of: History of California, Vol. V, 1846–1848*, and *California Pastoral, Vol. XXXIV, 1769–1848* (San Francisco: The History Co., 1886), offer information on participants in the action described in this biography. Other books used were Robert Glass Cleland, *The Cattle on a Thousand Hills, Southern California, 1850–1880* (San Marino, Calif.: The Huntington Library, 1969); R. H. Dana, Jr., *Two Years Before the Mast*, repr. (New York: P. F. Collier and Son, 1937); and Rev. Walter Colton, *Three Years in California* (Stanford, Calif.: Stanford University Press, 1949).

For Frémont's, and Carson's, part in the "conquest" of California, essential is Donald Jackson and Mary Lee Spence, eds., *The Expeditions of John Charles Frémont, Vol. I, Travels from 1838 to 1844*, and vol. 2, *The Bear Flag Revolt and the Court-Martial*

Bibliographical Essay

(Urbana: University of Illinois Press, 1970, 1973). These volumes contain Colonel Abert's written orders, Frémont's reports, and a great deal of additional information. Of several Frémont biographies, the best is Tom Chaffin, *Pathfinder: John Charles Frémont and the Course of American Empire* (New York: Hill and Wang, 2002). Also used were John Charles Frémont, *Memoirs of My Life*, repr. (New York: Cooper Square Press, 2001); Thomas Hart Benton, *Thirty Years View . . . from 1820 to 1850*, 2 vols. (New York: Appleton and Co., 1856); and Pamela Herr, *Jessie Benton Frémont* (Norman: University of Oklahoma Press, 1988). For Carson's longtime friendship with Maxwell, very useful is Lawrence R. Murphy, *Lucien Bonaparte Maxwell: Napoleon of the Southwest* (Norman: University of Oklahoma Press, 1983).

Carson's military career began in California with Frémont in 1846. Information on his trips to Washington with dispatches is scattered throughout Carter, ed., *"Dear Old Kit"*; Spence and Jackson, eds., *The Expeditions of John Charles Frémont*, vol. 2; Frémont, *Memoirs of My Life*; Harlow, *California Conquered*; Utley, *A Life Wild and Perilous*; Roberts, *A Newer World*; and Guild and Carter, *Kit Carson*. For information on Lt. Edward F. Beale and George D. Brewerton, see Gerald Thompson, *Edward F. Beale and the American West* (Albuquerque: University of New Mexico Press, 1983); and George Douglas Brewerton, *Overland with Kit Carson: A Narrative of the Old Spanish Trail in '48*, ed. by Stallo Vinton (New York: Coward-McCann, 1930). On Carson's 1842 trip to Missouri, essential is Lee Burke, "The Kit Carson–Ben Mills Story: Did Carson Really Buy Guns from Mills in Harrodsburg in 1842?" (*American Society of Arms Collectors Bulletin* 93; www.americansocietyofarmscollectors.org).

Other sources used for the army's and Carson's actions during this time are J. Patrick Hughes, *Fort Leavenworth: Gateway to the West* (Topeka: Kansas State Historical Society, 2000); William McKale and William D. Young, *Fort Riley: Citadel of the Frontier West* (Topeka: Kansas State Historical Society, 2000);

Bibliographical Essay

Leo E. Oliva, *Fort Union and the Frontier Army in the Southwest* (Santa Fe: National Park Service, Division of History, 1993); Howard Roberts Lamar, *The Far Southwest, 1846–1912: A Territorial History* (New Haven: Yale University Press, 1966); Dwight L. Clarke, *Stephen Watts Kearny: Soldier of the West* (Norman: University of Oklahoma Press, 1961); Dwight L. Clarke, ed., *The Original Journals of Henry Smith Turner: With Stephen Watts Kearny to New Mexico and California, 1846* (Norman: University of Oklahoma Press, 1966); Robert V. Hine and Savoie Lottinville, eds., *Soldier in the West: Letters of Theodore Talbot during His Services in California, Mexico, and Oregon, 1845–53* (Norman: University of Oklahoma Press, 1972); Lt. Col. W. H. Emory, *Notes of a Reconnoissance, from Fort Leavenworth . . . to San Diego, in California*, Ex. Doc. No. 41, U.S. 30th Congress, First Session (Washington: Wendell and Van Benthuysen, 1848); and "Journal of Capt. A. R. Johnston, First Dragoons," ibid., pp. 567–614.

For the army and the "Indian Wars" of Carson's later years, no book equals Robert M. Utley's *Frontiersmen in Blue: The United States Army and the Indian, 1848–1865* (New York: Macmillan, 1967). Other useful books are Robert W. Frazer, *Forts of the West: Military Forts and Presidios and Posts Commonly Called Forts West of the Mississippi River to 1898* (Norman: University of Oklahoma Press, 1965); Robert C. Ferris, series ed., *Soldier and Brave: Historic Places Associated with Indian Affairs and the Indian Wars in the Trans-Mississippi West* (Washington, D.C.: National Park Service, 1971); and Paul Andrew Hutton, ed., *Soldiers West: Biographies from the Military Frontier* (Lincoln: University of Nebraska Press, 1987). For the army mule, see Emmett M. Essin, *Shavetails and Bell Sharps: The History of the U.S. Army Mule* (Lincoln: University of Nebraska Press, 1997).

The American Indian side of the "Indian Wars" on the plains and in the mountains remains to be told in detail. Useful for this book were John D. McDermott, *A Guide to the Indian Wars of the West* (Lincoln: University of Nebraska Press,

1998); Ralph K. Andrist, *The Long Death: The Last Days of the Plains Indians* (New York: Collier Books, 1969); Stan Hoig, *The Sand Creek Massacre* (Norman: University of Oklahoma Press, 1961); Robert M. Utley and Wilcomb E. Washburn, *Indian Wars* (New York: Houghton-Mifflin, 2002); Elliott West, *The Contested Plains: Indians, Goldseekers, and the Rush to Colorado* (Lawrence: University Press of Kansas, 1998); and George Bird Grinnell, *The Fighting Cheyennes* (Norman: University of Oklahoma Press, 1956), and *The Cheyenne Indians: Their History and Ways of Life*, vols. I and II (Lincoln: University of Nebraska Press, 1972).

Carson's years as Indian agent occurred in a complicated and violent period. For this and related matters, useful was chapter 5, "Military and Civilian Policy," in Robert A. Trennert, Jr., *Alternative to Extinction: Federal Indian Policy and the Beginnings of the Reservation System, 1846–51* (Philadelphia: Temple University Press, 1975). Besides the biographical material already cited, other books useful for understanding this period are Janet Lecompte, *Pueblo, Hardscrabble, Greenhorn: Society on the High Plains, 1832–1856* (Norman: University of Oklahoma Press, 1978); Virginia McConnell Simmons, *The San Luis Valley: Land of the Six-Armed Cross*, 2nd ed. (Niwot: University Press of Colorado, 1999); David Meriwether, *My Life in the Mountains and on the Plains: The Newly Discovered Autobiography*, ed. by Robert A. Griffen (Norman: University of Oklahoma Press, 1965); Calvin Horn, *New Mexico's Troubled Years: The Story of the Early Territorial Governors* (Albuquerque: Horn and Wallace, 1963); Veronica E. Velarde Tiller, *The Jicarilla Apache Tribe: A History*, rev. ed. (Lincoln: University of Nebraska Press, 1992); and Virginia McConnell Simmons, *The Ute Indians of Utah, Colorado, and New Mexico* (Niwot: University Press of Colorado, 2000). Information on the later years of Kit's older brother Moses is found in James H. Tevis, *Arizona in the '50's* (Albuquerque: University of New Mexico Press, 1954). A remarkable background study is James F. Brooks, *Captives and Cousins: Slavery, Kinship, and Community in the Southwest Borderlands* (Chapel Hill: University of North Carolina Press, 2002).

For detail about and views of Mrs. White's murder, besides the Carson biographies cited earlier, see Donald Chaput, *François X. Aubrey: Trader, Trailmaker and Voyageur in the Southwest, 1846–1854* (Glendale, Calif.: Arthur H. Clark Co., 1975); and James F. Meline, *Ten Thousand Miles on Horseback* (Albuquerque: Horn and Wallace, 1966). Howard Louis Conard, *Uncle Dick Wootton: The Pioneer Frontiersman of the Rocky Mountain Region*, ed. by Milo Milton Quaife (Chicago: R. R. Donnelly and Sons Co., 1957), gives Wootton's information on the White murder. For the Maxwell Land Grant and material on Maxwell, Carson, the Beaubiens, and related matters, including the murder of Mrs. White, see María E. Montoya, *Translating Property: The Maxwell Land Grant and the Conflict over Land in the American West, 1840–1900* (Berkeley: University of California Press, 2002); and Jim Berry Pearson, *The Maxwell Land Grant* (Norman: University of Oklahoma Press, 1961).

From September 1861 until November 1867 Carson commanded volunteer soldiers during the Civil War and the Mescalero and Navajo campaigns. For information, useful are Donald S. Frazier, *Blood and Treasure: Confederate Empire in the Southwest* (College Station: Texas A&M University Press, 1995); William A. Keleher, *Turmoil in New Mexico, 1846–1868*, repr. (Albuquerque: University of New Mexico Press, 1982); John P. Wilson, *When the Texans Came: Missing Records from the Civil War in the Southwest, 1861–1862* (Albuquerque: University of New Mexico Press, 2001); John Taylor, *Bloody Valverde: A Civil War Battle on the Rio Grande, February 21, 1862* (Albuquerque: University of New Mexico Press, 1995); Don E. Alberts, *Rebels on the Rio Grande: The Civil War Journal of A. B. Peticolas* (Albuquerque: University of New Mexico Press, 1984); Marion Cox Grinstead, *Destiny at Valverde: The Life and Death of Alexander McRae* (Socorro, N.Mex.: Historical Society of New Mexico in association with the Socorro Historical Society, 1992); Jacqueline Dorgan Meketa, *Legacy of Honor: The*

Bibliographical Essay

Life of Rafael Chacón, a Nineteenth-Century New Mexican (Albuquerque: University of New Mexico Press, 1986); and Darlis A. Miller, *The California Column in New Mexico* (Albuquerque: University of New Mexico Press, 1982), and *Soldiers and Settlers: Military Supply in the Southwest, 1861–1885* (Albuquerque: University of New Mexico Press, 1989). For Carson's important part in the Mescalero campaign, besides sources cited, C. L. Sonnichsen's *The Mescalero Apaches* (Norman: University of Oklahoma Press, 1958) is very useful.

For Carson's part in the Navajo campaign, the best single source of documentary information remains Lawrence C. Kelly, *Navajo Roundup: Selected Correspondence of Kit Carson's Expedition Against the Navajo, 1863–1865* (Boulder, Colo.: Pruett Publishing Co., 1970). Two books offer Navajo views of this tragic affair. These are Broderick H. Johnson, ed., *Navajo Stories of the Long Walk Period*, repr. (Tsaile, Ariz.: Navajo Community College Press, 1973); and Tiana Bighorse, *Bighorse the Warrior*, ed. by Noël Bennett (Tucson: University of Arizona Press, 1990). Useful too are Charles Avery Amsden, *Navaho Weaving: Its Technic and History*, repr. (Glorieta, N.Mex.: Rio Grande Press, 1990); L. H. Bailey, *The Long Walk: A History of the Navajo Wars, 1846–68* (Pasadena, Calif.: Westernlore, 1978); Gerald Thompson, *The Army and the Navajo: The Bosque Redondo Reservation Experiment 1863–1868* (Tucson: University of Arizona Press, 1976); and Clifford L. Trafzer, *The Kit Carson Campaign: The Last Great Navajo War* (Norman: University of Oklahoma Press, 1982). An excellent primary source for the battle at Adobe Walls is George H. Pettis, *Kit Carson's Fight with the Comanche and Kiowa Indians* (Santa Fe: New Mexican Printing Company, 1908). See also Charles L. Kenner, *The Comanchero Frontier: A History of New Mexican–Plains Indian Relations* (Norman: University of Oklahoma Press, 1969). Excellent articles by Crawford R. Buell, Frank McNitt, and Andrew Wallace on the Mescaleros at Fort Stanton and the Navajo Long Walk appear in Albert H. Schroeder, ed., *The Changing Ways of Southwestern Indians: A Historic Perspective* (Glorieta,

273

N.Mex.: Rio Grande Press, 1973). Information on Colonel Carson and the peach orchards of Canyon de Chelly requires reading Stephen C. Jett, ed., "The Destruction of Navajo Orchards in 1864: Captain John Thompson's Report" (*Arizona and the West* 16, no. 4 [Winter 1974]: 365–78).

For Carson's last years at Camp Nichols, Fort Garland, and elsewhere I relied heavily on Marc Simmons, *Three Wives*; and Tom Dunlay, *Kit Carson and the Indians*. Also used, besides sources already cited, were Sandra L. Myres, ed., *Cavalry Wife: The Diary of Eveline M. Alexander, 1866–1867* (College Station: Texas A&M University Press, 1977); James R. Mead, *Hunting and Trading on the Great Plains, 1859–1875*, ed. by Schuyler Jones (Norman: University of Oklahoma Press, 1986); Edward S. Ellis, *The Life of Kit Carson*, repr. (Lake Wales, Fla.: Lost Classics, 1998); James F. Rusling, *Across America, or, the Great West and the Pacific Coast* (New York: Sheldon and Co., 1874); and Richard N. Ellis, *General Pope and U.S. Indian Policy* (Albuquerque: University of New Mexico Press, 1970). Clare V. McKanna, Jr., *Court-Martial of Apache Kid, Renegade of Renegades* (Lubbock: Texas Tech University Press, 2009), studies the challenge to Indian people of living trapped within their own, the army's, and the civil systems of law.

Indispensable reference works are Dan L. Thrapp, *Encyclopedia of Frontier Biography*, vols. I–III (Glendale, Calif.: Arthur H. Clark Co., 1988), and vol. IV, *Supplement* (Spokane: Arthur H. Clark Co., 1994); Ralph Emerson Twitchell, *The Leading Facts of New Mexican History*, vols. I and II, repr. (Albuquerque: Horn and Wallace, 1963); Howard R. Lamar, ed., *The Reader's Encyclopedia of the American West* (New York: Thomas Y. Crowell, 1977); and Lamar's revised *New Encyclopedia of the American West* (1998). One useful book offering information (and a questionable point of view) as yet uncited here is Henry Inman, *Stories of the Old Santa Fe Trail* (Kansas City: Ramsey, Millett, and Hudson, 1881).

Primary sources for a study such as this on Carson and his backgrounds are scattered across the country from the

Beinecke Library at Yale University and the National Archives in Washington to the Bancroft Library in Berkeley. Particularly rich are collections to be found in the Colorado Historical Society Archives, Denver; the Colorado Springs Pioneers Museum, Colorado Springs; the Missouri Historical Society Archives, St. Louis; the Howard B. Lee Library, Brigham Young University, Provo; and, in New Mexico, the Center for Southwest Research, University of New Mexico, Albuquerque; the Fray Angélico Chávez History Library, and the New Mexico State Records Center and Archives, Santa Fe; and the various collections on Carson in the Kit Carson Historic Museums, Southwest Research Center, Taos. I am indebted to Joy L. Poole and to the Yale Collection of Western Americana, Beinecke Rare Book and Manuscript Library, for the use of the Rowland Willard–Elizabeth S. Willard Papers.

Index

References to illustrations appear in italics.

Abert, James W., 130
Abert, John J. (colonel), 105, 107, 108, 117, 120, 147–48
Adobe Walls, 89, 178–79; Kiowa-Comanche campaign and, 232–34, 235, 236
Albuquerque, 216; First Infantry in, 207–209, 218
Alexander, A. J., 238
Alexander, Eveline (Evy), 238, 248
Allande, Pedro Maria, 41
Amick, Mrs. Leander, 95
Ancotash, 249, 250
Apaches, 53, 55–56, 164, 169–70, 177, 199, 210, 231, 232. *See also* Jicarillas; Mescalero campaign
Arapahos, 89, 104–105, 244
Arkansas River, 112, 147; winter camp on, 71–77
Armijo, Manuel, 101, 113, 114

Army of the West, *142*, 165–66; in California, 170–72; journey of, 168–70
Arny, W. F. N., 195
Asero, José, 60–61
Ayers, John, 207

Baca, Luis Maria C. de, 56
Bancroft, George, 149, 154
Barboncito, 223, 227
Barclay's Fort, 184
Baylor, John, 207, 209–10
Beale, Edward F., 85, 100, 172, 173, 175, 192
Beall, Benjamin Lloyd, 179
Bear Flag Revolt, *141*, 152–53, 161–62; dispatches about, 163–65
Beaubien, Maria de la Luz. *See* Maxwell, Maria de la Luz Beaubien
Beaubien, Narciso, 90, 101

277

Index

Index

Index

Waa-nibe, 82, 83–84, 85
Wakara (friendly Paiute chief), 177
Waldo, Lawrence, 90
Walker, Joe, 89, 130, 151, 152
Walker Lake, 150, 151
Walpole, Frederick, on Frémont in Monterey, 161–62
Warfare: Indian, 69–70, 153–54, 179, 181–84; Navajo–New Mexican, 222–23. *See also* Civil War; Kiowa-Comanche campaign; Mescalero campaign; Navajo campaign
Warner's Ranch/Warner's Springs, 170–71
War of 1812, 35, 36–37
Washington, D.C., 174; Ute trip to, 255, 257–58
Weatherhead, Samuel, 186
Westport, Mo., 97, 98

White, Ann: death of and effect on Carson, 181–83; Ute view of, 183–84
White, James, 181, 183–84
White, Virginia, 181–82, 183
Whitlock, J. W., 220–21
Wichitas, 245
Wilmot, Luther, 205
Wind River Range, 108–109
Wolfskill, William, 44, 45–46, 52, 55, 57
Wootton, Uncle Dick, 182
Workman, David, 38, 39, 43, 44–45, 51
Wynkoop, Edward ("Ned"), 207–208, 214

Young, Ewing, 44, 51, 52, 53–54; fur-trapping parties of, 55–64
Yount, George, 44, 55, 89

289